VEGETABLES:

A Love Story

Happy cooking!

René

VEGETABLES:
A LOVE STORY

92 Heartwarming Recipes
from the Kitchen of
Sweetsugarbean

RENÉE KOHLMAN

TOUCHWOOD

TouchWood Editions
touchwoodeditions.com

The information in this book is true and complete to the best of the author's knowledge.
All recommendations are made without guarantee on the part of the author or the publisher.

Edited by Lesley Cameron
Cover and interior design by Tree Abraham

CATALOGUING DATA AVAILABLE FROM LIBRARY AND ARCHIVES CANADA
ISBN 9781771513401 (hardcover)
ISBN 9781771513418 (e-book)

TouchWood Editions acknowledges that the land on which we live and work is within the traditional territories
of the Lkwungen (Esquimalt and Songhees), Malahat, Pacheedaht, Scia'new, T'Sou-ke and W̱SÁNEĆ
(Pauquachin, Tsartlip, Tsawout, Tseycum) peoples.

We acknowledge the financial support of the Government of Canada through the Canada Book Fund,
and the province of British Columbia through the Book Publishing Tax Credit.

This book was produced using FSC®-certified, acid-free papers, processed chlorine free,
and printed with soya-based inks.

Printed in China

25 24 23 22 21   1 2 3 4 5

For my darling Dixon.
You're the best.

CONTENTS

Introduction

Everybody loves a good love story, and a love story surrounded by food? Even better. Love is at the core of our very existence. It brings us into the world, and when we've lived a life that's full and good, it will see us out in the end. Food is also central to our lives. It gives us strength, sustenance, and satisfaction. When enjoyed fully and completely, good food lingers in the memory long after the dishes have been done and the floor swept. This book is both a love story about food and a food story about love. And, I'm overjoyed to say, the main characters in this story are vegetables. Never before have I been so intrigued by their nuance of flavour, their various textures, and the endless possibilities they offer in the kitchen. When you come to the final page of this book, I hope you'll feel the same way too.

On our first date, Dixon gave me a bundle of asparagus, tied with a slip of twine. I knew then and there that he was the person I'd been looking for all my life. I also knew that my second cookbook had to be about vegetables. Don't ask me how I knew—I just did. My darling man is the inspiration for the cookbook you are holding now, as many of the recipes are meals we've shared together since May 2016 when our love story began. Dixon Simpkins and his family grow vegetables for a living, on 20 acres of land near Saskatoon, and, lucky for me, many of them end up in my kitchen, in the recipes you are about to read. When the asparagus first bursts out of the earth, Dixon brings those pretty green spears to me, their points tightly closed, so I can sauté them in butter to go along with our breakfast of sunny-side-up eggs, crispy maple bacon sausages, and hot buttered toast. Sweet and juicy, fresh local asparagus is a joy to eat, and when the man who grows it is sitting across the table from you, grinning widely because he loves that you love asparagus, the joy is multiplied tenfold. In the summer months Dixon shows up at my door with baskets full of cucumbers, baby potatoes, zucchini, cabbage, green beans, tomatoes, and peas. Sometimes he'll even have broccoli and cauliflower. The lovely heads of these brassicas taste so much better than the ones that have to travel thousands of miles to get to the store. Dixon loves corn as much as I do, so he makes sure there is always some stocked in the refrigerator, ready to be boiled and bathed in butter. As the weather cools and the leaves begin to change, various squashes and all the root vegetables arrive. Sweet carrots, ruby red beets, earthy parsnips, humble potatoes, beautiful squash, and pungent onions keep coming throughout the winter, as Dixon has a root cellar that reaches far into the Saskatchewan prairie. Preparing meals with vegetables that Dixon has nurtured from seedling to harvest adds an extra element of joy. He adores everything I make, from a simple toasted tomato sandwich to heartier soups, pastas, and casseroles. His gratitude is shown with kisses and offers to do the dishes—neither of which I'll ever turn down.

Of course, as with any good love story, there's also a significant backstory. Food was my lover long before Dixon made eyes at me over bowls of Burmese chicken soup on our first date. There's also the love story between my mom and me, the food she fed me as a child, and the recipes we've exchanged over some 30 years. As a young child, barefoot and happy, I ran through the vegetables gardens she grew on our Saskatchewan farm. The rows of corn were great places to run and run, my small arms outstretched, shaking the leaves of the vegetable giant, the summer sunlight that dappled through, imprinting itself on my memory. The green beans she planted blew my mind when they were simply boiled straight from the garden, then swaddled in butter and fresh dill. Her tomatoes, which would ripen in boxes covered with newspaper on late summer days, were delicious, thickly sliced and layered between slices of white bread, slick with mayonnaise. She was the first person to teach me how to unearth potatoes, scraping away the dirt to find the gems left behind. When given a handful of fresh peas, she showed me how to slip the green orbs out of their pods and into a bowl, but they usually made their way to my mouth instead. The delight of those summer days, in the garden with my mom and the vegetables, has never left me, and I suspect it never will.

Food shared with friends, be it a budget-friendly vegetable stew or a platter of black bean tostadas, is another important part of this love story. The first kitchen I ever cooked in, besides the one run by my mom, was in a drafty third-floor walk-up apartment in Montreal in the early 1990s, otherwise known as my art school days. My roommate, Josée, and I would buy groceries at the markets on our way home from school. Not having a car, we didn't do huge grocery runs but quick stops for whatever we needed and would fit into our backpacks. We would trudge up the narrow, winding staircase to the top floor, put the radio on to CBC, unpack the groceries, and begin to cook. Josée also came from a home where delicious, home-cooked meals were really important. We weren't vegetarians but being on tight budgets, meat was more of a luxury item than a staple for us. We happily dove into *Moosewood* and Mollie Katzen cookbooks to meal-plan for the week. Oh, how well we ate for students! Tarts of phyllo pastry loaded with wilted greens and feta! Vegetables simmered in spicy peanut sauce! Cheesy enchiladas of black beans and zucchini! New friends gathered around our second-hand table, and long into the night we would share stories and laugh until the cheap wine was gone and the plates were scraped clean, taking up residence in the kitchen sink. I can still see those happy, smiling faces of the friends of my youth. How we talked of dreams and goals, along with dissecting plot lines of *Beverly Hills, 90210* and deciding if we would rather date so-and-so or so-and-so. Those dinner parties were where I really, really fell in love with cooking and feeding people. Only a few short years later, I would trade in my paint brush for a chef's knife and enter culinary school. The rest, as they say, is history.

I've been a solo eater for over half of my life. Except for a couple of years in Montreal, I've lived alone, and largely eaten alone, for a very long time. Even today, my darling Dixon has his little farmhouse outside of Saskatoon, and I have my little house in the city. We share meals about 65 percent of the time, and this is a routine that works very well for us. Given the considerable amount of cooking I've done for myself, I'd like to take this opportunity to note that it's important to love yourself by taking the time to feed yourself well. That last word is important. Even when I was busy working in restaurants for 20-plus years, I took the time to prepare fresh, simple meals at home. People, especially co-workers, were like, "How can you go home and cook after you've been doing it all day?" They had a fair point, but, honestly, I love to cook, and I love to eat good food. Long before self-care was a buzzword used to sell books and get clicks on social media, I was taking care of myself the best way I knew how: by making meals that were simple, delicious, and healthy. Eating well was a priority instilled in me from a young age, and I never shrugged it off. More importantly, I took the time to cook. We all choose how we want to spend our precious time, and I choose to spend it in the kitchen, developing recipes along the way. I've heard people say, "Oh, I'm not going to cook myself anything special because it's only just for me." This makes me so sad! You should cook something special ESPECIALLY if it's just for you.

The recipes in *Vegetables: A Love Story* are pulled from notebooks of long ago and yesterday, from my mom's memory, from my popular food blog *Sweetsugarbean*, and, most importantly, from my heart. I've loved creating every single vegetable-focused recipe, and I hope this book will inspire you in your own gardens, kitchens, and love stories.

NOTES FROM MY KITCHEN TABLE

If you're wondering where to get the best vegetables, how I feel about eating asparagus in the winter, or why there is no spinach in this cookbook, you're about to find out!

The Vegetables

I realize not everyone has a handsome farmer showing up at their front door with an armload of just-harvested vegetables. The next best thing would be to grow as much of your own veg as you're able to. Whether it's a pot of tomatoes on the patio or a half-acre plot bursting with vegetables (lucky you!), when you grow your own food, it tastes better—and you also connect with the earth, which is never a bad thing. If you have kids, get them involved, too. Show them the magic that can happen when a tiny seed is planted in the dirt.

But what if you have neither a handsome farmer nor a handy growing space? Fret not! Get thee to a local farmers' market or purchase a CSA subscription from a local vegetable farmer. This is the best way to find out what vegetables are in season where you live. Ask the farmers questions. Ask how they like to prepare their parsnips or when the corn was picked. Most farmers love talking about their vegetables. When you connect with the people who produce your food, you not only gain a greater appreciation of where your food comes from but also become aware of the hard work that goes into all the pretty vegetables you see at the market.

If you can't get to a farmers' market, then shop locally as much as possible—even if "local" ends up being Canada, rather than the actual town you live in. Look for the Product of Canada labels on fresh vegetables and on the bags of frozen. All over Canada, hard-working farmers are producing some of the best food on the planet. Support them as much as you can.

Eat Seasonal . . .

. . . as much as possible. In the Prairies, where I live, there are basically four to five months of the freshest, just-picked vegetables, and, even then, there may only be several weeks for asparagus, peas, beans, corn, and tomatoes. These are the things I happily gorge on when they're in season. I eat them simply, not wanting to fuss much with their sun-ripened flavours. When I shell fresh peas, I often don't bother doing anything other than boiling them in a little water until tender. Drain, stir in a pat or two of butter and some chopped dill, and season. Boom. Done. I like to do the same with green beans, but I also really love transforming their flavour with the heat from a skillet and some miso paste or a turn in the oven with melted mozzarella and crispy bread crumbs. Corn on the cob is heavenly with butter, salt, and pepper, though grilling and slathering it with garlic mayonnaise is also a front-runner for me. A garden-fresh tomato is one of the best things about summer, and about life, really. How I love to arrange juicy, ripe slices on a pretty plate, where they are then drizzled with good olive oil and become acquainted with torn basil leaves and fresh mozzarella. A flicker of flaky salt makes everything come together. I live and breathe their fresh flavours in the summer because those vegetables don't taste like that in February. So, what do I eat in February? Everything from avocados to zucchini, though I understand that choosing Canadian-grown produce is considerably more difficult at this time. Just do your best. Sometimes the greenhouse-grown cherry tomatoes taste pretty decent, but I honestly don't eat that many fresh tomatoes in the winter. I'll get my tomato fix from canned: the crushed ones transformed into sauces and the whole ones into soups and stews. Frozen peas, beans, and corn are a winter staple, though in my opinion the budget brands often don't have the same taste and quality as the premium brands. I watch when they go on sale and stock up. With frozen veg, you get what you pay for. And sometimes frozen just doesn't cut it. I don't even try to eat asparagus in the winter, for example, as it's just not the same vegetable I devour in spring. I like to think that when Sinéad O'Connor sang "Nothing Compares 2 U" she was singing about the sweetest springtime asparagus.

When it comes to choosing organic or non-organic produce, I pick a little bit of both. For me, the most important thing is that the produce is local, but when that's not an option, I'll choose whatever looks the best—and fits within my grocery budget.

This Is a Cookbook About Vegetables, but It's Not a Vegetarian Cookbook

That's right. The recipes in this book are vegetable-focused, but not exclusively vegetarian. There is a smattering of meat and fish here and there, but not everywhere. Bacon—oh, how I love bacon—is a good friend of so many vegetables, but if you don't eat it, don't add it in the recipes. I won't be sad, I promise. However, if the recipe does not call for bacon and you want to add it, then I think we could be friends for life. This book reflects the way I eat, which is lots of veg (obviously), a little meat and fish, and plenty of pulses. My love of lentils and beans started in that Montreal kitchen in the early 1990s, and I've been crushing hard on them ever since. Inexpensive, nutritious, and oh so versatile, pulses offer up amazing health benefits, and so they're still a major part of my diet. Not all recipes call for beans and lentils, but if you want to include them, we must be kindred spirits.

But You Wrote an Award-Winning Cookbook About Sweet Things, What Do You Know About Vegetables?

Plenty, as it happens. While baking has a sweet spot in my heart, and in the latter years of my professional culinary career it has been my primary focus, I've been cooking and loving vegetables for a very long time—as you now know. I just knew that my second cookbook would not be about sweet things, as I shared most of my favourite baked-goods recipes in *All the Sweet Things*. So I've got plenty to say about vegetables, especially after meeting my darling Dixon. The bulk of my professional cooking career involved either running a line in a restaurant or intensive catering. I've cooked everything from intimate dinners for two to Christmas dinner for over 1,000. Yes. One. Thousand. People. That's a lot of mashed potatoes, let me tell you. Plus, in recent years, I've been developing recipes for brands and commodity groups, and I take pride in having my recipes turn out every single time. I'm very particular about that, which is a good quality to have if you're a cookbook author. When I was touring around with *All the Sweet Things* (thanks so much to those of you who came out—hope to see you again!), lots of people asked when I would be writing a cookbook about something other than baking. You spoke, I listened. In many ways, *Vegetables: A Love Story* is the savoury companion to *All the Sweet Things*. It's full of heart and humour—and seriously good recipes that I hope will become favourites in your own home.

Why You Won't See Any Spinach or Rutabaga in the Recipes

I once loved spinach. I mean, I really, really loved it. I worked in a bistro in Edmonton around 1999–2000, and we had a super-good spinach salad on the menu. There was bacon (of course), some slices of hard-boiled egg, and a creamy honey Dijon dressing, if I'm remembering correctly, but who knows, it was a long time ago. Anyway, the main thing is I loved this salad. I had it every day for my lunch. That is, until I started feeling not so well in the afternoon. At first I thought it could be the dressing. Maybe it was too rich? But then a friend made me a spinach quiche and a spinach salad for dinner one night, and that just about did me in. I was on the couch, curled up in a ball, my stomach aching, and my body riddled with chills, almost like I had the flu. It wasn't the flu. It was the spinach. I'd eaten so much that my body was tapped out. Like, no more girl, you've had your fill for a lifetime. And I really had. These days, I can handle a few leaves tucked into mixed greens, but that's about it. Everything in moderation is a real thing. So, instead of spinach, I love up on the other greens like arugula, chard, and kale. But not too much, and not every day.

About the rutabaga. There is one recipe in the book that uses a wee bit of rutabaga, and it's only because Dixon said that if anyone could make it taste good, it would be me. The recipe turned out fantastic, but I still don't have enough love for the 'baga to give it its own chapter. How do I put this diplomatically? Rutabaga is not pleasing to my palate. I don't like it very much at all. I've tried, oh how I've tried, to find some room for it in my heart, but I'm not feeling it. Sure, you can boil it, then mash it with copious amounts of butter and cream to make it somewhat palatable. But I didn't want to waste the time or ingredients on a vegetable that I just don't like. The good news is that *Vegetables: A Love Story* contains over 90 tried-and-tested recipes that use vegetables that I really, really adore. My apologies to rutabaga lovers. But here is my pledge to you: if you have a recipe that you really think could change my mind on this one, let me know and I'll try it!

So, how did I decide which vegetables to include? I narrowed it down to the veg I like to eat (which is most veg) and then wrote recipes where they're the star of show. Garlic, for example, features in many dishes, but it's usually a supporting actor rather than a key player, so there's no chapter for garlic. Same goes for celery. I'm inspired to cook more with these unsung heroes of the vegetable world, so you never know what will happen. Stay tuned!

NOTES FOR THE COOK

I tried very hard to make the recipes as simple and straightforward as possible. The ingredient lists don't have anything too hard to find, and most of the stuff is likely in your pantry or refrigerator already. The fanciest I got may be smoked paprika, miso paste, za'atar, and ditali pasta. I know, wild and crazy. Some recipes require multiple pots and pans, while others need only one. Some recipes take a bit of time to prep, while others can be completed in under 30 minutes. There's a little bit of everything here: recipes for entertaining, for feeding a family, for eating on the couch while watching *Ozark*, and for sitting solo at the kitchen table while reading a book. Whether you've been cooking for 50 years or you're just starting out, I'll be your cheerleader along the way. Think of me sitting in your kitchen, with a glass of red, applauding like crazy as you pull a pan of Mom's Cabbage Rolls (page 61) from the oven. And imagine me high-fiving you as you stir all of that cheese into Cheesy Butternut Squash Rigatoni (page 219). I'm just so happy that you're cooking from this book. If I learned anything from writing *All the Sweet Things*, it's how positively awesome it was to see so many copies of my first cookbook in your kitchens, the pages splattered and sticky from use. It's truly humbling to see how you've made memories with your own families using my sweet recipes, and I hope the same happens with this, my second book baby. These pages are filled with all the vegetable dishes I've loved cooking over the years, and some new recipes that Dixon and I have fallen in love with as we've built our life together. Dixon, with a little cajoling on my part, offers up some insight on each vegetable, too. Be it a growing tip or harvesting tip, a story, or even a recipe (!!), I'm sure you'll enjoy reading the Dixon Says portion of each chapter as much as I have.

I'm hoping *Vegetables: A Love Story* will be a fixture in your kitchen as you make dinner for yourself or your family, and on your nightstand as you curl up to read before going to sleep. Many recipes in this cookbook conjure up memories for me, and I'm honoured to share them with you. The way the house smells when I cook Vegetable Stew in a Spicy Peanut Sauce (page 75) makes me feel like I'm 20 years old again, in a brand new city, and in many ways living a brand new life. Replicating my mom's Lazy Perogie Casserole (page 213) takes me back to the Sunday suppers of my childhood and falling in love with that glorious combination of carbs on carbs on carbs. Every time I make Mushroom Risotto Cakes (page 153) I think of a certain young woman, happily living solo and slowly stirring the chicken broth into the rice, breathing in the aroma and the moment. Cooking those first verdant spears of Asparagus and Eggs (page 25) is a lovely reminder of what can happen when you ask a cute boy out on a date, and he says yes. Who knew he'd bring me a bundle of my favourite vegetable to that Burmese restaurant on our first date? And, somehow, that bundle of asparagus was the impetus for this cookbook. Most good love stories have a certain amount of magic in them; mine just also happens to contain vegetables.

PANTRY NOTES

My pantry is generally well-stocked with a wide variety of items. Every time I look inside and see that it's full, I'm grateful that I have the privilege to afford ample amounts of good-quality ingredients.

At any given time, I have the following in my precious cupboard of dry goods. (Note that not everything here is used in the recipes in this book—that doesn't make them any less important to me.) There are also plenty of coffee beans, tea, and chocolate, otherwise known as a cookbook author's best friends. And while I try to cook from scratch as much as possible, I love a good shortcut when I see one. For me, this means packaged gnocchi and tortellini. Both products are readily available and great time savers!

- Cans of chickpeas, black beans, kidney beans, white beans
- Cans of whole, diced, and crushed tomatoes; tomato paste
- Cans of tuna, salmon (look for the MSC blue fish label to ensure sustainability and quality)
- Boxes of low-sodium chicken broth and vegetable broth
- Cans of evaporated milk (full-fat) and coconut milk (full-fat)
- Dry pasta, various types including gnocchi and couscous
- Dried beans and lentils
- Grains such as oats, barley, bulgur
- Rice, particularly basmati (use a good quality brand), long-grain brown, and Arborio
- Flour, particularly all-purpose, whole wheat, and spelt

- Seeds such as quinoa, flax, sesame, pumpkin, and sunflower
- Cornstarch
- Cocoa powder
- Cornmeal
- Baking soda
- Baking powder
- Sugar: granulated, brown, and icing
- Honey
- Yeast (never again shall I be without)
- Panko bread crumbs
- Tortilla chips
- Extra-virgin olive oil
- Canola oil
- Other oils such as camelina oil and cold-pressed canola oil for salads, dips, spreads
- Vinegars such as apple cider, red wine, sherry, rice, and white wine
- Fine sea salt (for cooking) and flaky salt (such as Maldon, for finishing certain dishes)
- Black peppercorns (I use only freshly ground black pepper)
- Variety of dried spices, particularly smoked paprika, garlic powder, dry mustard powder, chili powder, ground cumin, ground coriander, curry powder, ground turmeric, sumac, za'atar, cayenne, cinnamon, ground ginger, and onion powder
- Dried herbs, such as oregano, basil, Italian seasoning, bay leaves, sage, thyme, and rosemary, though I do prefer to use fresh whenever possible
- A bottle of sherry (I don't cook with a lot of booze, but sherry really works well with vegetables!)
- Onions and garlic
- Dried fruit such as cherries and cranberries (but never raisins or sultanas—I'm so not a raisin person!)

REFRIGERATOR NOTES

I only use full-fat dairy, and that's what I used when I tested recipes for this book.

Milk (3.25%)

Buttermilk (be sure to shake it before measuring)

Yogurt is plain Greek (5% or higher, but never lower)

Mayonnaise

Sour cream

Cheese: extra-old cheddar, mozzarella, bocconcini, cream cheese, ricotta, feta, brie, and real Parmesan, not the powdered stuff

Butter (salted unless stated otherwise)

Eggs (large and free run)

Fresh lemons and limes

Pickles

Olives

Oil-packed sun-dried tomatoes

Real maple syrup

Peanut butter

Tahini

Dijon mustard, grainy and smooth

Anchovy paste

Mild Indian curry paste and Thai red curry paste

White miso paste

Hot sauce, such as Sriracha, Frank's RedHot, and green jalapeño Tabasco

Tamari or low-sodium soy sauce

Worcestershire sauce

Salsa

White wine (I specify dry when it makes a difference to a dish)

FREEZER NOTES

Meat and poultry (locally sourced as much as possible—it pays to find a real butcher and to use good meat)

Shrimp (look for the MSC Blue Fish symbol on packaging)

Fish (I buy locally sourced white fish, pike, steelhead trout, or MSC-certified wild sockeye salmon)

Tortillas: corn and whole wheat

Naan

Vegetables such as peas, corn, green beans (I prefer premium brands for taste and quality)

Thick-cut bacon

Nuts such as peanuts, chopped walnuts, pecan halves, and sliced almonds

Phyllo pastry

All-butter puff pastry

Ginger (I just chop/grate what I need then put it back in the freezer)

Frozen berries and fruit

MY FAVOURITE KITCHEN TOOLS

KITCHEN SCALE This is the best $25 you will ever spend on kitchen equipment. I measure everything from dried pasta to potatoes with this thing.

LIQUID MEASURE CUP It's so much easier to measure liquids this way—less chance of spilling!

CUTTING BOARDS Try to have one specifically for meat.

KNIVES You only need three types of knives. Splurge on a chef's knife, purchase an inexpensive serrated bread knife, and have a few paring knives. Keep your knives sharp. You're more likely to slice your finger on a dull knife than a sharp one.

RIMMED BAKING SHEETS (13- x 18-inches) I have three and use them all the time.

NON-STICK SKILLETS It's good to have a small one (7-inch diameter) for quick things like eggs and a large one (12-inch diameter) for pancakes, stir-fries, etc.

CAST-IRON SKILLETS I use these all the time, in various sizes such as 10-inch, 12-inch, 14-inch. Yes, you can use warm soapy water to clean them. Just don't let them soak overnight.

DEEP-DISH CAST-IRON BRAISER (12-inch) I use this for baked pasta dishes and casseroles.

DUTCH OVEN (5 to 6 quarts) I love my blue Le Creuset so much. If my house is ever on fire, I'm taking this with me.

LARGE SOUP/STOCKPOT (7 quarts or larger) This is a must for big-batch recipes like chili, soups, and broths.

BAKING DISHES/CASSEROLE DISHES in assorted sizes, such as 9- x 13-inch, 9- x 11-inch, 7- x 11-inch, 10-inch square, 8-inch round, 3-quart oval. I have a bit of an addiction to these types of dishes. Send help.

ENAMEL ROASTING PAN I picked up a 9- x 13-inch gem at a vintage store for a steal, and I use it for roasting vegetables and baking casseroles.

PARCHMENT PAPER It's a godsend.

FOOD PROCESSOR AND MINI-CHOPPER For big things like hummus and pesto, I'm all about the food processor, but for small jobs, I whip out the mini-chopper.

IMMERSION BLENDER A must for blitzing soups and sauces.

WOODEN SPOONS Use these on cast-iron, enamel, and non-stick cookware.

SILICONE SPATULAS Various sizes, for scraping out jars, bowls, and what have you.

METAL TONGS I use these all the time for tossing salads, pulling veg off the grill, flipping items over on sheet pans, you name it.

MICROPLANE Perfect for grating citrus peel or hard cheeses.

FINE-MESH SIEVE A must for rinsing things like rice, quinoa, barley, and for making mascarpone/ricotta cheese.

TIPS AND TRICKS FOR SUCCESSFUL COOKING

Be sure to read the recipe through before proceeding. Make sure you have all of the ingredients on hand so you don't have to make any quick trips to the store for tomato paste. Pay attention to things like reserving pasta water or chilling a filling before proceeding with the recipe.

Have your vegetables prepped before starting the recipe. This is called mise en place, and it's a great habit to get into.

When I say "chopped," I mean the vegetables should be cut into bite-sized pieces. "Diced" is smaller than that, like ¼-inch pieces. "Minced" is very finely chopped.

When you're putting a pot of cold water on to boil, cover it with a lid and the water will come to a boil faster.

Line those baking sheets with parchment paper for easy cleanup. If you wet it first, then wring it out, the parchment becomes super malleable and fits in the pan easily. (There won't be much surface water on it, so it's no biggie if you're adding ingredients that have been tossed in oil.)

Be mindful when handling raw meat and fish. If you touch raw meat and fish, wash your hands in hot, soapy water. If raw chicken and fish juices dribble on the counter, wipe them up with a bleach-water solution or disinfectant wipes. Be aware of any potential bacteria like salmonella and E. coli that could be on your hands, and what your hands touch. I once worked with a cook who would handle raw chicken and then go around touching other things. Not one to keep my mouth shut when I see bad stuff going down, I would call him out on his reckless and dangerous behaviour all the time. Don't be that guy. Raw meat and its juices can make you very sick. Be smart when handling it.

Wash vegetables thoroughly under cool running water. Don't cut into a vegetable before washing it, as any bacteria on the peel will be transferred to the inside.

Change your dishcloths daily. This might seem like common sense, but you'd be surprised at how many people don't. I know someone who went away for three weeks, leaving behind a roommate. Upon her return, the same dishcloth was still clinging to the sink tap, and she could smell it before she even walked into the kitchen. She's surprised the darn thing didn't walk itself to the washing machine on its own. Same goes for tea towels. Change those daily, too.

Have a meal plan of some sort. It saves time and money overall, plus takes away the 4 PM stress of "What the heck am I going to cook for dinner?"

Avoid food waste as much as possible. Go through your refrigerator a couple of times a week and pay attention to those items that need to be used up. Don't let leftovers linger for more than three days. You can freeze most things, but be sure to label them first; otherwise, you'll have a really annoying guessing game on your hands. Plan to cook from the refrigerator at least once a week. Clean-out-the-fridge meals make me feel like I'm on *Chopped*, but I don't have to use ingredients like gummy candies or tripe. (Meal-planning also helps with this.)

The recipes in this book were tested on my gas range; I don't have convection. Keep this in mind when it comes to baking/roasting times, as your oven may run hotter than mine.

Set a timer! Whether it's love or cooking, timing is everything.

VEGETABLE STORAGE NOTES

When a particular vegetable is in season, I like to stock up, especially if I know I can freeze any surplus. I'd love to give you a seasonal guide to veg, but Canada being the size it is, seasons can vary widely across the country—and even within single provinces. However, I can give you a quick guide to best practices for storing vegetables. Humidity drawers (a.k.a. crispers) in your refrigerator play an important role in extending the edible life of your vegetables. Setting the dial to the middle position won't do you or your vegetables any favours! As a rule of thumb, the high humidity setting will cut off air flow to the drawer, allowing the contents to sit in the humidity and the gases they produce. This acts like a closed window. Most vegetables go in this drawer, including leafy greens. The moisture will keep them crisp. The low humidity setting acts like a window that has been cracked open, allowing the gases to escape. This is great for most fruits like apples and peaches. Vegetables aren't suitable for this drawer. Citrus fruits prefer very low humidity and often do better when stored in the main part of the refrigerator.

> VEGETABLES LAST LONGER IF THEY ARE NOT WASHED BEFORE REFRIGERATED. AS SOON AS WATER HITS THEM, USE AS SOON AS POSSIBLE.

ASPARAGUS: Best eaten as soon as you bring it home. *Refrigerating:* Wrap spear ends in damp paper towel and store in an unsealed plastic bag, or, if you have room, stand the bunch upright in a jar filled with water. Use within 3 to 4 days. *Freezing:* Wash thoroughly, trim the ends, cut into 1½-inch pieces, and blanch (plunge into boiling water for 2 minutes, then transfer to ice-cold water). Drain off excess moisture and pack into resealable plastic bags. Can be frozen for up to 1 year.

AVOCADOS: Ripen on the counter. This will happen faster if they're in a paper bag. *Refrigerating:* Once ripe, store in the refrigerator for up to 3 days. *Freezing:* Place the flesh of 1 avocado and 1 Tbsp of lemon juice in a blender or mini-chopper. Purée until smooth. Pack the purée into a small resealable plastic bag and freeze for up to 5 months.

BEETS: *Refrigerating:* Store in a loosely closed plastic bag for up to 2 weeks. If the greens are attached, leave them on until ready to use. *Freezing:* Raw beets don't freeze well. To freeze cooked beets, wash and trim the beets, leaving a ½-inch stem. Boil whole beets, covered, until tender. Slip off the skins once cool. Slice or chop and store in resealable plastic bags for up to 1 year.

BROCCOLI: *Refrigerating:* Store in a loosely closed plastic bag in the crisper for up to 5 days. *Freezing:* Follow the instructions for asparagus to freeze for up to 1 year.

BRUSSELS SPROUTS: *Refrigerating:* Store in a loosely closed plastic bag for 3 to 5 days. *Freezing:* Keeping the sprouts whole, follow the instructions for asparagus to freeze for up to 1 year.

CABBAGE: *Refrigerating:* Store in a loosely closed perforated plastic bag for up to 2 months. *Freezing:* Plunge the cabbage leaves (or thin wedges of cabbage) into boiling water for 2 minutes, then transfer to ice-cold water. Drain off excess moisture and pack into resealable plastic bags. Freeze for up to 1 year.

CARROTS: *Refrigerating:* Store in a loosely closed plastic bag in the crisper for up to 3 to 4 weeks. If you have a root cellar or a cold room, leave the dirt on the carrots and they will last for up to 8 or 9 months. *Freezing:* Peel and cut the carrots into 1-inch pieces. Boil for 2 minutes, then transfer to ice-cold water. Drain off excess moisture and pack into resealable plastic bags. Freeze for up to 1 year.

CAULIFLOWER: *Refrigerating:* Store in an open plastic bag in the crisper for up to 1 week. *Freezing:* Follow the instructions for asparagus to freeze for up to 1 year.

CELERY: *Refrigerating:* Store in a loosely closed plastic bag for up to 1 week. *Freezing:* Follow the instructions for asparagus to freeze for up to 1 year.

CORN: *Refrigerating:* Store with the husks on for up to 2 days. *Freezing:* Husk the corn, remove the silk, and wash. Boil whole cobs for 4 minutes, then transfer to ice-cold water. Drain, cut the kernels off the cobs, and pack the corn into resealable plastic bags. Freeze for up to 8 months.

CUCUMBERS: *Refrigerating:* Store in a loosely closed plastic bag for up to 1 week. *Freezing:* Do not freeze.

GARLIC: Store in a dry, cool, well-ventilated area, away from heat. The warmer the room, the shorter the shelf life. *Refrigerating:* Don't refrigerate whole garlic bulbs, as they'll start to sprout. Once garlic is peeled and chopped, it can be refrigerated in an airtight container for up to 5 days. *Freezing:* Do not freeze.

GREEN BEANS: *Refrigerating:* Store in a tightly closed plastic bag for up to 5 days. *Freezing:* Follow the instructions for asparagus to freeze for up to 1 year.

GREEN ONIONS: *Refrigerating:* Store in a loosely closed plastic bag for up to 5 days. *Freezing:* Wash and dry thoroughly. Chop and place in a resealable plastic bag for up to 10 months.

KALE: *Refrigerating:* Store in a loosely closed perforated plastic bag in the crisper for 5 to 7 days. *Freezing:* Wash and remove tough centre ribs and stems. Boil for 2 minutes, then transfer to ice-cold water. Drain off excess moisture and pack into resealable plastic bags. Freeze for up to 10 months.

LETTUCE: *Refrigerating:* Store in a loosely closed plastic bag for up to 5 days. *Freezing:* Do not freeze.

MUSHROOMS: If purchasing in plastic-covered containers, keep them there until ready to use. Use them within 5 days. *Refrigerating:* If buying in bulk, store in a paper bag in the refrigerator for 5 to 7 days. *Freezing:* Sauté sliced mushrooms in butter for 2 minutes. Let cool, then pack into an airtight container. Freeze for up to 10 months.

ONIONS: Store in a cool, dry place away from potatoes, as both will spoil sooner when they're close to each other. Keep onions away from plastic and store in a mesh bag or basket so air can circulate. Stored properly, they'll be good for up to 2 months. *Refrigerating:* Chopped raw onions can be stored in an airtight container in the refrigerator for up to 1 week. *Freezing:* Peel and chop onions, then pack into a resealable plastic bag and freeze for up to 8 months.

PEAS: Fresh green peas are best enjoyed as soon as they're picked. *Refrigerating:* Once shelled, use them within 2 to 3 days. *Freezing:* Boil shelled peas for

90 seconds, then transfer to ice-cold water. Drain off excess moisture, pack in resealable plastic bags, and freeze for up to 1 year.

POTATOES: Store in a cool, dry place away from onions for up to 3 weeks. If you have a root cellar or a cold room, leave the dirt on the potatoes and they will last for up to 8 or 9 months. *Refrigerating:* Do not refrigerate. When potatoes are refrigerated, the starches turn to sugars, and the potatoes develop a sweet taste and darken when cooked. By the same token, don't leave potatoes in a cupboard for too long in the summer. The smell of rotten potatoes is not one you want to have to ever encounter. *Freezing:* Raw potatoes don't freeze well, and I'm not a fan of frozen cooked potatoes either as the texture is quite mushy.

RADISHES: *Refrigerating:* Remove the green tops, then store in a container of water (be sure they are covered with water), for up to 1 week, changing the water daily. *Freezing:* Do not freeze.

SQUASH: Store in a cool, dry place for up to 2 months. *Refrigerating:* Do not refrigerate. *Freezing:* Raw squash doesn't freeze well. To freeze cooked squash: Peel, chop, boil until tender, mash, let cool, and then pack into resealable plastic bags. Freeze for up to 1 year.

SWEET POTATOES: Store in a cool, dry place for up to 1 month. Use a basket or mesh bag so air can circulate. Avoid storing in plastic. *Refrigerating:* Do not refrigerate whole sweet potatoes, as their texture becomes very firm and they develop an unpleasant taste in the refrigerator. Submerge peeled, chopped sweet potatoes in water and refrigerate for 1 day. *Freezing:* Raw sweet potatoes don't freeze well. To freeze cooked sweet potato, peel, chop, boil until tender, mash, add a small amount of lemon juice to prevent discolouration,

let cool, and then pack into a resealable plastic bag and freeze for up to 1 year.

SWISS CHARD: *Refrigerating:* Store in a plastic bag for up to 4 days. *Freezing:* Separate the leaves from the stems, blanch them separately (boil stalks for 2 minutes; leaves for 1 minute), transfer to ice-cold water, drain off excess moisture, and package separately. Freeze for up to 1 year.

TOMATOES: For best flavour, store at room temperature, out of direct sunlight, for up to 1 week. *Refrigerating:* If they're very ripe, pop them into the refrigerator and store for up to 1 week, and allow them to sit at room temperature for at least 30 minutes before eating. *Freezing:* Wash tomatoes and pat dry. Leave the tomatoes whole or chop them, lay them in a single layer on a baking sheet, and place in the freezer. Once frozen, transfer them into resealable plastic bags and freeze for up to 3 months. If the skins bother you, plop the raw whole tomatoes in boiling water for 30 seconds, remove the skins, and freeze as above.

ZUCCHINI: *Refrigerating:* Store in a plastic bag for up to 6 days. *Freezing:* See page 264 on how to freeze grated zucchini. Otherwise, wash and slice zucchini into ½-inch pieces, boil for 2 minutes, then transfer to ice-cold water. Drain off excess moisture and pack into resealable plastic bags. Freeze for up to 10 months.

WASTE NOT, WANT NOT: MY SECRET VEGETABLE BROTH RECIPE

When you cook with as many vegetables as I do, there will be kitchen scraps, and plenty of them. To avoid these peels and trimmings from ending up in the compost or garbage, I like to make a flavourful broth, which, in turn, will go into soups, stews, and other dishes. I keep a large resealable plastic bag in the freezer, and every time I have vegetable remains, I toss them in the bag. When the bag is full, about 8 cups of scraps, I make a big batch of broth. Not only does this cut down on my kitchen waste, it also saves me money. And I like saving money—especially on my grocery bill. You can use most scraps, but the popular ones in my house are the trimmings from carrots, onions, celery, mushroom stems, bell peppers, zucchini, leeks, garlic, tomatoes, and squash and tired herbs—especially parsley. I generally avoid anything too pungent (broccoli, kale, cabbage, Brussels sprouts), and it should be noted that potato peels will make your broth muddy, so add them to the compost. Also, make sure the scraps aren't mouldy or rotten. I put the frozen vegetable scraps in a large stock pot and cover them with plenty of cold water (about 5 quarts). I toss in 4 cloves of garlic, which I smash first; 2 bay leaves; 2 tsp salt; ½ tsp black peppercorns; and a pinch of whole cloves, if I have them on hand. Cover the pot with a lid and bring everything to a boil over high heat. Turn down the heat to medium and simmer the broth, uncovered, for about 1 hour. Let the broth cool to lukewarm. Using tongs, I like to pick out the large scraps first, discarding them into the organic waste. Then I'll strain the broth through a fine-mesh sieve into a large bowl. I let it cool completely at room temperature, then I pour it into freezer-safe containers. The broth can be refrigerated for up to 5 days, but mine mostly goes into the freezer. It's cool to hang out here for 6 months. This makes about 3 quarts of broth.

In the middle of May, Dixon will utter the most beautiful words to me: "Babe, the asparagus is ready to be picked!" His reward for such an announcement is a little squeal of joy from me, accompanied by hugs and kisses. When this much-loved vegetable is fresh from the fields, it tastes of spring, fresh air, and renewal. In my opinion, it's one of the very best things to come from the earth, and because its growing period is rather short, I thoroughly enjoy every spear that comes into my kitchen. Whether it's swirled in a pan with hot butter and garlic, roasted with olive oil and lemon juice, stirred into pasta, or chopped into a salad, fresh, local asparagus is absolute magic. Those six weeks in late spring are pure bliss, and the fleeting nature of asparagus season is much like life: savour every second of it while you can.

Harvesting asparagus is back-breaking work, though, and I always feel badly for Dixon when he has to cut so much of it at once. He gets extra back rubs in May and June! Asparagus plants are pretty neat, and, over the years, I've learned a fair bit about them. Hanging out with Dix has been an education. Like, did you know that asparagus are the young shoots of the cultivated lily plant that grows out from an underground stem or rhizome? Some plants can produce asparagus for 15 to 20 years! There are about 20 varieties of edible asparagus, and they're divided into three groups: green asparagus, which is the most common; white asparagus, which is the result of asparagus growing underground or being deprived of light; and violet asparagus, which has a distinctive fruity flavour. It's an aquatic plant, and it needs plenty of water to produce those delectable, verdant spears. Given the tendency for dry growing conditions around Saskatoon, I always do a little happy dance when the rain falls on the fields. It means more asparagus for me! All types of asparagus pack a nutritional punch, with high levels of vitamins A and C, potassium, iron, and calcium.

Dixon Says: I have a love/hate relationship with asparagus. I love eating it and I love the money it brings in, but the novelty of cutting it almost every day wears off pretty quickly! The season for asparagus is very brief. Usually we harvest it from Mother's Day to Father's Day. After that, I might rob a few spears for dinner, but it needs some time to grow for itself, recharging the roots for next year. It's a great early season crop, however, and it's a great seller during the time when stored vegetables are running low and other planted crops aren't ready yet. It grows fast when the weather's warm—as much as 6 inches per day. To cut an asparagus spear, hold it near the tip, bend it over slightly and, using a sharp knife, cut near the ground on the side away from the hand holding it. We cool our asparagus with cold water as soon as possible to remove the field heat so it doesn't spoil, but if you're eating it right away, there's no need. The cut end will likely be a little tough and stringy. I like to cut it off with a sharp knife; start at the cut end and gently test with a sharp knife. If there's resistance, move a little further up the spear until you feel the knife would cut through the spear without effort. It's possible to remove the cut end simply by bending it until it snaps, but I find that you lose a little of the nice stuff on the wrong side.

ASPARAGUS

Our First Date

It was early 2016, and I was in the thick of writing *All the Sweet Things*. Creating a cookbook takes a massive amount of work, and the project was using all of my mental and physical energy. I was largely hunkered down at home, and I only left the house to get groceries and go to my job every Sunday at the Saskatoon Farmers' Market, where I would sell fruit wines made by my friends at Living Sky Winery. Those Sundays were slow paced, and I thoroughly enjoyed the break from my book and the chance to talk to folks other than my cats. Then, one Sunday, sometime in February, I noticed a handsome farmer who had his table of root vegetables set up in the next aisle. There were a few things that immediately caught my attention about Dixon. I liked how he was always doing something, be it packaging his carrots and potatoes or rearranging the display. He was always busy, and I liked that. He wasn't lazy, and I liked that even more. Then there was the way he talked to customers and other vendors. He was always smiling. He seemed happy! I'd previously dated a couple of men who were rather morose, and Dixon's good-natured personality gave my intuition a gentle yet persistent nudge. Then there was Dixon himself. I noticed how his broad shoulders and strong back moved in his somewhat snug T-shirt. The rest of him looked pretty good, too. I would catch myself sneaking furtive glances his way throughout those Sundays in the winter of 2016, and then I decided to finally do something about it.

Saturdays were always big bake days, as I was feverishly recipe testing for *All the Sweet Things*, and any extra product (I could not eat all of those cookies and cakes myself!) was taken to the market the next day, where I would give away samples to fellow vendors. This is how I broke the ice with Dix. Every Sunday I would come laden with chocolate chip cookies, granola bars, slices of cranberry orange cream cheese loaf, and banana bread, you name it. I would pass by Dixon's table, toss him a smile, and casually ask if he wanted to try some baking. He always said yes, with a big smile. Dixon likes to interject at this part of the story and say that he was disappointed when he found out that others were sampling my wares too. I told him that I did not want to be too obvious about my intentions. Plus, I had a lot of baked goods to unload!

So, with the cookies and cakes breaking the ice, and my manuscript completed on April 1, I decided to take things to the next level. Dixon was very sweet, and a little shy. I knew I would have to be the one to ask him out on a date. I too am a little shy, but there comes a point in your life when you just gotta take a big breath and jump. And so it was the final Sunday in April, just a day or two after my 43rd birthday, when I came up to him, took a big breath, and blurted out: "Hi, Dixon! I write restaurant reviews for *The StarPhoenix* and I was wondering if you would like to come out for dinner with me sometime?" His response was an immediate and joyful YES! Then came the awkward inputting of numbers into phones, more shy smiles, and a date set for two days later. Two days! What the heck was I going to wear?

next cookbook would be about vegetables! And Love! Because goddammit, after searching half my life for a man who would not let me down/break my heart/let me go, here I was sitting across from him. My true love. I know it sounds corny (this is a cookbook about love and vegetables—things were bound to get corny eventually), but all those people who told me that I'd know when the Right One came along were right.

Over the next few hours, the air crackled with electricity between us. Sparks were shooting out all over the place. Delicious food would arrive, and we would slurp the soup and nibble on the noodles. It only took 30 minutes for Dixon to suggest a second date for the

"HI, DIXON! I WRITE RESTAURANT REVIEWS FOR *THE STARPHOENIX* AND I WAS WONDERING IF YOU WOULD LIKE TO COME OUT FOR DINNER WITH ME SOMETIME?" HIS RESPONSE WAS AN IMMEDIATE AND JOYFUL YES!

The restaurant we were meeting at was a Burmese spot I knew would be quiet and cozy—two factors that seemed important for our first date. Dixon was the first to arrive, and I spotted him immediately, tucked away in a corner, wearing a soft, yellow-checkered shirt. I took a seat opposite him, and then it happened. Dixon, blushing as all get out, handed me a bundle of fresh asparagus, the spears gathered together with a slip of twine. He told me he'd picked the asparagus himself that morning, and that he thought I would like it more than flowers. He was right. That moment changed everything. It was like something in the universe shifted. No longer was I going to be alone; my soul would now be attached to Dixon's, and that's all there was to it. I was so touched by his offering of that bundle of verdant spears, I immediately thought of how great this scene would be in my next cookbook. And! My

following week. We were equally smitten. Three hours breezed by, and finally the very kind owner of the restaurant came to our table, told us that he had to close up, and asked us to pay. We were getting kicked out! After the bill was paid, we took our leave to the parking lot, where we proceeded to talk for another 30 minutes. We all know that point at the end of a first date, when you wonder if there will be a kiss, and who will make the first move, and should it be a lip kiss or a cheek kiss? Mine landed somewhere on Dixon's cheek, close to his ear, just as he was going in for a hug. It couldn't have been more awkward! I felt like Molly Ringwald in a John Hughes movie, but it was all good. We just smiled and said our goodbyes. It was like we both knew that there would be plenty of time to get the kisses right. And that is that is how this love story began. Five years and counting, the kisses are magnificent.

Asparagus and Eggs

In the early days of May, the sun will warm the earth enough to tease the first spears of asparagus bursting out of the ground. This is the first vegetable to be harvested at Dixon's farm, and those gloriously green spears are carefully bundled up and driven into Saskatoon. At my doorstep, I greet both the man and the vegetable with multiple kisses. Sweet springtime asparagus is a treasure to behold, often not needing much more than a swirl in the pan with hot butter, a sprinkle or two of salt, and a fresh grinding of black pepper. This is the dish I made with that bundled-up bunch of asparagus Dixon gifted me on our first date. I remember taking a photo of my breakfast and texting it to him, with the hopes that soon, very soon, I would be making a similar breakfast for the both of us. I wasn't wrong!

Warm a large non-stick skillet over medium-high heat. Toss in 2 Tbsp of the butter. Give the pan a shake as it melts. Add the asparagus and cook until the spears turn bright green. Gently toss now and again. Depending on how thick the asparagus is, this could take anywhere from 5 to 8 minutes. When you're satisfied with the doneness, squeeze in some lemon juice to taste and season with salt and pepper.

Meanwhile, in another skillet, melt the remaining 2 Tbsp butter, crack in the eggs, and cook them however you like them. If you'd rather poach the eggs, that's equally wonderful.

Divide the asparagus between two plates and nestle the eggs around the spears. Serve with hot buttered toast. What a feast!

SERVES 2

4 Tbsp butter, divided

1 medium bunch of asparagus, about ½ pound, tough edges trimmed

½ lemon, juiced

Salt and pepper

4 large eggs

Hot buttered toast, for serving

A Tart of Asparagus, Bacon, and Cheese

This simple tart showcases the beauty of fresh asparagus, which pairs well with its good friends bacon and cheese. Serve the tart warm or at room temperature as an appetizer, or cut the slices larger and serve them alongside a green salad for a light supper. I'm rather partial to the latter, especially with a glass of chilled Sauvignon Blanc close at hand. A tumble of mint or basil leaves not only makes the tart look pretty but also adds the final flourish of flavour. Fresh and delicious, this tart will surely put smiles on those gathered around your table in the spring when asparagus tastes its absolute best.

Preheat the oven to 400°F. Place the oven racks in the highest and lowest positions. Line two rimmed baking sheets with parchment paper.

In a medium bowl, toss together the whole asparagus spears, oil, lemon zest, and salt and pepper to taste. Let the asparagus marinate while you prepare the pastry (that should take about 5–7 minutes).

Unroll the sheets of puff pastry (or roll out each one out to roughly 10 × 12 inches). Use a paring knife to score a line around the perimeter of each pastry sheet, about 1 inch from the edge. Place a sheet of pastry on each baking sheet. Using a fork, poke holes all over the pastry within the border. This will ensure that this part remains flat during baking, while the border will puff up.

Crumble half of the Boursin over each piece of puff pastry. Scatter Asiago and bacon over top. Place the marinated asparagus evenly on top. (I line it up in pretty rows.) Using a pastry brush, spread the egg wash along the border. Bake until golden, about 20–22 minutes. Rotate the pans from top to bottom at the halfway point.

Remove the tarts from the oven and cut each into eight pieces, if serving as an appetizer, or into four if serving as a main alongside a salad. Garnish the slices with fresh herbs. Serve warm or at room temperature.

SERVES 4–8

1 large bunch (about 1 lb) of medium-sized asparagus, tough ends trimmed

1 Tbsp extra-virgin olive oil

Grated zest of 1 lemon

Salt and pepper

1 package (16 oz/450 g) frozen puff pastry, thawed in the refrigerator

1 box of herb and garlic Boursin cheese

1 cup grated Asiago (or Parmesan) cheese

8 slices thick-cut bacon, cooked and chopped

1 egg, beaten with a little water for egg wash

Small handful of mint (or basil) leaves

✳ *This recipe is very easily divided in half to make a single tart.*

Asparagus, Prosciutto, and Brie Flatbreads with Spiced Honey Drizzle

These little asparagus flatbreads are great for just two people, but you can double, even triple the recipe if you're having people over for appetizers and cocktails. The prosciutto is a wonderful partner for the asparagus, as it's salty, savoury, and best when it's crispy. In fact, you may want to roast more asparagus than the amount I've listed, because, if you're like me, you'll be plucking it off the baking sheet before it even has a chance of making it onto the flatbreads. By draping the prosciutto over the asparagus as it roasts, you're adding even more flavour to the vegetable. Two birds, one stone, and all that. When it comes to the cheesy bread, be sure to toast the mini naan first to avoid soggy bottoms, as no one likes that. You could use Camembert or Cambozola instead of the brie, with excellent results. The sweet heat of the honey really loves up on the creamy brie, salty meat, and garlicky asparagus. It's a sensory circus in the very best way.

Preheat the oven to 400°F. Line two rimmed baking sheets with parchment paper.

Place the naan on one of the prepared baking sheets and toast until slightly crispy, about 5–6 minutes.

Meanwhile, toss together the asparagus, oil, garlic, and salt and pepper to taste in a medium bowl. Spread these on the second baking sheet and top with the slices of prosciutto, making sure they don't overlap. Roast until the prosciutto is crispy and the asparagus is tender, about 10–12 minutes. I like to remove the prosciutto from the asparagus and place it alongside the spears during the last 2 minutes of cooking, just so things can crisp up nicely.

Top each crispy naan with brie and return to the oven until the brie is melted, about 4–6 minutes.

Stir together the honey, vinegar, and a pinch of red pepper flakes in a small bowl.

To assemble the flatbreads, top each brie toast with three or four spears of asparagus and one slice of prosciutto. Arrange on a platter and drizzle with the honey mixture. Garnish with fresh basil leaves. Serve immediately.

SERVES 2

4 pieces mini naan

12–16 fresh asparagus spears, tough ends trimmed

2 tsp extra-virgin olive oil

1 clove garlic, minced

Salt and pepper

4 slices prosciutto

4 small slices brie, cut in half

1 Tbsp liquid honey

1 tsp apple cider vinegar

Red pepper flakes

Fresh basil leaves, for garnish

* *The amount of asparagus required depends on the length of the spears rather than their weight for this recipe. If they're long, you can cut them in half. It's always good to cook more asparagus than you need, though, because you might want to nibble on it before it gets to the bread!*

* *If you want to use regular naan instead of mini, then you'll have naan pizza, which is a favourite around here, too. The cooking time will be around the same.*

Cream of Asparagus Soup

This soup makes me feel super posh—like I should be having lunch with the Queen or something. The asparagus flavour really shines through here, with garlic, lemon, and just a wee bit of mustard along for the ride, and the colour is quite pretty. Normally, I would encourage you to use an immersion blender as I dislike washing more dishes than necessary. However, if you're going to go posh, then really go posh, and by this I mean: No one wants to eat stringy asparagus soup. Ever. A good blender will remove most, if not all, of those annoying bits, leaving you with a pot of the silkiest asparagus soup ever. Fit for a queen, even.

Trim the tips from 12 asparagus spears (about 2 inches from the top) and cut them in half lengthwise if thick. Set aside for garnish.

Cut the remaining asparagus, including the leftover bits from the previous step, into ½-inch pieces.

Warm the butter in a Dutch oven over medium heat. Stir in the onion and cook until softened, about 5 minutes. Stir in the garlic and cook just until fragrant, about another 1–2 minutes. Add the asparagus and mustard powder. Season generously with salt and pepper. Cook, stirring often, for 5 minutes. Add just enough broth to cover—about 3½ cups. Bring to a boil and simmer, covered, until the asparagus is very tender, about 15–20 minutes.

While the soup simmers, cook the reserved asparagus spears in a small pot of boiling salted water just until tender, about 2 minutes. Drain and rinse under cold water.

Purée the soup in a blender. (I do it in three batches.) Transfer the purée to a large bowl. Be careful! Hot liquid! Return all of the puréed soup to the pot, stir in the cream, and thin to your desired consistency with more broth. You may need to warm the soup over low heat as you do this. Stir in the lemon juice and season to taste with more salt and pepper.

Divide the soup into bowls and garnish with the asparagus tips.

SERVES 4

2 lb fresh asparagus, tough ends trimmed

3 Tbsp butter

1 small yellow onion, chopped

2 garlic cloves, minced

½ tsp dry mustard powder

Salt and pepper

4½ cups low-sodium chicken or vegetable broth

½ cup whipping (35%) cream

1 Tbsp lemon juice

Beets are a vegetable that I have come to love, though there was a time in my youth when I would not have put one on the end of my fork. Ah, the wisdom that comes with age! Besides being delicious, beets are super good for us. They are low in calories, yet high in valuable vitamins and minerals. In fact, they contain a bit of almost every single vitamin and mineral that your body needs to be its best, beautiful self. And don't toss out the tops! Many nutrients are found in the stalks and leaves.

I have come to admire not only the beet's jewel-like beauty but also its earthy sweetness. Beets are quite lovely when roasted. I like to toss chunks of beets in a little bacon fat (or canola oil), with chopped rosemary and thyme leaves, slices of shallot, and generous pinches of salt and pepper. Roast at 375°F until the beets are tender. The roasting time will depend on how large your beets are, but allow for about 30–45 minutes. If I'm feeling fancy, I'll crumble goat cheese or feta on top before serving. A marvellous side if there ever was one.

One of my favourite things about beets has to be harvesting them alongside Dixon. I'll never forget our first harvest together, when the snow had arrived way too early—in September!—and we were plucking beets and carrots out of the cold muck. Clad in rubber boots, layers of long johns, and fleece, I saw first-hand the amount of hard work it takes for a small vegetable-growing family like Dixon's to get food from the farm to the table. With the cold, biting wind swirling around us, I would stop and stare at my beloved, clad in the same attire as I. He was grinning his face off. When I asked him why (I was hoping he would say it's time for coffee break), he just said that there's no place he'd rather be and nothing else he'd rather be doing. And that's when I fell a little deeper in love with him. And then he said, "Let's go warm up in the truck."

Dixon Says: Beets are almost a never-fail crop for me. The seeds can be directly planted into the ground, and, if the beets are too thick, they can be thinned by picking them out for greens, which are great steamed or in a salad. When the beet root starts to form, I start to pick them for bunched beets at the market. I usually go over a patch a couple of times so that by the time fall rolls around, the beets are thinned and have room to size up for the autumn harvest.

BEETS

Beet Borscht with Lots of Dill

Borscht is one of those soups that you probably think you make the best. Or your mom does. Or your grandma. And I'm not going to fight you on that. There are as many borscht variations as there are beets growing in Dixon's garden! Me? I like my borscht heavy on the beets and dill. This recipe is vegetarian, but you could easily use beef or chicken broth as your base and add any leftover cooked meat you have in the refrigerator, if that's your style. Borscht really is one of those soups where you can do whatever the heck you like. Leave out potatoes and add white beans instead. Don't like cabbage? Don't add cabbage! In the summer, when the beets come with their lovely greens attached, I stir them in at the end, as they add extra nutrition, and I hate throwing away perfectly good greens. But let's face it: borscht isn't borscht without a generous dollop of sour cream. And a good handful of dill. One of the prettiest soups to ever come out of my kitchen, each bowlful is almost a masterpiece.

Warm the oil in a very large soup pot over medium-high heat. Add the onion and carrot. Cook, stirring often, until softened, about 5 minutes. Stir in the beets, cabbage, and garlic. Cook for another 5 minutes. Add the broth, diced tomatoes and their juice, tomato paste, and paprika. Stir well. Cover, bring to a boil, then turn down the heat to medium-low and simmer, covered, until the beets have softened, for about 20 minutes.

Stir in the potatoes and simmer, covered, until all of the vegetables are tender, about 20–25 more minutes. Add the beet greens, as well as the dill, vinegar, honey, salt, and pepper. If the soup is too thick, add more broth or water.

Turn down the heat to low and simmer, covered, until the greens are tender, about 5 minutes. Adjust the seasonings to taste with more salt, pepper, vinegar, honey, etc. Ladle into soup bowls and garnish with a healthy amount of sour cream and dill.

SERVES 8–10

2 Tbsp canola oil

1 large yellow onion, diced

1 large carrot, chopped

4 medium beets, trimmed, scrubbed, and grated

2 cups thinly sliced green or purple cabbage

3 garlic cloves, minced

8 cups low-sodium vegetable broth

1 can (28 oz/798 mL) diced tomatoes

1 can (5½ oz/156 mL) tomato paste

1 Tbsp smoked paprika

2 large Yukon Gold or your favourite waxy white potatoes, chopped (2½ cups)

2 cups chopped beet greens or Swiss chard

½ cup chopped fresh dill, plus more for garnish

¼ cup apple cider vinegar

1 tsp honey

1½ tsp salt

¼ tsp pepper

Sour cream, for garnish

✳ *Seeing as this soup contains potatoes and potatoes don't freeze well, do not freeze this soup. If you think that you won't be able to eat it all up within 5 days, substitute a can (19 oz/540 mL) of white beans, drained and rinsed, for the potatoes. If beans aren't your favourite, add 1 cup of rinsed whole green lentils when you add the broth. The cooking time remains the same. The soup will freeze nicely then!*

Beet and Pomegranate Salad
with Lemon Poppy Seed Dressing

I love serving this salad in the autumn and winter for all of the big feast days like Thanksgiving and Christmas. It's a little sweet, a little savoury, it has plenty of textural contrast, and, oh boy, is it pleasing to the eye. The beets and dressing can be prepared up to three days ahead of time, so there's no stress on the day of feasting. Be sure to use that pretty platter from the china cabinet—the one you never use but always want to. This is a lovely salad to look at, especially when the dressing bleeds into the deep purple of the beets. The poppy seeds and pomegranate arils add a little crunch to satisfy those of us who like texture, and the little sprigs of dill are a tasty finishing touch. This salad proves that beets are good for more than borscht. They too like to get dressed up and show off a little!

Place the beets in a large saucepan and cover with cold water. There should be about 2 inches of water above them. Add a pinch of salt. Cover, bring to a boil over medium-high heat, then turn the heat down to medium-low and simmer, covered, until the beets are tender. This could take anywhere from 45 minutes to 1 hour, depending on the size of your beets. Pierce with a knife to check for doneness.

Drain the beets and let them cool enough so that you can slip the skins off without burning yourself. Trim off and discard the root ends. Let the beets continue to cool.

Meanwhile, whisk together the oil, lemon juice, mayonnaise, yogurt, poppy seeds, mustard, honey, ½ tsp salt, and pepper. Taste and adjust seasonings as necessary.

When the beets are at room temperature, slice them into ¼-inch-thick rounds and arrange on a pretty platter. Drizzle the dressing over top. Add the pomegranate arils and fresh dill sprigs. Serve immediately.

SERVES 6–8

2½ lb medium red beets, scrubbed (about 6–8 beets)

½ tsp, plus a pinch of salt

2 Tbsp canola oil

2 Tbsp fresh lemon juice

2 Tbsp mayonnaise

1 Tbsp plain Greek yogurt

1 Tbsp poppy seeds

2 tsp Dijon mustard

1 tsp honey

¼ tsp pepper

½ cup pomegranate arils

2 Tbsp fresh dill sprigs, for garnish

✳ *This salad tastes best when served at room temperature. The beets can be cooked and sliced ahead of time. Just let them come to room temperature before plating the salad.*

✳ *For added visual interest, use a combination of golden and red beets.*

Barley Risotto with Beets and Ricotta

Barley is a grain that deserves way more attention. Hearty and wholesome, it's high in nutrients such as fibre, something that all of us need more of in our diets. I'm almost 50. These are the things I think about! Barley also has a lovely chewiness that lends itself well to traditional rice dishes such as risotto. Don't worry, butter and wine are still key players, but I changed the game with a burst of colour from beet purée. It's so pretty! And red! Yes, the risotto is fine on its own, with a lovely, chewy texture, and it's all aromatic with the fresh thyme, and it's very, very fancy because it's, well, red. But when you get a bite of the ricotta with the beet-barley combo, there may be a smacking of lips. Partner this risotto with any roasted meat for one dandy of a meal.

Place the broth in a medium saucepan over medium-high heat. Cover and bring to a boil. Turn down the heat to low and keep warm.

Melt 2 Tbsp of the butter in a large saucepan over medium heat. Add the garlic and shallot. Cook until fragrant, about 1 minute. Add the barley and stir until glossy, another minute or so. Add the wine and stir constantly until the barley has absorbed it, about 2–3 minutes.

Add ½ cup of the warm broth. Stir often until the barley has absorbed most of the liquid. Continue adding the broth ½ cup at a time and stirring until the barley is soft yet tender to the bite (softer than al dente). Start testing for doneness once you've added 4 cups of the broth and then add more as required. (If it's still not ready after you've added 5 cups of broth, add a splash or two of warm water.) Turn the heat down to medium-low, so the risotto is just simmering.

Stir in the beet purée and thyme. Turn down the heat to low. Stir in the remaining 2 Tbsp butter and season to taste with salt and pepper. The entire stirring and cooking process will take about 40–45 minutes. The risotto should be slightly saucy but not soupy. Serve immediately, with a generous dollop of ricotta over each serving.

SERVES 4–6

4–5 cups low-sodium chicken or vegetable broth, divided

4 Tbsp butter, divided

2 garlic cloves, minced

1 shallot, diced

1 cup pearl barley, rinsed

¾ cup white wine

¾ cup beet purée (see note)

1 tsp chopped fresh thyme leaves

Salt and pepper

½ cup ricotta (or more!)

✳ *You can use canned beets for the purée, or you can boil/roast 2 medium beets (see page 32 for a rough guide to roasting them) until very tender. Peel when cool, place in a food processor with about 2–3 Tbsp of water, and process until very smooth and thick but not runny. You may need to add more water when puréeing.*

Oh, broccoli. How you love to go from very good to very bad in just the shortest amount of time. I suspect many of us can recall with horror the boiled-too-long-broccoli of our childhood. The colour and texture had vanished out of the vegetable, transforming it into khaki moosh. This sad excuse for broccoli was pushed around from one corner of the plate to the next. And no wonder. There's nothing exciting about broccoli when it's boiled to death. That is broccoli done wrong. But broccoli done right can be a revelation. You know about the wonders of roasted broccoli, complete with addictive crispy bits, right? Sprinkle some super-fragrant spices such as coriander, cumin, or chili powder over broccoli florets and toss them in some canola or olive oil. Spread on a baking sheet and roast at 425°F until the edges start to get crispy, about 20 minutes, shaking the pan once or twice. Squeeze some lemon juice over top, toss around a little, and it's good to go. Or add broccoli florets to a screaming-hot, oiled skillet and cook them for a few minutes in your favourite stir-fry sauce. Be sure to leave some crunch intact. The only time I enjoy boiled broccoli is when it's been simmered in a soup and partnered with plenty of cheddar cheese and cream: cozy comfort in a bowl, saltines on the side. Raw is not my first choice when it comes to ways of consuming this cruciferous vegetable, though I'm more likely to undertake the task if there is a creamy dip involved.

Dixon Says: When I was growing up on the farm, we would harvest the broccoli heads and then let the plant flower and go to seed before it got roto-tilled. Nowadays, we grow varieties that continue producing additional, though smaller, florets of broccoli, allowing multiple cuttings. We start cutting the broccoli from mid- to late July, and it's usually finished producing by early September. I remember, as a little kid, finding the flowering broccoli plants and their attending swarms of bees intensely fascinating. Being the brilliant four-year-old that I was, I found it immensely fun to catch the bees. I did this by cupping my hands and quickly clapping them together above the broccoli flowers, inevitably catching a bee or two. It was really neat to feel a bee buzzing around inside my hands before I let it go!

You can see where this is going, I'm sure. Eventually, one of the bees didn't take kindly to being played with and stung my hand. I ran back to the house, crying. My mom wasn't terribly impressed with me, but we got a dishpan and some warm water and went out to the garden. She scooped some soil into the water and made a muddy paste and told me to put my hand in it. I don't know if it was magic or an old wives' thing or just something to distract me, but it did help soothe the sting! After a while, I brushed the dried mud off my hands and went on my merry way again. I've never tried to catch a bee since. This is perhaps more a story about bees rather than broccoli, but whenever I think of broccoli—or bees—I remember that sunny day in the garden.

BROCCOLI

Tempura Broccoli and Friends

Whenever I think of tempura, I think of a romantic evening Dixon and I enjoyed together in Montreal. It was August 2016, just a few months into our relationship, and our love was all fresh and new. I'd won a trip to this beautiful city (that's a fun story for another time), and one of the perks was staying a few nights in the absolutely stunning Hôtel Place d'Armes. It was across the street from the Notre Dame Basilica, right in the heart of Old Montreal, so we're talking fancy. There was a Japanese restaurant connected to the hotel, and on our first night there, we devoured most of the menu, including all things tempura, which happens to be one of my favourite things to eat. We still talk about that magical night, often as we're eating homemade tempura. There are some rules to follow when you're making your own, so read the recipe thoroughly—twice—before you start frying.

Line a rimmed baking sheet with paper towel.

Prepare the vegetables: Cut the broccoli into small-medium florets, leaving lots of stem attached. Scrub the sweet potato and cut it into ⅛-inch-thick slices. Cut the zucchini on the bias into ¼-inch-thick slices. Cut the eggplant into ¼-inch-thick rounds. Cut the onion into wedges. Be sure all of the vegetables are patted dry completely.

Prepare the dipping sauce: In a small bowl, whisk together all of the dipping sauce ingredients. Taste and adjust the seasonings if necessary.

Warm the oil in a Dutch oven or deep-sided pot over medium-high heat until the temperature reaches 360°F. Try to maintain this temperature. Dip your thermometer into the oil now and then to check it.

While the oil is warming, prepare the batter: Mix the batter right before you want to deep-fry. I like to have my dry ingredients ready in a mixing bowl and when the oil is at the right temperature, I whisk in the sparkling water. Whisk until the batter is smooth and runny, but some lumps are okay. You don't want to overmix. The batter should be as cold as possible. I add a few ice cubes to keep it cold and to thin it out, if need be.

When the oil is hot, quickly dip the vegetables in the batter, shake off the excess, then using your hands, carefully sink five to six pieces into the hot oil. Don't overcrowd the pan. Cook them, turning frequently, until they're golden brown, about 2–3 minutes. The harder vegetables take about 3 minutes, so add them first; the softer vegetables need only 2 minutes. Using a slotted spoon, remove the vegetables from the oil and drain them on the prepared baking sheet. Sprinkle generously with flaky salt. Repeat with the remaining vegetables and batter.

Serve immediately with the dipping sauce. If you need to warm the tempura before serving (the first pieces may have cooled down), simply pop them in a 350°F oven for 3 minutes.

✳ *Other vegetables that work well here are asparagus spears, cauliflower florets, whole mushrooms, or even slices of squash (not spaghetti squash, though!).*

SERVES 4-6

Vegetables

1½ lb assorted vegetables, such as broccoli, sweet potato, zucchini, eggplant, onion

Dipping Sauce

¼ cup tamari (or reduced-sodium soy sauce)

¼ cup rice vinegar

1 Tbsp granulated sugar

2 tsp fresh lime juice

1 tsp finely chopped fresh ginger

1–2 tsp Sriracha (or chili garlic sauce)

1 Tbsp finely chopped cilantro

Batter

4–5 cups canola oil, for deep frying

½ cup all-purpose flour

½ cup cornstarch

½ tsp baking powder

½ tsp salt

¾ cup ice-cold sparkling water, such as Perrier

A few ice cubes

Flaky salt, for sprinkling

Mediterranean Flaxseed Flatbread with Broccoli

I've been asked numerous times to create a gluten-free pizza or flatbread crust, and here it is! Keeping things both simple and nutritious was my key aim, so I reached for the jar of flaxseed that I always have sitting on the kitchen shelf. The rest of the crust ingredients are Parmesan cheese, eggs, and some seasonings. That's it! This is a great crust that belongs more to Crackerland than Breadland, and, yes, it has a fabulous amount of fibre. There's unarguably a touch of healthful goodness to this flatbread, but there's still plenty of richness, thanks to the melty cheese. I love how the Mediterranean flavours embrace the roasted broccoli, but feel free to play around with whatever toppings you like. I'm also a huge fan of crumbled chorizo, chopped pineapple, and thin slices of jalapeño pepper. Instead of feta, I sometimes add torn bocconcini, and it's so good! There really are endless possibilities for this flatbread (see the notes).

Preheat the oven to 375°F.

Prepare the dough: In a large bowl, stir together the flaxseed, Parmesan, oregano, garlic powder, pepper, salt, and a pinch of red pepper flakes. Stir in the eggs and mix well. Let the dough rest, uncovered, at room temperature for 10 minutes.

Grease a rimmed baking sheet with the oil and sprinkle on the cornmeal. Place the flax dough in the centre and press it into a 9- × 11-inch oval. The dough will be sticky, so use some oil from the sun-dried tomato jar to grease your hands as you shape and pat it into an oval. Bake on the lower rack of the oven for 8 minutes.

Remove the crust from the oven. Increase the heat to 400°F.

Add the toppings: Spread the pizza sauce on the crust. Sprinkle on the mozzarella, and top with the broccoli, sun-dried tomatoes, red onion, olives, and feta, in that order. Bake on the top rack until the cheese is lightly browned and the broccoli is slightly charred, about 15–20 minutes.

Remove the flatbread from the oven and let cool in the pan for 5 minutes before serving. Serves 2–3 as a main with a side salad or 4–6 as an appetizer.

* Purchase flaxseed already ground, or grind your own in a coffee grinder.

* To make a quick pizza sauce, purée ½ cup canned diced or whole tomatoes, without their juice, and season with ¼ tsp garlic powder, ¼ tsp oregano, and a pinch each of salt, pepper, and sugar. Adjust seasonings to your taste.

* Use whatever toppings you like for this flatbread, but don't add more than 1½ cups of raw vegetables. If you're using softer veg such as zucchini or mushrooms, sauté them first so they don't release too much liquid while on the pizza. Thin slices of red pepper, very small cauliflower florets, cherry tomato halves, and shaved asparagus can go on the flatbread as is.

SERVES 4–6

Flatbread Dough

1 cup ground flaxseed

½ cup grated Parmesan cheese

1 tsp dried oregano

1 tsp garlic powder

¼ tsp pepper

⅛ tsp salt

Red pepper flakes

2 large eggs, lightly beaten

1 Tbsp canola oil

1 Tbsp cornmeal

Toppings

½ cup pizza sauce or marinara sauce

½ cup shredded mozzarella

1½ cups chopped (no bigger than 1-inch pieces) broccoli

¼ cup oil-packed sun-dried tomatoes, sliced

¼ cup thinly sliced red onion

¼ cup sliced Kalamata olives

½ cup crumbled feta cheese

Charred Broccoli with Coconut Milk and Peanuts

I don't think I'd ever eaten a whole pound of broccoli by myself in ONE DAY until I developed this recipe. As soon as it was all charred and the sweet/sour/spicy coconut milk mixture had glazed the florets, my fingers were in the pan, tipping the blackened broccoli into my mouth. What a revelation! So much flavour in each bite! And then I made it look all pretty on a platter, my willpower in full force as I tried not to eat it all at once after the photograph was taken. I failed. With a pot of rice to soak up the sauce, I was in heaven. I love it when vegetables surprise me, and this recipe did just that.

In a small bowl, whisk together the coconut milk, lime juice, fish sauce, honey, Sriracha, ginger, and salt.

Warm the oil in a 12-inch cast-iron skillet over high heat. When it's smoking hot, add the broccoli in a single layer as much as possible. Let the broccoli cook undisturbed until the bottom is nicely charred, about 2–3 minutes. Now give it a stir, trying to have the non-charred side facing down as much as possible, and cook for 2 more minutes, without stirring.

Turn off the heat, pour in the coconut milk mixture, and stir to evenly coat. The sauce will thicken up as soon as it hits the heat. Once all of the broccoli is glazed, transfer it and any remaining sauce to a serving dish and scatter the peanuts, green onions, and red pepper, if using, over top. Serve immediately.

SERVES 4

⅓ cup full-fat coconut milk

3 Tbsp fresh lime juice (from about 2 limes)

1½ tsp fish sauce

1½ tsp honey

1½ tsp Sriracha

1½ tsp finely minced fresh ginger

½ tsp salt

2 Tbsp canola oil

1 lb broccoli (1 medium head), cut into large florets, using as much stem as possible

2 Tbsp canola oil

¼ cup roughly chopped roasted and salted peanuts

1 Tbsp thinly sliced green onions

1 red chili pepper, such as serrano, thinly sliced (optional)

❋ *If you're serving this to kids, perhaps dial back on the heat by skipping the chili pepper and decreasing the amount of Sriracha.*

❋ *I know you guys hate opening cans of coconut milk and not using the whole amount. I've got you covered! Use the rest of the coconut milk in the Coconut Rice with Shrimp and Peas on page 187, the Curried Butternut Squash Soup with Coconut Milk on page 223, or the Lentil and Chickpea Curry with Cauliflower and Coconut Milk on page 95. You can also freeze the coconut milk in ⅓-cup amounts for future charred broccoli consumption.*

When it comes to Brussels sprouts, most people are either on Team Love or Team Hate. If you find yourself on the latter, chances are you ate them supremely overcooked until they were mushy and grey. Not a good look on any vegetable, especially one that can be a little, um, pungent. In fact, a few years ago I was wandering through Pike Place Market in Seattle—one of the most beautiful markets I've ever been to—and a vendor selling vegetables had a sign saying "Little Green Balls of Death" right below the Brussels sprouts. I'm guessing they aren't a fan! But, if handled correctly and creatively, the Brussels sprout can elevate any dish and, dare I say, become a vegetable you adore.

Brussels sprouts look a bit like baby cabbages. That's because they're both part of the brassica family. With cabbages, we eat the head that grows out of the ground. Brussels sprouts, on the other hand, are buds that grow along the length of a thick, fibrous stalk. But why do they smell so bad? Actually, they only get really stinky when they're overcooked—especially when boiled—and release *glucosinolate sinigrin*, an organic compound that contains sulphur but also happens to be responsible for some of the Brussels' super-nutritional characteristics. In fact, Brussels sprouts are an excellent source of a whole range of nutritional goodies, so snap 'em up! Buy ones with dense, firm bright green heads. Give the wilted, tired-looking sprouts a pass and be sure to remove and discard any damaged or yellowed leaves before cooking.

So, how to cook Brussels sprouts so they become a fan favourite in your house? Roasted, they become almost sweet and nutty, and will up your side-dish game—especially if you toss them in a little bacon fat before they hit the oven. Bacon and Brussels sprouts are very good pals. That combo will turn even the biggest non-believers into fans of the little cabbage look-alikes. If raw is more your style, think about shaving them into a salad with a grainy mustard dressing, crumbled blue cheese, and (wait for it) bacon. I also like to thinly slice the sprouts, toss them in oil, and roast until the edges are crispy. Put them in a bowl with toasted walnuts, grated Parmesan, and a squeeze of lemon, and I'll surely eat the whole darn thing just like that.

Dixon Says: Brussels sprouts aren't my favourite. Sure, I'll eat them because they're chock-full of good-for-you stuff like fibre and vitamins C and K, but before Renée, I hardly ate them at all. When I was little, I thought they were like tiny baby cabbages, which they are in a way, so they were fun, if not particularly to my taste. Now, though, as Renée prepares them with her special touch, I eat as much as I can. We don't grow Brussels sprouts because like other brassicas, they're prone to infestation from cabbage worms and root maggots, and, being so tiny, it doesn't take much to render them unsellable. Other vendors at the market have better luck with them. Typical peak season here in Saskatchewan is late August and September.

BRUSSELS

SPROUTS

Skillet Brussels Sprouts and Gnocchi with Bacon

As far as I'm concerned, this is a skillet of happiness. It starts off with bacon, followed by the sizzling symphony of onion and garlic—one of the best smells ever. When the Brussels sprouts are added to the pan, they develop lovely brown bits and heaps of flavour. Packaged gnocchi is admittedly a cheat, but a forgivable one in my opinion. It simmers in chicken broth until it's pillowy soft and a splash of cream brings everything together. I won't lie. I've eaten half the skillet waiting for Dixon to arrive for supper. And then he eats the other half while I sit across from him, sipping wine and smiling like someone who's just won the lottery. Brussels sprouts haters take note: Dixon would not go near them until he tried this dish. I think the bacon helped!

In a large skillet over medium-high heat, cook the bacon until almost crispy. Using tongs, place it on a paper towel-lined plate. When it has cooled, chop it up. You should have about 2 Tbsp of bacon fat in the skillet. If you don't, add enough canola oil to make up the difference. Stir the onion into the hot bacon fat and cook until it's soft, a few minutes or so. Stir in the garlic, cook for 30 seconds, then stir in the Brussels sprouts, the salt, and a pinch of red pepper flakes. Cook over medium heat, stirring often, until the sprouts have some nice brown bits, about 8 minutes.

Stir in the gnocchi and then the broth. Increase the heat to medium-high and bring to a boil. As soon as it reaches a boil, turn down the heat to medium-low and simmer, stirring often, until the gnocchi are cooked through and most of the liquid has reduced, about 5–7 minutes.

Turn down the heat to low and stir in the cream, Parmesan cheese, chopped bacon, and fresh thyme leaves, in that order. Cook for a couple of minutes just to bring everything together. Season to taste with more salt and some pepper. Serve with more grated Parmesan on top.

SERVES 4

5 slices thick-cut bacon

1 Tbsp canola oil (optional)

½ cup diced yellow onion

2 garlic cloves, minced

2 cups trimmed, halved Brussels sprouts

½ tsp salt

Red pepper flakes

1 package (1 lb/500 g) gnocchi

1¾ cups low-sodium chicken broth

¼ cup whipping (35%) cream

½ cup grated Parmesan cheese, plus more for garnish

1 tsp chopped fresh thyme leaves

Pepper

✳ *If bacon isn't your thing (what?), just sauté the onion in 2 Tbsp canola oil and proceed with the recipe.*

Shaved Brussels Sprouts Salad with Crispy Chickpeas

As much as I adore a crispy-edged Brussels sprout, there is something quite lovely about this ballsy brassica when it's raw and very thinly sliced. How you get those slices so thin is up to you. I get the shivers every time I look at a mandolin, so I'm on Team Chef's Knife. The shaved Brussels sprouts get loved up real good with a lemony tahini dressing, while the pretty pomegranate arils bring not only some colour but also their trademark tangy sweetness. The roasted chickpeas add plenty of crunch (because texture!), and they're so good you may want to make a double batch just to have some on hand for healthy snacking. There's definitely a Middle Eastern vibe happening here, and I'm super into it. Given the festive visual appeal of this salad, it's a natural fit for holiday feasts, where it can get cozy with some sliced turkey or tofurkey. Whatever floats your (gravy) boat.

Preheat the oven to 375°F. Line a rimmed baking sheet with parchment paper.

Prepare the salad: In a medium bowl, stir together the chickpeas, oil, 1 tsp of the za'atar, the smoked paprika, garlic powder, salt, and pepper. Spread the chickpeas onto the baking sheet in an even layer. Roast for about 35 minutes, stirring occasionally. They should be crispy, but not hard as rocks. Let cool completely before adding to the salad.

Place the shaved Brussels sprouts in a large bowl.

Prepare the dressing: Whisk together the dressing ingredients with 1½ Tbsp water in a medium bowl. Adjust the seasoning with more maple syrup and salt, if necessary. Pour the dressing over the sprouts and sprinkle on the remaining 1 tsp of za'atar. Use your hands to toss everything together very well. Be sure that all of the sprouts are evenly coated with the dressing.

Stir in the pomegranate arils and roasted chickpeas. Season to taste with more salt and pepper. Serve immediately.

SERVES 6

Salad

1 can (19 oz/540 mL) chickpeas, drained, rinsed, and patted dry

1½ Tbsp canola oil

2 tsp za'atar, divided

½ tsp smoked paprika

½ tsp garlic powder

½ tsp salt

¼ tsp pepper

1 lb Brussels sprouts, bottoms trimmed, outer leaves removed, very thinly sliced

Dressing

¼ cup fresh lemon juice (from about 2 lemons)

2½ Tbsp tahini

1 Tbsp canola oil

2 tsp pure maple syrup

½ tsp salt

¼ tsp pepper

For Garnish

⅔ cup pomegranate arils

✳ *You'll find za'atar in the international foods aisle of the supermarket. Za'atar is the name of a wild herb and also the name of a spice mixture that can include that herb along with sumac, sesame seeds, thyme, salt, and other spices. The za'atar blends can vary by origin and by the person who is mixing the blend. I like to sprinkle it on everything from eggs to roasted potatoes to salads.*

Brussels Sprouts Pizza with Prosciutto and Bocconcini

The days of me greeting the pizza delivery dude in my pajamas are probably long gone, thanks to the fact that I'm pretty much obsessed with always having pizza dough on hand. And if I feel like getting in an arm workout, I knead it by hand instead of entrusting it to my stand mixer. Brussels sprouts may be an unusual pizza topping, but don't be scared. You might just want to eat them out of the bowl as is! But wait! There's plenty of cheese, plus prosciutto, and a honey drizzle that brings some sweet heat. If you don't want to make your own pizza dough, purchase 1 lb of dough from the deli, or, if you really want to cheat, spread the toppings on naan. It's all good! It's pizza!

To prepare the dough by hand: Stir together the water, yeast, and sugar in a large bowl. It should bubble and froth after about 5 minutes. (If it doesn't, you'll need to open a new package of yeast and start again.) Add 2½ cups of flour, the salt, and then the oil and stir until the dough comes together. On a lightly floured surface, knead the dough until it's elastic, about 8 minutes. Add a bit more flour if it's too sticky.

To prepare the dough in a stand mixer: Using a spoon, mix together the water, yeast, and sugar in the bowl of a stand mixer. It should bubble and froth after about 5 minutes. (If it doesn't, you'll need to open a new package of yeast and start again.) Attach the dough hook and add 2½ cups of flour, the salt, and then the oil and beat the dough on medium speed until it's elastic, about 5–6 minutes. Add a bit more flour if it's too sticky.

When the dough is ready, place it in a large greased bowl, being sure to turn it over a few times so it's evenly greased. Cover the bowl with plastic wrap or a clean kitchen towel and let it rest in a warm, draft-free place for about 1 hour or until doubled in size.

Punch the dough down, cover it again, and let it rest for 5 minutes. Divide it in half and place one half of the dough in a resealable plastic bag for future pizza use. It can be refrigerated for up to 4 days or frozen for up to 1 month. You'll use the other half of the dough for the following pizza recipe. (This recipe makes enough dough for two 12-inch pizzas.)

To prepare the toppings: In a 12-inch skillet, warm the canola oil over medium-high heat. Stir in the onion and cook for a few minutes. Stir in the Brussels sprouts and cook until softened and some of the edges are beginning to caramelize, about 7–8 minutes. Stir in the garlic and cook for another minute. Season with the salt and pepper. Spoon the mixture into a shallow bowl and stir in the lemon juice. Let cool to room temperature.

(continued on page 57)

MAKES 6 SLICES

Simple Pizza Dough

1 cup warm water (110°-120°F)

1 package (2¼ tsp) active dry yeast

1 tsp granulated sugar

2½–3 cups all-purpose flour, plus more for kneading

1 tsp salt

1 Tbsp extra-virgin olive oil, plus more for greasing bowl

Toppings and Assembly

2 Tbsp canola oil

1 small onion, diced

10 oz Brussels sprouts, stem removed and very thinly sliced (about 2½ cups)

2 garlic cloves, minced

¼ tsp salt

¼ tsp pepper

1 Tbsp fresh lemon juice

4 Tbsp extra-virgin olive oil, divided

1 portion of Simple Pizza Dough (or 1 lb of store-bought pizza dough)

1 Tbsp sesame seeds (optional)

2 cups shredded mozzarella

1 container (4 oz/125 g) baby bocconcini cheese

4 slices prosciutto, chopped

2 tsp honey

2 tsp water

Red pepper flakes

(continued from page 55)

Preheat the oven to 450°F.

Grease a 12-inch pizza pan with 2 Tbsp of the olive oil. On a lightly floured surface, roll the pizza dough into a 12-inch circle and then stretch it into the prepared pan. Brush the crust with the remaining 2 Tbsp olive oil. Scatter the sesame seeds (if using) around the edge of the pizza crust. You want to create a 1-inch border. Scatter the mozzarella all over the crust, avoiding the border. Top with the Brussels sprouts, then the bocconcini cheese and prosciutto.

Place the pan on the bottom rack of the oven and bake for 10 minutes. Transfer to the top rack and bake for another 10 minutes, or until the cheese is melted and browned and the crust is golden brown. Stir together the honey, water, and a pinch of chili flakes in a small bowl. Brush this over the hot crust and dab any leftover honey mixture on top of the cheese. Let the pizza rest for about 5 minutes before removing it from the pan to slice and serve.

✳ *If you find your oven runs a little on the hotter side, turn down the temperature to 425°F and check to see if the pizza is done around the 15-minute mark.*

When I'm out for a wander in Dixon's vegetable garden in the late summer, I spend a great deal of time admiring the cabbages. I love their perfectly formed round heads, and how the outer leaves unfurl, not unlike a Georgia O'Keeffe painting. The colours are extraordinary: deep sea greens crashing into misty blues; majestic purples merging with moody maroon. It doesn't come as too much of a surprise to me that the German origin of my surname translates into "Cabbage Farmer." Seeing as I have a head of cabbage in my refrigerator more often than not, I come by my roots honestly.

I'm a firm believer that cabbage doesn't get enough love. It's super low-cal—just 25 calories per 4 ounces—rich in antioxidants and Vitamins C, B, and K, and high in fibre, which is a good thing when it comes to digestion, and it helps keep inflammation in check. Cabbage is also wonderfully affordable, and affordable is what I'm looking for when it comes to my grocery bill. It's a great vegetable to pick up on my weekly shopping trip, as it can last in the refrigerator for up to a couple of months. Unlike with tender greens, there's no pressure to use it up right away.

So, cabbage is pretty much a wonder vegetable, and you can do so much more with it than make cabbage rolls, coleslaw, and sauerkraut. It's terrific in cozy casseroles and stews or simmered in soups alongside sausage and potatoes. When it's raw, it's perfect for adding crunch to salads and tacos. Braised cabbage is also delicious, especially if red wine and bacon are involved. But I particularly adore cabbage when it's hit with some intense heat. You can slice it into wedges, drizzle it with a little olive oil, add a smattering of salt and pepper, and roast it in a 400°F oven until it's browned at the edges and tender in the middle, about 30 minutes. Cabbage emits a lovely sweetness when it's cooked at high heat, and when those edges become caramelized, this humble brassica, so often overlooked in the produce department, is elevated into the top tier of vegetable deliciousness.

Dixon Says: Cabbages, like other cruciferous vegetables, aren't particularly difficult to grow, but they do take some time and need care and attention over the growing season. We start the seedlings in the greenhouse to get them going in March or early April and transplant them in the garden once the risk of frost is gone, around early June. They're favourites of insects, though, particularly root maggots and cabbage butterflies, so it's a good idea to protect the young plants with row covers. There's not a lot of difference in growing red or green cabbage—just the colour!

CABBAGE

Mom's Cabbage Rolls

When I was in the planning stages of this book, the first recipe I knew I had to include was my mom's cabbage rolls. Prepared for holidays and Sunday suppers, hers are the best I've ever had, and the ones by which I judge all other cabbage rolls. Mom says the most important thing is to get a round, tight head of good locally grown cabbage. Her trick is to use uncooked rice in the filling, and she pumps up the flavour with herbs (parsley, mint) and spices (allspice, cumin), along with plenty of garlic, like any good cook would. Yes, these take some work, but enlist another set of hands to help, even if it's just to wash the dishes or peel off the cabbage leaves while you roll. I have so many memories connected to the smell of cabbage rolls wafting out of the oven, and, for those alone, I'll treasure this recipe always.

Prepare the sauce: Warm the oil in a medium saucepan over medium-high heat. Add the onion and sauté until translucent, about 5 minutes. Stir in the garlic, bay leaf, and thyme. Cook until the garlic is golden, another 2 minutes or so. Stir in the crushed tomatoes, rinse out the can with about ½ cup water, and add this tomatoey water as well. Turn down the heat to medium-low and stir in the sugar, salt, and pepper. Cover and simmer for 30 minutes, stirring occasionally. Season with more salt and pepper, if needed. Discard the bay leaf. The sauce can be made a few days ahead of time or frozen for up to 2 months.

Prepare the filling: In a large bowl, combine the meat, rice, onion, garlic, herbs, and spices, and mix well with your hands.

Prepare the cabbage rolls: Remove the core from the cabbage, leaving the inside hollow. Heat a very large pot of water to boiling. (You want the pot about half-full.) There needs to be enough room for the cabbage to float. When the water comes to a boil, place the head of cabbage into the pot. Cover with a lid and occasionally stir the cabbage so it steams evenly. After a few minutes, turn down the heat to medium, so the water continues to simmer. Once the leaves begin to come away from the head (this can take around 7–10 minutes), use tongs to remove the leaves from the water and drain them in a colander. Let each leaf cool a little bit before you work with it. Remember to keep the pot covered and check on the remaining leaves as you make the cabbage rolls so they don't overcook. To be clear, you are assembling the cabbage rolls while the cabbage is cooking. This is why it's a good idea to have someone looking after the cabbage while someone else is assembling the meat filling inside the leaves.

Each cabbage leaf should be about 4 × 6 inches. The outer leaves of the cabbage may be large and you'll have to cut them. Using a sharp knife, remove the centre rib of the cabbage leaf, as it can be tough.

When the cabbage leaves are ready, lay them on a cutting board and place about 2 heaping soup spoons of the meat mixture at the bottom (narrow) edge of the

(continued on page 63)

MAKES 20–25 ROLLS

Tomato Sauce

2 Tbsp extra-virgin olive oil

1 medium yellow onion, diced

1 garlic clove, minced

1 bay leaf

½ tsp dried thyme leaves

1 can (28 oz/796 mL) crushed tomatoes

2 tsp brown sugar

¾ tsp salt

¼ tsp pepper

Filling

1 lb lean ground beef (or pork, or a combination)

¾ cup uncooked long-grain white rice

1 small yellow onion, finely diced

3 garlic cloves, minced

2 Tbsp chopped fresh mint leaves

2 Tbsp chopped fresh parsley leaves

1¾ tsp salt

½ tsp pepper

½ tsp ground cumin

½ tsp ground allspice

(continued from page 61)

cabbage leaf. Roll once, just to encase the filling, then tuck in the sides and continue to roll. Don't roll too tightly, as the cabbage rolls will expand when they cook. There's raw rice inside, remember. The rolls will be about 1½ × 3½ inches once they're rolled up. Place the finished cabbage rolls seam side down in a baking dish just large enough to hold them without crowding. (A 9- × 11-inch baking dish will hold about 15 cabbage rolls, and a 3- × 6-inch baking dish will hold about 6.) Be sure not to pack them in too snugly, as they'll swell as they cook. Continue to stuff and roll the cabbage leaves.

Preheat the oven to 350°F. Pour most of the tomato sauce over the rolls, being sure to cover them evenly. There will be about 1 cup of sauce remaining, which you can use as a base for pizza, etc. Cover the baking dishes tightly with their lids or aluminum foil. Bake the cabbage rolls until the rice and meat are fully cooked, about 1 hour. (They'll look compact when they're done.) Remove from the oven and let stand 10 minutes before serving. The cabbage rolls are best served with sour cream, and you can garnish them with fresh dill sprigs, if you like.

The cabbage rolls freeze very well, making this a great make-ahead recipe for busy weeknights. Simply place the uncooked cabbage rolls (covered in sauce) in disposable aluminum roasting dishes, or whatever you have on hand that's freezer safe. Just be sure the containers are sealed very well so air can't get in. When it comes time to bake the frozen cabbage rolls, thaw them in the refrigerator, then bake as above. If the cabbage rolls are a little frozen when you bake them, add about 10–15 minutes onto the cooking time. This recipe makes about 20–25 cabbage rolls, depending on the size of the leaves. It can be easily doubled.

Cabbage Rolls

1 medium head of green cabbage

Sour cream, for serving

Fresh dill sprigs, for garnish

✱ *Any leftover cooked cabbage can be used in a stir-fry or chopped up for soup. If you can't use it right away, freeze it for future use (see page 17).*

A Tale of Two Cabbage Rolls

Ask around and you'll find almost everyone has thoughts on cabbage rolls. How big they are, what's inside, and how they are cooked varies by nationality. Some like them small, like the size of a pinky, and stuffed with rice only. Some add bacon. Or meat. Others add dill. Some cook them with canned tomato soup; others with a light tomato sauce. It's all relative, but everyone has an opinion, and everyone thinks their cabbage rolls are the best. The one thing everyone agrees upon is that cabbage rolls are delicious. And they are best when served with sour cream.

I grew up eating my mom's German-style cabbage rolls—as big as a pencil case and stuffed with ground meat (usually beef) and rice. Both the meat and the rice are uncooked. How's that for a revelation? The rolls swell when they're baked in a simple tomato sauce and become perfectly compact and delicious bundles of gastronomic joy. The first thing I love about cabbage rolls is the smell that wafts out of the oven as they cook. The sweetness of the cabbage marries with the fat of the meat, while the brightness of the herbs, particularly the mint, makes these meat and rice cabbage parcels anything but ordinary. The smell of cabbage rolls will always remind me of my mom, and

what a damn fine cook she is. How lucky I've been to have a mother who loves food and loves to cook from scratch as much as I do. Her influence on my culinary education has been immeasurable, and for that, I'm eternally grateful.

When Mom is rolling up the cylinders of cabbage goodness, I look at her hands and see my hands. Both pairs are rather large, with trimmed, unpainted nails. Our fingers are long and wide, the palms creased with lines that tell stories and hold secrets. These hands have had to clasp on tight, with all their might, and they've also known when to open up and let go. These hands are not without scars, but both sets have long, strong lifelines, and for that I am glad. When I look at my mom's hands, I see hard work. And sacrifice. I see the hands of a woman who lost both her mother and her husband too soon. I see the hands of a woman who loves to dig in the dirt and sow seeds, knowing that planting a garden is all about hope and better things to come. Mom's hands are the first hands that held me tight, that wiped away my tears, that showed me how to stir a cake batter, and how to shell peas. I love my mom's hands. I especially love them when they're making cabbage rolls.

When I moved away from home for the first time, I missed my mom so very much. Our weekly long-distance phone calls were largely about food, and whenever she told me they'd had cabbage rolls for supper that night, I'd let out a deep, heavy sigh. I would have given anything to be around that table, sliding my knife into stuffed cabbage leaves. Considering that I was halfway across the country, I couldn't just pop home to Saskatoon for Sunday dinner then scoot back to Montreal for school the next day. If only there were magical time/space transportation devices invented for homesick daughters who missed their mothers. Craving cabbage rolls like crazy, I had to come up with my own version of Mom's recipe, though in a much less labour-intensive way. Twenty-year-old Renée was not into boiling cabbage, let alone stuffing it with meat and rice. That took too much time! And it was too much work! What I could do was chop some cabbage and layer all of the other ingredients in a casserole dish, throw it in the oven, and come back a couple of hours later, and it would be ready. My apartment smelled like my faraway home, and that was exactly what I was looking for. This simple, lazy cabbage rolls casserole has become my own tradition, and, while it lacks the visual appeal of the stuffed cabbage rolls, the taste is right up there with my mom's. Both ways of amalgamating the meat, rice, cabbage, and tomato sauce are delicious. And so are the memories that go with them.

I LOOK AT HER HANDS AND SEE MY HANDS. BOTH PAIRS ARE RATHER LARGE, WITH TRIMMED, UNPAINTED NAILS. OUR FINGERS ARE LONG AND WIDE, THE PALMS CREASED WITH LINES THAT TELL STORIES AND HOLD SECRETS. THESE HANDS HAVE HAD TO CLASP ON TIGHT, WITH ALL THEIR MIGHT, AND THEY'VE ALSO KNOWN WHEN TO OPEN UP AND LET GO.

Cabbage Rolls Casserole

I've been making this delicious deconstructed cabbage rolls casserole for years and years. When the craving for cabbage rolls hits you hard (all my German/Russian/Ukrainian/Polish peeps know what I'm talking about), but you don't have a mama near you to make them, or you don't have the time to make them yourself, this casserole is the next best thing. All of the traditional flavours are here but with just the fraction of the work involved. Who doesn't love the sound of that? Just slide the dish in the oven, let it bake for 2 hours (don't stir!), and before you know it, you're tucking into a comfy feast of meat, cabbage, rice, and tomato sauce. It's peasant food, for sure, and I make absolutely no apologies for that. My German/Russian soul does a little dance every time I take a bite.

In a large bowl, mix together the beef, rice, onion, garlic, ¾ tsp of the salt, and ¼ tsp of the pepper.

In a medium bowl, stir together the crushed tomatoes, vinegar, sugar, mustard, the remaining ½ tsp of salt, and the remaining ¼ tsp of pepper. Rinse out the tomato can with about ¾ cup water and add this tomatoey water as well.

Layer one-third of the cabbage in the bottom of a 3-quart casserole dish, or something of a similar size. I use my 12-inch deep-dish cast-iron braiser. Arrange half of the beef mixture on top. Cover with half of the remaining cabbage, then top with remaining beef, followed by the remaining cabbage. Pour the tomato sauce over top, but do not stir. Cover with a tight-fitting lid or aluminum foil and let sit at room temperature for 20 minutes.

Preheat the oven to 325°F. Bake the casserole for 2 hours without stirring. Let stand 5 minutes before serving. Sprinkle with parsley and serve with plenty of sour cream.

SERVES 4–6

1 lb lean ground beef

¾ cup uncooked long-grain white rice

1 large yellow onion, diced

3 garlic cloves, minced

1¼ tsp salt, divided

½ tsp pepper, divided

1 can (28 oz/796 mL) crushed tomatoes

¼ cup apple cider vinegar

2 Tbsp packed brown sugar

2 tsp dry mustard powder

8 cups chopped green cabbage (about ½ head)

2 Tbsp chopped parsley (flat-leaf or curly), for garnish

Sour cream, for serving

✱ *I like to use basmati rice in this casserole—it cooks up nice and fluffy. Brown rice may need a longer cooking time.*

Caramelized Cabbage Wedges
with Tomato Miso Butter

This side dish will make you think twice about cabbage. After you try this recipe, you'll want to serve it to your favourite people, just so you can show off a little. Dixon was like, "This is cabbage? It's so good!" The secret is heat. Searing the cabbage in an incredibly hot pan gives it a smoky depth and teases out the sweetness of the leaves. The tomato miso butter enhances the flavour of the vegetable even more. Because the cabbage needs to be basted with the miso concoction, this is not a hands-off recipe, but it's so worth the effort. Once fully caramelized, the cabbage is so soft, so ethereal, a knife slides through it like butter. A squeeze of lime juice at the end makes all of the flavours burst to life. One pound of cabbage is a very small head, which can be difficult to find. You may want to purchase a 2-lb head and just use half of it for this recipe. Or get two skillets into action and double the miso butter. The more the merrier when it comes to this way of cooking cabbage, if you ask me.

SERVES 4

Cabbage

1 lb cabbage

Miso Butter

2 Tbsp butter, softened

1½ Tbsp light miso paste

1 Tbsp tomato paste

1 tsp ground cumin

¼ tsp red pepper flakes

2–3 Tbsp canola oil, divided

1 lime

Flaky salt

Preheat the oven to 400°F.

Cut the cabbage into four wedges, being careful to leave the core intact in each wedge. The wedges should be about 2½–3 inches thick.

In a small bowl, stir together the butter, miso paste, tomato paste, cumin, and red pepper flakes.

Place a 12-inch ovenproof skillet over high heat and pour in 2 Tbsp of the canola oil. When the oil is hot, place the cabbage wedges in the pan cut side down. Don't overcrowd the pan. Leave the cabbage wedges in the pan without turning until the bottom sides are charred and lightly blackened, about 2–3 minutes. If the cabbage has absorbed most of the oil, pour in the remaining 1 Tbsp oil.

Flip the cabbage wedges over onto their other cut side and spread the miso butter on the caramelized sides, dividing it evenly. Cook for another 2–3 minutes, so the other side of the cabbage can get caramelized on the bottom, too.

When both cut sides are seared, place the skillet in the oven and roast the cabbage for 20 minutes, basting the wedges with the melted tomato miso butter every 5 minutes. I just tilt the skillet and spoon some of the melted goodness over each wedge. Carefully flip the wedges over onto their other cut side at the 10-minute mark. After 20 minutes in total, the cabbage should be very tender and deeply caramelized.

Squeeze the lime juice over the wedges and sprinkle with flaky salt.

Cabbage and Pork Egg Rolls

Around the turn of the century (how fun to say that—I feel like I should be wearing petticoats or something), my mom started making egg rolls. She likely found the recipe in a newspaper or magazine article (she can't remember which one) and thought she would try it out. Since then, these egg rolls have made an appearance each Christmas and have become something I look forward to eating every year. Sitting around the glowing tree, nibbling on these deep-fried delights, is one of my favourite holiday traditions. Once the filling is prepped, be sure to let it cool down completely before assembling the egg rolls. And it may take a little bit of effort to get the rolls right, but this is one of those recipes where practice will make perfect. It's tempting to overfill, but you'll have greater success if the rolls aren't overstuffed. This is a team event, so buddy up and have someone roll while someone else fries. Those who cook also get the first taste—and it's a good one!

MAKES 28–30 ROLLS

2 Tbsp canola oil

1 lb ground pork

3 garlic cloves, minced

1 Tbsp minced fresh ginger

4 cups very thinly sliced green cabbage

1 cup grated carrot

1 package (10 oz/300 g) fresh bean sprouts, rinsed well and thoroughly dried

1 tsp salt

¼ tsp pepper

Red pepper flakes

2 packages egg roll wrappers (found in the produce department)

¼ cup milk

Canola oil, for deep-frying, about 6 cups

Sweet chili sauce, for serving

Warm the 2 Tbsp of oil in a large skillet over medium-high heat. Add the pork, garlic, and ginger. Brown the pork for about 5 minutes, breaking the meat up with the back of a wooden spoon. Stir in the cabbage and carrot. Cook just until the cabbage begins to wilt, 2 minutes, then stir in the bean sprouts. Season with the salt, pepper, and a pinch of red pepper flakes. Cook until the vegetables have softened a little but are still crunchy, about 3 more minutes. Adjust the seasonings to taste. Let cool completely before assembling the egg rolls. I like to spread the filling out on a baking sheet so it cools quickly. You can also pop the filling into the refrigerator to get things moving along faster. It can be made up to 2 days ahead, but be sure to drain off any excess juices that may have accumulated before using.

To assemble the egg rolls, brush the edges of a wrapper with milk. Have the wrapper placed so that one of the points is facing you (like a diamond shape). Place 2 heaping soup spoons of filling in the centre of the wrapper. Fold the sides over the edge of the filling so that it's nice and snug. Now roll it up tightly, starting with the point closest to you. Fold completely over the filling. Roll and seal by brushing milk onto the underside of the edge. Be sure to wrap the egg rolls tightly to prevent splatters when frying. Place the finished rolls on top of a damp tea towel and cover with another damp towel until you're ready to deep-fry. It's easiest if there's one person rolling and one deep-frying.

Line a baking sheet with paper towels. In a pot that's at least 6 inches deep, such as a Dutch oven or a wok, pour in about 3 inches of canola oil. You want the oil to cover the egg rolls completely. Heat the oil very carefully over medium-high heat to about 375°F. If you don't have a thermometer, drop a small piece of bread into the hot oil. If it sizzles, the oil is hot enough. Using your hands, carefully slide in about five or six egg rolls, one at a time. Don't overcrowd the pot, as this will bring down the temperature of the oil. Using long tongs, or a slotted spoon, carefully move the egg rolls around, flipping them over, if need be, so they brown evenly. They should be a dark golden brown. This should take about 4 minutes. Drain them on the prepared baking sheet while you cook the rest of the egg rolls. (You don't need to give the oil time to warm up between batches.) If you're serving all of the egg rolls at once, and some of them have cooled down, warm them in a 250°F oven for 10 minutes.

---

* *Let the oil cool down completely before saving for a similar deep-fryer project (maybe the Tempura Broccoli and Friends on page 43). Strain the oil to remove any egg roll particles, and only reuse it once.*

* *Do not stack egg rolls before or after frying.*

* *Egg rolls freeze great! Just wrap cooked egg rolls in aluminum foil and place them in a resealable plastic bag. Freeze for up to 2 months. Thaw them in the refrigerator before warming them in the oven at 325°F for 10 minutes.*

* *You'll likely have egg roll wrappers left over. Just wrap the package tightly in plastic wrap, put it into a resealable freezer bag, and freeze for up to 1 month. Thaw the wrappers in the refrigerator before using. See page 73 to make a vegetarian filling for these egg rolls.*

Vegetarian Filling for Egg Rolls

Warm 1 Tbsp of the oil in a 12-inch skillet over medium-high heat. Add the mushrooms, ¼ tsp of the salt, the garlic powder, and a pinch of pepper. Cook, stirring often, until the mushrooms have released their liquid, about 5–7 minutes. Stir in the tamari and cook for another minute. Remove the mushrooms from the skillet and place them in a large bowl.

Warm the remaining 1½ Tbsp of oil in the skillet over medium-high heat. Stir in the bok choy, cabbage, carrot, garlic, ginger, and red pepper flakes. Cook, stirring frequently, until the cabbage begins to wilt, about 3 minutes. Add the remaining ½ tsp of salt and the ¼ tsp of pepper. Stir in the bean sprouts and cook for another 2 minutes. Add the cabbage mixture to the bowl of mushrooms. Stir. Adjust the seasonings to taste. Let cool completely before assembling the egg rolls. I like to spread the filling out on a baking sheet so it cools quickly. You can also pop the filling into the refrigerator to get things moving along faster. If the vegetables are too juicy, strain the liquid out. If the filling is too "wet" there will be much splattering when deep-frying.

✳ *For additional tips on how to stuff and fry egg rolls, see recipe on page 71–72.*

MAKES 20 ROLLS

2½ Tbsp canola oil, divided

3 cups sliced button and/or shiitake mushrooms

¾ tsp salt, divided

½ tsp garlic powder

¼ tsp pepper, plus a pinch

2 tsp tamari (or reduced-sodium soy sauce)

2 cups chopped bok choy

2 cups thinly sliced green cabbage

1¼ cups grated carrot

2 garlic cloves, minced

1 Tbsp minced fresh ginger

Red pepper flakes

1 package (10 oz/300 g) bean sprouts, rinsed very well and thoroughly dried

Vegetable Stew in a Spicy Peanut Sauce

This recipe has been in my life and in my kitchen for 25 years. In fact, it was one of the very first dishes I ever cooked for friends way back when I was learning how to cook. This comforting conglomeration of vegetables was on heavy rotation, not only because it tasted delicious, but also because it was easy on a student's chequing account. The bulk of the stew is made of cabbage and potatoes, so there you go. As far as heat goes, feel free to adjust the quantity of jalapeño to your liking. The best part of making this stew is when the peanut butter is stirred in at the end. It creates a smooth, almost velvety texture with a richness that binds the vegetables together. It's kind of like a group hug with your favourite people. You can elevate the protein by adding a cup or two of cooked lentils or chickpeas or you can serve the stew as is, over bowls of steaming rice. What this vegetable stew lacks in visual appeal, it surely makes up for in flavour.

Warm a Dutch oven over medium-high heat. Add the oil. When it's warm, sauté the onion for about 5 minutes. Stir in the garlic, ginger, and jalapeño pepper and cook until fragrant, 3–5 minutes. Add the cabbage and potatoes. Cook for another few minutes, just to marry everything together.

Stir in the tomato juice, broth, and then the tomatoes. Cover and turn the heat down to medium. Simmer until the potatoes are fork-tender, about 15 minutes. Stir in the zucchini and cilantro and cook, uncovered, for 5 minutes longer.

Turn down the heat to low, stir in the peanut butter and simmer gently, uncovered, for 5 minutes. Add more tomato juice or broth if you find it's too thick. Season with salt and pepper. Add some cayenne pepper for more heat, if you like. Garnish with more chopped cilantro. Serve over bowls of steamed rice or quinoa, or on its own. Leftovers taste even better the next day.

SERVES 6

2 Tbsp canola oil

1 large yellow onion, chopped

3 garlic cloves, minced

2 Tbsp minced fresh ginger

1–2 chopped jalapeño peppers, seeds removed unless you want it super spicy

3 cups chopped green cabbage

3 cups cubed (1-inch pieces) red potatoes

3 cups tomato juice

1 cup vegetable broth (homemade, see page 19, or store bought)

2 cups chopped fresh Roma tomatoes

2 cups chopped (½-inch pieces) zucchini

½ cup chopped cilantro, plus more for garnish

½ cup smooth peanut butter (natural is optimal)

Salt and pepper

Cayenne pepper (optional)

Homemade Sauerkraut

My mom makes the best sauerkraut in the world. I grew up eating this stuff, often with fried perogies and onions, braised with juicy pork chops, and set atop grilled sausages, snug in their buns. Mom usually cranks out jars of this stuff in the autumn, when she hunts around for the best deal on heads of cabbage, though honestly, anytime is a good time for making the sauerkraut. But be warned, this isn't the kind of sauerkraut that's packed into a crock and left to ferment. Mom's version is thinly shredded cabbage, packed into sterile jars, with a little vinegar brine action added to aid in fermentation. After about 3 weeks, you can crack open a jar and add it to dishes like the ones mentioned above or get creative and make your own family favourites. For a fantastic feast, serve this alongside the Lazy Perogie Casserole (page 213). And if you want to make a lot of sauerkraut, this recipe also doubles easily.

Wash four 1-quart jars and their lids in hot soapy water. Rinse with boiling water. Having clean, sterilized jars and lids is very important! If you have a dishwasher, I suspect that would do the job for you. Have I ever mentioned that I don't have a dishwasher?

Slice the bottom off the cabbage and remove the tough core inside. Cut the cabbage into four pieces. Slice the cabbage as thinly as possible, using a very sharp chef's knife. Place all of the cabbage into a large non-reactive bowl (see note below). When your bowl is half full, toss in 1 Tbsp of the pickling salt. Toss the cabbage around. As you add the cabbage to the bowl, continue to toss it around with your hands.

Place 1 tsp each of pickling salt, sugar, and vinegar into EACH clean jar. Lightly pack the shredded cabbage into each jar. You don't want to pack it in too tightly. It's okay if your jars aren't packed fully to the top. Pour warm, not hot, previously boiled water into each of the jars so that it fully covers the cabbage, leaving 1 inch of headspace. Screw on the lids, then gently shake each jar to move the salt, sugar, and vinegar around.

Place the jars on top of a couple of clean tea towels in a warm space where they can sit undisturbed. Cover with another tea towel. The sauerkraut has to be kept out of direct sunlight. When the cabbage starts to do its thing, there is a good possibility that the liquid will run out of the tops of the jars (hence, the tea towels underneath). When this happens, you'll need to add more brine to the jars so that the cabbage is always covered with liquid. To make this brine, place 1 tsp EACH of pickling salt, granulated sugar, and vinegar into a glass 2-cup measuring cup. Fill with 1¾ cups of previously boiled warm water and stir to dissolve. Top up the jars of sauerkraut with this brine, then screw the lids back on. If any brine is left over, refrigerate it in case you need to top up the jars again.

The sauerkraut is ready to eat 3 weeks after it is made. Transfer the jars to the refrigerator. Once a jar is opened, eat the sauerkraut within 4 weeks. Unopened jars of sauerkraut can be refrigerated for up to 6 months.

MAKES 4 QUART JARS

1 large head of green cabbage

2 Tbsp, plus 2 tsp pickling salt

5 tsp granulated sugar, divided

5 tsp white vinegar, divided

Boiled water that has slightly cooled for filling jars

* *Don't use freshly picked cabbage for sauerkraut. Let it cure for at least 1 week after it is picked. If you're buying cabbage from the farmers' market, be sure to ask when it was picked.*

* *A non-reactive bowl is one made from a substance that won't react chemically with the foods placed in it. Reactive bowls are made from copper, aluminum, cast iron, or plastics that stain easily. Good examples of non-reactive bowls are stainless steel, glass, ceramic, and non-staining plastic.*

Carrots are one of the first foods to hit our taste buds. Boiled and mashed, or spooned from a jar, they've been coaxed into wee baby mouths by exhausted parents for centuries. Naturally sweet, it's easy to see why the young ones get hooked on this nutritious root vegetable. And I mean nutritious! Loaded with beta carotene (hence the orange colour), vitamin A, antioxidants, and fibre, crunching on carrots is where it's at.

As someone who cooks a lot, carrots are always in my crisper, and I'm fortunate to have a handsome farmer boyfriend who grows the best carrots around. The Extra Sweet Nantes are the Simpkins family's biggest cash crop, and for good reason. Saskatonians will search out their carrots specifically because they are so sweet, juicy, and delicious—even in the middle of winter.

Lord knows I've purchased enough supermarket carrots in my lifetime, and nothing compares to Dixon's carrots. I've worked in restaurants where the delivery truck drops off a 50 lb case of carrots, and no lie, some of them have been as big as a small child's arm. They make for great quick peeling, but their taste is pretty lacklustre. Simpkins carrots are fairly legendary around my city, and I know you all want to hop a plane right now and come to Saskatoon just to see what I'm talking about, right?!

Carrots are the base of many savoury recipes as they add a subtle sweetness and are compatible with so many other vegetables. One of my favourite ways of eating them is roasted alongside wedges of onion and chunks of potato. Give them a good amount of olive or canola oil to sizzle in, salt and pepper, and a smattering of whatever herbs you have around—I like twiggy rosemary and thyme. I call this concoction the Big Three because it's just so basic, it goes well with any roasted meat, and it's mega-delicious. Carrots are also fantastic when they are grated into slaws, puréed into soups, and baked into cakes smothered with cream cheese icing. If you have my first cookbook, you'll know that the carrot cake recipe is to die for!

✳✳✳✳✳✳✳✳✳✳✳✳✳✳✳✳✳✳✳✳✳✳✳✳✳✳✳✳✳✳✳✳✳✳✳

Dixon Says: Carrots can be a difficult crop to grow. Their seed is tiny, and they take quite a while to germinate. They're best grown in sandy soil, and, because of their tiny size, they need to be seeded shallowly and watered frequently enough that the soil is damp for 2 to 3 weeks. Once established (a couple of inches tall), regular watering, about 1 inch per week, should see them grow to a suitable and tasty size. Through the summer, carrots are easily harvested by hand after a watering or rainfall when the soil is still moist. In the autumn, when you're harvesting them for storage, wait for the temperature to dip down below freezing for a few nights to sweeten them up. Your carrots will amaze you! Remove the green tops and leave any soil on them when putting them into storage. Keep the temperature as low as you can without freezing them.

CARROTS

Maple Mustard Glazed Carrots

The trick to cooking a good boiled carrot is to not cook the bejeezus out of it. Simmer just until the carrots are tender, with a little bit of life left in them, and don't be shy with seasoning. I like this little pot of carrots because there's no draining off of liquid—the carrots self-glaze in butter, maple syrup, and Dijon. Dixon's eyes always light up when I serve these carrots—he's a survivor of the Overboiled Carrot Club—and he likes how these are nothing like the roots of his youth. There's nothing fancy to see here, just a good, solid carrot recipe that is sure to please even the pickiest eaters.

Place the carrots, maple syrup, mustard, salt, and pepper in a medium saucepan with ¾ cup of water. Stir well. Bring the carrots to a boil over high heat, uncovered. Turn down the heat to medium, cover, and simmer the carrots until they're almost tender, but not quite, about 5–6 minutes.

Remove the lid and continue to simmer the carrots until almost all of the liquid has disappeared, about 8 minutes. Stir in the butter and dill. Season to taste with more salt and pepper, if you like.

SERVES 4

1½ lb carrots (about 7–8 medium) peeled and sliced ¼-inch thick on the diagonal

1½ Tbsp pure maple syrup

2 tsp grainy Dijon mustard

½ tsp salt

¼ tsp pepper

1 Tbsp butter

1 Tbsp chopped fresh dill

Honey-Roasted Carrot Tart with Ricotta and Feta

If you've ever wondered what to make with those pretty heirloom carrots you see at the farmers' market, this is it! Dixon always saves some of the purple carrots he grows so I can make us this tart. It's got loads of wow factor, and it's fun to pull out of the oven when you have guests gathered around the table. There are a couple of steps here, but it's worth the work. Roasting the carrots first with a little honey and spices deepens their flavour and ensures some tenderness in the finished tart. I like adding greens to almost everything, so it's no surprise that they're nestled in the ricotta/feta cheese filling. Bonus vitamins! I love walking out to my herb garden and picking the aromatic leaves as a garnish for the tart. Carrots and mint forever!

Preheat the oven to 400°F. Line two rimmed baking sheets with parchment paper.

On a lightly floured surface, roll the puff pastry into a 10- × 14-inch rectangle about ⅛-inch thick. Using a sharp paring knife, score a border around the perimeter of the pastry about ½ inch away from the edges. Carefully place the pastry on one of the baking sheets. Prick the area inside of the border very thoroughly with a fork to prevent puffing in the centre. Brush the border lightly with the egg wash. Bake on the top rack of the oven until the pastry is lightly golden, about 20–22 minutes. Remove from the oven and let cool. If the pastry does puff up in the centre, take a sharp knife and poke a few holes in it to help it deflate.

Meanwhile, in a large bowl, toss the carrots with the oil, honey, cumin, paprika, ½ tsp of the salt, and ¼ tsp of the pepper. Spread in an even layer on the second baking sheet. Roast the carrots on the bottom rack of the oven until they are golden brown around the edges and more tender than crisp, about 25–28 minutes. Be sure to give them a stir a couple of times. It's better to have carrots a little on the softer side than the firmer side. Stir in the the lemon zest, and let them cool to room temperature before assembling the tart.

Warm a large skillet over medium-high heat and add the greens with a splash of water. Cook until they're wilted, about 2 minutes. Remove the greens from the skillet and place them in a large bowl to cool down. (Use the same bowl the carrots were in.)

In a food processor fitted with a metal blade, blend the ricotta, feta, and garlic until smooth. Scrape into the bowl along with the cooled greens. Add the remaining ½ tsp of salt, the remaining ¼ tsp of pepper, the egg, lemon juice, and thyme. Stir just until everything is evenly mixed.

To assemble the tart, spread the cheese filling onto the puff pastry shell right up to the border. Arrange the roasted carrots in a single layer on top of the cheese. Bake until the carrots are very tender and the cheese filling has set, about 30 minutes. Remove the tart from the oven and let rest 10 minutes before serving. Garnish with fresh mint leaves. The tart is best enjoyed while warm. Makes 8 slices.

SERVES 4–6

1 package (14 oz/400 g) frozen puff pastry, thawed in the refrigerator

1 egg, beaten with a splash of water, for egg wash

1¼ lb multi-coloured carrots, of similar thickness, scrubbed and sliced in half lengthwise

1 Tbsp extra-virgin olive oil

1 Tbsp honey

1 tsp ground cumin

½ tsp smoked paprika

1 tsp salt, divided

½ tsp pepper, divided

Grated zest of 1 lemon

3 cups baby greens, such as kale, chard, or spinach

1¼ cups ricotta cheese

1 cup crumbled feta cheese

2 garlic cloves, smashed

1 large egg

2 Tbsp fresh lemon juice

2 tsp fresh thyme leaves (or 1 tsp dried)

Fresh mint or basil leaves, for garnish

Balsamic Roasted Carrots with Gorgeous Greens Pesto

First off, let's talk about the pesto. It's gorgeous stuff. Also, making pesto is a great way to use up any wilted greens in the crisper. I love how the boldness of the kale is taken down a notch by the toasty nuts, aromatic herbs, and salty cheese. When I have a jar of this in the refrigerator, it goes on all sorts of things, like roasted vegetables, hot pasta, pizza (base and topping), dips, and sandwiches. The pesto is also a fabulous companion to the caramelized balsamic carrots. Dix and I regularly polish off a whole platter just between the two of us! The sweetness of the carrots is tempered by the herbaceousness of the pesto—and just look at how pretty they are together. When I plan on making this recipe, I ask Dixon to bring me carrots with the tops attached, as that little green nub at the top makes for a great presentation. No tops? No problem! They'll still taste great.

Prepare the pesto: Place the kale, pecans, mint, garlic, lemon juice, salt, and pepper in a food processor fitted with a metal blade. Pulse until smooth. Scrape down the bowl. With the motor running, gradually pour in the oil. Stop and scrape down the bowl. Add the cheese and process just until smooth. Taste and adjust the seasonings. Scrape into a jar. The pesto keeps well in the refrigerator for up to 10 days, or you can freeze it for up to 6 months. Makes about 1¼ cups.

Prepare the carrots: Preheat the oven to 375°F. Line a rimmed baking sheet with parchment paper.

Place the carrots in a large bowl. Add the rest of the ingredients (balsamic vinegar through thyme) and toss well. Transfer to the prepared baking sheet, being sure to scrape all of the oil and herbs from the bowl. Spread the carrots out into an even layer. Roast until the carrots are very tender and easily pierced with a fork, stirring four times, about 40–50 minutes.

Place the roasted carrots on a serving platter and spoon about ¼ cup of pesto over top. Serve immediately.

SERVES 4

Pesto

3 cups packed chopped kale, centre ribs removed (or use spinach, chard, arugula, or a mix)

½ cup toasted pecans (or almonds, walnuts, hazelnuts)

¼ cup fresh mint (or basil or parsley leaves, or a combination)

2 garlic cloves

2 Tbsp fresh lemon juice

½ tsp salt

¼ tsp pepper

¾ cup extra-virgin olive oil

¾ cup grated Parmesan cheese (or Asiago or pecorino)

Carrots

1 lb carrots, little green tops attached, cut in half lengthwise

2 Tbsp balsamic vinegar

1½ Tbsp canola oil

½ tsp garlic powder

½ tsp salt

¼ tsp pepper

6 fresh thyme sprigs (or 1 tsp chopped fresh thyme, or ½ tsp dried thyme)

✳ *Be sure that the carrots are around the same size so they cook evenly. You may have to slice some into quarters instead of in half.*

A Comforting Casserole

My mom is the casserole queen. She's always giving me a hard time about how I don't make enough casseroles. And, of course, she's right. This comforting casserole has been in Mom's rotation for decades, and it makes for a cozy, heartwarming supper. This tasty melange of meat, vegetables, and rice is something that you can throw together in one pan and then pretty much forget about for an hour and change, though the aroma coming from the oven will likely lead you into the kitchen a little sooner. I love the simplicity of the ingredients and the method—something my mom would have needed when she had four kids to feed and no one around to help with meal prep. High-five to the single parents and the creator of casseroles!

Preheat the oven to 375°F. Lightly grease a 9- × 13-inch casserole dish that's at least 2 inches deep or a 12-inch round braising pan with canola oil.

In a large bowl, combine the meat, vegetables, rice, Worcestershire sauce, and seasonings. Pour in the crushed tomatoes. Rinse out the can with about 1 cup water and add this tomatoey water as well. Mix well. Transfer to the prepared baking dish and cover tightly with a lid or aluminum foil.

Bake for 1 hour and 15 minutes, then test to see if the vegetables are tender and the rice is cooked. If not, bake for another 10 minutes. Remove the foil, stir, and bake, uncovered, for 5 more minutes to crisp up the top a little. Garnish with parsley and serve.

SERVES 4–6

1 lb lean ground beef

2 cups chopped (½-inch pieces) carrots

2 cups chopped (1-inch pieces) red or yellow potatoes

2 celery stalks, chopped small (but not diced)

1 large yellow onion, diced

2 garlic cloves, minced

½ cup white basmati rice, rinsed

1 Tbsp Worcestershire sauce

1½ tsp salt

1 tsp dried thyme leaves

1 tsp dry mustard powder

½ tsp pepper

2½ cups canned crushed tomatoes

2 Tbsp chopped fresh parsley (flat-leaf or curly), for garnish

✳ *If your potatoes are lookin' good on the outside, feel free to keep their skins on. Otherwise, peel them. Waxy potatoes work well in this.*

Let's have a little flashback, shall we, to the early weeks of 2016. Just as the price of oil was plummeting, the price of our beloved creamy white brassica (Canada is the second-largest importer of cauliflower in the world) was doing the opposite. Rumours of cauliflower heads selling for $7.99 (for one!) flooded the internet. Cauli-lovers everywhere shuddered in horror. Thanks to the variables of not having enough of the stuff on the market to meet the demand, bad weather in the prime cauliflower-growing areas in Mexico and the United States, and it being a fussy crop to grow to begin with, it's easy to see why a head of cauliflower was costing almost as much as a pound of grass-fed ground beef. Thankfully, the price has come down a bit, and we can get back to putting it in our shopping carts, without even flinching at the $2.99 price sticker. The question now is, how do you want to cook it?

A duvet of creamy cheese sauce is a well-known tool for getting kids to eat their vegetables—just ask cauliflower's verdant cousin, broccoli. Cauliflower is also quite delicious simmered in soups and stews. Being a fairly mild-tasting vegetable makes it great for soaking up the more vibrant flavours of an Indian curry or a Moroccan stew. Roasting it transforms it into something nutty, almost sweet, and the charred bits are really the best part. I often toss cauliflower florets with olive oil, lemon juice, garlic powder, salt, and pepper. Roast them in an even layer on a baking sheet at 425°F for half an hour, stirring once, then hit them with ½ cup grated Parmesan and roast for about 7 more minutes. When the cauliflower comes out of the oven, I sprinkle fresh lemon zest over top and garnish with fresh herbs. It makes a supremely tasty side dish, if it even gets that far off the sheet pan. The caramelized edges lend a sweetness to the cauliflower, which is then balanced out by the acidity of the lemon and the saltiness of the Parmesan. I treat broccoli this way as well (same timing, same temperature), and it's good, good stuff.

Let's all cross our fingers that we don't see another nightmare price increase of this popular vegetable. Or any other vegetable, for that matter.

Dixon Says: Who doesn't love a good cauliflower—am I right? While there are many different coloured varieties out there, my favourites are the good old-fashioned white ones, like fluffy white crunchy clouds! To keep the heads that beautiful snow-white, you need to keep them protected from sunlight, as the light turns the head a kind of unappealing yellow colour. To this end, when it looks like the head is starting to form, carefully choose an appropriately sized inner leaf and snap the stem so it folds nicely over the head. Check on it periodically, and when it meets your satisfaction, cut and enjoy!

CAULIFLOWER

Christmas Eve Cauliflower

Cauliflower and cheese sauce is a classic combo. I've gussied it up a little here by roasting a whole head of the creamy white vegetable slathered in the aforementioned cheese sauce. It becomes a bit of a spectacle, especially when presented to a table of guests. They will ooh and ahh at all of its bubbling golden glory—just like Mom and Dix did when I prepared it for Christmas Eve one year. Stick a small carving knife in the head before you bring it to the table, and they'll be talking about your dinner party for years! I like to slice the cauliflower at the table and tell guests to help themselves to wedges. Just be sure that everyone gets some of the sauce. If there's any left over, I'll take a slice of bread and dunk it in the skillet, wiping up all of that cheesy, garlic goodness.

Prepare the cauliflower: Bring a very large pot of water to a boil. The pot needs to be large enough so the cauliflower can float. Stir in the lemon, garlic, 1 Tbsp of the oil, the salt, peppercorns, and bay leaf. Put the cauliflower into the pot with the core facing up. Cover, turn down the heat to medium-low, and simmer until the cauliflower is fork-tender, 10 minutes. Carefully remove the head from the water and drain it in a colander. This step can be done a day in advance. Just cover and refrigerate the cauliflower head until you're ready to proceed.

Preheat the oven to 375°F.

Prepare the cheese sauce: Place a medium saucepan over medium heat. Melt the butter, then stir in the flour so it makes a paste (yes, that would be a roux). Cook, stirring constantly, for 2 minutes. Gradually whisk in the wine, milk, and cream, being careful to scrape along the inside edges of the pot. The sauce will thicken after about 8 minutes or so. Stir in the cheese, mustard, paprika, salt, pepper, and a pinch of red pepper flakes. Keep stirring until the cheese is melted and smooth. Remove from the heat and season to taste.

Place the cauliflower head in a 10-inch ovenproof skillet or baking dish. Rub the head with the remaining 2 Tbsp olive oil and sprinkle with the dried thyme. Pour half of the cheese sauce over top and snuggle in the whole cloves of garlic around the bottom of the cauliflower. Bake, uncovered, for 20 minutes. Remove from the oven and pour over the remaining cheese sauce. Bake, uncovered, until the cauliflower is tender and golden, about 10–12 more minutes.

Cut the cauliflower into wedges and spoon some sauce over each wedge.

SERVES 6

Cauliflower

1 lemon, sliced

1 head of garlic, cloves smashed

1 Tbsp extra-virgin olive oil

2 tsp salt

1 tsp black peppercorns

1 bay leaf

1 medium head of cauliflower, outer leaves removed and core trimmed so it sits flat

Cheese Sauce

2 Tbsp butter

2½ Tbsp all-purpose flour

¼ cup white wine

1 cup milk

½ cup whipping (35%) cream

1½ cups shredded extra-old cheddar cheese

¼ cup grated Parmesan cheese

1 tsp Dijon mustard

½ tsp smoked paprika

½ tsp salt

¼ tsp pepper

Red pepper flakes

Finishing the Dish

7 whole garlic cloves, peeled

2 Tbsp extra-virgin olive oil

½ tsp dried thyme

Roasted Cauliflower Soup with Brie

Cauliflower soup is like a warm hug from the inside out. On the frigid days that hit Saskatoon in January and February, I need all of the hugs I can get. Dix is a great hugger, by the way, but so is soup. When it's this cold, you don't mess around. You go from A to B, then home again. Grocery shopping is put on hold, and supper is built from whatever is hanging around inside the refrigerator and pantry. This soup came to be because at the back of the refrigerator there was a head of cauliflower, and the crisper held one of Dixon's sweet carrots and a stalk of somewhat sad celery. I roasted some of the vegetables for the soup, while others were cooked in a bit of butter directly in the soup pot. Together they became one, with fresh dill and cream rounding things out nicely. That brie, though! It's a little luxury that goes a long way on a cold winter's day.

Preheat the oven to 425°F. Line a rimmed baking sheet with parchment paper.

In a large bowl, toss together the cauliflower and carrot in the oil. Scrape the contents of the bowl into an even layer on the baking sheet and roast for about 25 minutes, stirring once or twice. You want the cauliflower to have some browned bits. Remove from the oven and reserve about ½ cup of the small florets for garnish.

Meanwhile, warm a Dutch oven over medium-high heat. Melt the butter, stir in the onion and celery, and cook until the vegetables are softened, about 5 minutes. Stir in the garlic and bay leaf. Cook until the garlic is fragrant, 1–2 minutes.

Stir in the roasted cauliflower and carrot. Pour in the broth and then the mustard, a generous dash of hot sauce, a generous dash of Worcestershire sauce, and a pinch of nutmeg. Bring to a boil over medium-high heat, then turn the heat down to medium-low and simmer, covered, until the vegetables are softened, about 10 minutes. Remove the pot from the heat. Discard the bay leaf. Stir in the cream.

Purée the soup with an immersion blender. You can leave some chunky bits, if that's your preference, or you can purée until it's completely smooth. It's up to you. Stir in the dill and season with salt and pepper. If you find the soup too thick, thin it out with a bit of broth, milk, or water.

Ladle the soup into bowls. Garnish each with a slice of brie, a few sprigs of fresh dill, and the reserved roasted cauliflower florets. If you want to be sneaky, you can put the brie in the bottom of the bowls then spoon hot soup over top. Either way is amazing!

SERVES 4–6

1 medium head of cauliflower, chopped into florets (about 5–6 cups)

1 medium carrot, chopped into ½-inch chunks

2 Tbsp canola oil

2 Tbsp butter

1 large onion, chopped

1 celery stalk, chopped

2 garlic cloves, minced

1 bay leaf

4 cups low-sodium chicken or vegetable broth

1 Tbsp Dijon mustard

Hot sauce (your favourite)

Worcestershire sauce

Ground nutmeg

1 cup whipping (35%) cream

2 Tbsp finely chopped fresh dill, plus some larger sprigs, for garnish

Salt and pepper

1 small wheel of brie, sliced, for garnish

✱ *If you're not fond of brie (who are you?), then substitute grated Parmesan or sharp cheddar cheese for garnish.*

Lentil and Chickpea Curry with Cauliflower and Coconut Milk

I've been making a variation of this curry for years and years—since my days as a rosy-cheeked art student in Montreal. Pulses such as lentils and chickpeas are inexpensive sources of protein, so you can see why they're good friends of the budget-minded cook. I really love how the cauliflower absorbs all the lovely curry flavour, and the peas that are lingering in the back of the freezer finally have a home! (See also pages 185–189 for more ideas about using frozen peas.) The coconut milk mellows the warm spices and adds richness, and, really, it is nectar of the gods, isn't it? This recipe makes a rather humongous batch, so it's perfect for feeding friends. Any leftovers taste even better the next day, or you can pop them into the freezer for future lunches. Don't forget to warm up some naan —it's made for curry scooping!

In a large Dutch oven, warm the oil over medium-high heat. Add the onion and carrots. Cook until softened, about 4 minutes. Stir in the garlic, ginger, curry paste, cumin, coriander, salt and cayenne. Stir well and cook for a couple of minutes.

Stir in the crushed tomatoes and coconut milk. I like to rinse out each can with water and add this (about 1½ cups of water in total) as well. Add the lentils, chickpeas, and honey. Bring to a boil, then turn down the heat to low so the curry can simmer. Cover. Stir every 10 minutes or so. It takes about 30–40 minutes for the lentils to fully cook.

When the lentils are soft and tender, stir in the cauliflower florets and cook for 5 minutes. Stir in the peas and cook just until the cauliflower is tender and the peas are warmed through, about 4–5 more minutes.

If the curry is too thick, thin it with a bit of veggie broth or water. Stir in the cilantro. Adjust the seasonings with more salt, pepper, and, if you like it spicy, some hot sauce.

Scoop the curry into bowls and garnish with dollops of plain yogurt, cilantro leaves, and a bit more hot sauce, if you're so inclined. Serve with warm naan.

✱ *This curry freezes very well. Just portion it into freezer-safe containers, label, and date.*

SERVES 8

3 Tbsp canola oil

1 large yellow onion, diced

2 medium carrots, diced

3 garlic cloves, minced

2 Tbsp minced fresh ginger

3½ Tbsp mild Indian curry paste

1 tsp ground cumin

1 tsp ground coriander

1 tsp salt

½ tsp cayenne pepper

1 can (28 oz/796 mL) crushed tomatoes

2 cans (each 14 oz/398 mL) coconut milk

2 cups uncooked whole green or black beluga lentils, picked through and rinsed

1 can (19 oz/540 mL) chickpeas, drained and rinsed

2 Tbsp honey

1 medium head cauliflower, chopped into small florets (about 5–6 cups)

1 cup frozen peas

Vegetable broth (optional)

½ cup chopped cilantro, plus more for garnish

Plain Greek yogurt, for serving

Hot sauce, for serving

As a kid, I remember running through rows of tall, tall corn. It was fun to get lost among those vegetable giants, and even more fun to nibble on the crunchy, sweet, buttery cobs at suppertime. These days, I don't do too much running through fields of corn, but I still adore eating fresh, sweet corn. There's really nothing quite like it. In the middle of winter, the frozen stuff in bags will do in a pinch, but come August and September, I eat all of the corn I can get my hands on. This also means a lot of flossing, and I know my dentist will be happy to hear that.

For many of us, the simplest way to cook corn is often the best. Simmer the cobs until tender, slather them heavily with butter, and finish with a good sprinkling of salt and pepper. It's pretty much perfection, isn't it? Bits of corn and butter mess up your face, but it doesn't matter. It's summer and it's fresh hot corn. You want to buy it as fresh as possible, with the husks still on. Corn starts converting its sugars to starch as soon as it's picked, which is why you don't want it to linger in the refrigerator for too long before cooking it. The best place to buy fresh, sweet corn is, of course, the farmers' market. Here you can look the farmer in the eye and ask when it was picked. Chances are they'll tell you exactly what kind of corn it is, where it was grown, and that it was picked the day before, if not that very morning. This is the story you want to hear. Look for plump, green ears that have fresh-looking cuts at their stems and slightly sticky brown silk at the top. If the supermarket is your only option, you'll have to pull back the husks and inspect the kernels. They should be firm and shiny. If not, keep looking. When buying corn, there's one golden rule: Never buy shucked corn. This trick hides the evidence of old corn: dried cuts on the stems, lacklustre husks, and wilting silk. Dixon is very picky about his corn, and he'd be so disappointed if you bought the shucked stuff!

Corn on the cob is fantastic, but I also love corn roasted. It imparts a smokiness that's very appealing in things like salsa, chili, tostadas, and fritters. And the best part is, if you have a gas stove and are too lazy to turn the barbecue on, you can roast the corn over the flame of your burner, rotating often for even cooking. Let it cool, then slice off the ends to make them flat and shear the kernels into a Bundt pan. All of the kernels get trapped and you aren't losing any on the counter or floor. How's that for kitchen hacks?

Dixon Says: Renée asked me one evening, "What vegetable are you most excited about in the garden?" One jumped out at me immediately. For as long as I can remember, I've loved watching corn grow. It starts out as a tiny little sprout and grows into a tiny little stalk and then a great big stalk! "Knee-high by the fourth of July!" my dad would always say, as a good benchmark. Corn loves the heat, so hot weather and adequate moisture—about an inch over the course of a week—gives you a really nice corn patch. And I love picking corn. There is almost nothing as satisfying as the clean snap-twist of a perfect pick. Then, awkwardly carrying an armful of cobs to put in the wheelbarrow. And I'm not gonna lie. Even counting cobs as they're bagged is a fun activity. But the best times of picking corn come at the end of a long, hot day in the garden. Walking along, feeling the tips of the cobs for those perfect ones, to pick and take back to the house for supper, the anticipation slowly growing. Minutes later: shuck 'em and into the corn pot.

CORN

Roasted Corn and Black Bean Tostadas

This recipe is in the hand-scrawled notebook I began when I first moved away from home back in 1993. Cans of black beans could be found for under $1 each, and corn tortillas were only a few bucks for a large stack, which meant these tostadas were cheap and cheerful. And delicious. I haven't swayed from the original recipe too much, except by adding roasted corn to the party. Because we're all friends here, I like to eat these with my hands, no fork required. Just pick up and chomp away. Be sure to have napkins at the ready, though, because things could get messy. But these are so good that a little salsa on the face is worth every bite.

MAKES 8 TOSTADAS

In a large saucepan over medium-high heat, warm 2 Tbsp of the oil. Stir in the onion and sauté just until the onion is translucent, 5 minutes. Stir in the jalapeño pepper, garlic, and a good pinch of salt. Cook for another minute. Stir in the black beans, tomatoes, orange juice, orange zest, cumin, coriander, oregano, and 1 tsp of the chili powder. Add 2 Tbsp water. Cover, turn down the heat to low, and cook for about 20 minutes, stirring occasionally. If the mixture seems too thick, add a bit more water. Stir in the cilantro and season to taste with salt and pepper. Remove from the heat and let the mixture cool to room temperature, stirring it once in a while. This step can be done up to 3 days ahead. Refrigerate the filling in an airtight container and let come to room temperature before making the tostadas.

Preheat the oven to 400°F. Line three rimmed baking sheets with parchment paper.

In a medium bowl, stir together the remaining 1 Tbsp canola oil, the remaining 1 tsp chili powder, the corn, and generous pinches of salt and pepper. Spread onto one of the prepared baking sheets and roast for 10–12 minutes, stirring occasionally. The corn should be lightly roasted. Remove from the oven.

Arrange 4 corn tortillas on each of the other two baking sheets. Spread about ⅓ cup of the black bean filling on top of each corn tortilla, leaving about a ½-inch border. Top each one with some roasted corn and shredded cheddar. Place one pan on the top rack of the oven and one on the bottom. Bake for 4 minutes, rotate the pans from bottom to top, and bake until the cheese is melted, another 4–5 minutes. Serve with guacamole, salsa, sour cream, extra cilantro, and pickled red onions, if you like. Leftover black beans can be refrigerated for up to 5 days or frozen for up to 1 month.

Tostadas

- 3 Tbsp canola oil, divided
- 1 yellow onion, diced
- 1 jalapeño pepper, diced (remove seeds for less heat)
- 2 garlic cloves, minced
- Salt
- 1 can (19 oz/540 mL) black beans, rinsed and drained
- 1 cup chopped fresh Roma tomatoes
- 1 Tbsp fresh orange juice
- 1 tsp grated orange zest
- 1 tsp ground cumin
- 1 tsp ground coriander
- 1 tsp dried oregano
- 2 tsp chili powder, divided
- ½ cup chopped cilantro
- 2 cups fresh or frozen corn (thawed)
- Pepper
- 1 package 6-inch soft corn tortillas, yellow or white
- 1⅓ cups shredded extra-old cheddar cheese

For Serving

- Guacamole
- Salsa
- Sour cream
- Cilantro (optional)
- Pickled Red Onions (page 165, optional)

---

* *If you're using fresh corn, take a sharp knife, and shave the kernels off the cobs.*

* *If you're making these tostadas in the summer and you don't want to turn the oven on to roast the corn, just give it a light sauté with the same ingredients in a 10-inch skillet over medium heat until lightly toasted.*

* *For extra crunch, garnish with thinly sliced radishes.*

Grilled Corn with Garlic Mayonnaise, Feta, and Lime

There's nothing wrong with straight-up corn on the cob: butter, salt, pepper, done. But you can up your game and try corn this way. (If you've been to Mexico and enjoyed elote, it's very similar.) Mayonnaise might seem like an odd thing to add to corn, but trust me, when it's slicked onto hot grilled cobs, there is some sort of magical reaction. Like butter, the mayonnaise adds a richness to the cob, and, after it slightly melts, it finds its way into all of the nooks and crannies that corn is well known for. I spiked mayonnaise with garlic powder and smoked paprika, and it tastes so much better than the stuff straight from the jar. The lime juice squeezed right onto the cobs brings a welcome bit of acidity that balances out their sweetness. Be sure to serve a wedge or two alongside so folks can add more if they like. I swear Dixon looks forward to summer just so he can eat this grilled corn, then rave about it until I make it again, and so on and so forth.

Preheat the grill to medium. Brush the cobs evenly with the oil. Grill for about 8–10 minutes, turning frequently. The corn will have some charred spots and be fork-tender when it's ready to come off the grill. Meanwhile, stir the mayonnaise with the paprika and garlic powder.

Place the grilled corn cobs on a large platter and brush each cob with the spicy mayonnaise. Squeeze lime juice over the corn and scatter the feta cheese on top. Sprinkle with the chili powder and some cilantro. Serve immediately with lime wedges on the side.

SERVES 4

4 cobs fresh sweet corn, shucked

2 tsp canola oil

¼ cup mayonnaise

½ tsp smoked paprika or chili powder

½ tsp garlic powder

1 fresh lime, juiced

¼ cup crumbled feta cheese

1 tsp chili powder

Torn cilantro leaves or flat-leaf parsley, for garnish

Lime wedges, for serving

Corn Chowder with Salmon and Dill

Dixon brings me plenty of fresh, sweet corn in the summer. I know, I'm a lucky duck. Any of the corn that doesn't get eaten up right away (it happens!) is shaved off the cobs and frozen for winter. What a treat it is to pull a package of corn out of the freezer in February, a perfect month for a fish chowder if ever there was one. I like my chowders thick and creamy, bursting with vegetables. Bacon adds a smoky richness, which makes a great starting point for this soup, but it can be left out, if you prefer. I like to finish the chowder with plenty of fresh dill and a bit of lemon zest, just to marry the flavours. Dixon and I devour deep bowls of this hearty soup when we need a reminder that summer will return one day, glorious corn cobs and all.

SERVES 6

5 slices thick-cut bacon, chopped

1 leek, cleaned and sliced

2 celery stalks, diced

2 medium carrots, diced

3 cups chopped (¾-inch chunks) Yukon gold or waxy white potatoes

4 cups low-sodium chicken (or vegetable) broth

¾ tsp salt, divided

½ tsp pepper, divided

½ tsp smoked paprika

2 cups corn, fresh or frozen

1 lb boneless skinless salmon fillet, cut into ¾-inch cubes

2 Tbsp all-purpose flour

1 Tbsp canola oil

¾ cup whipping (35%) cream

2 Tbsp chopped fresh dill

Grated zest of 1 lemon

Warm a Dutch oven over medium-high heat. Add the bacon and cook until browned but not too crispy and most of the fat is rendered out, about 5 minutes.

Stir in the leek, celery, and carrots. Cook for 5 minutes, then stir in the potatoes, followed by the broth, ½ tsp of the salt, ¼ tsp of the pepper, and the paprika. Cover. When the soup begins to simmer, turn down the heat to medium-low and gently simmer until the vegetables are tender, about 10–13 minutes. Stir in the corn.

Meanwhile, place the salmon cubes in a bowl. Toss with the remaining ¼ tsp salt, remaining ¼ tsp pepper, and the flour. Warm the oil in a large non-stick skillet over medium-high heat. Cook the salmon until lightly browned on both sides, about 2 minutes per side. It doesn't need to be cooked through, just browned.

Spoon the fish into the soup, then stir in the cream, dill, and lemon zest. Gently simmer for a few minutes. Season to taste with salt and pepper.

❋ *The chowder will thicken up as any leftovers cool in the refrigerator. If you find it too thick, thin it with a bit of milk or chicken broth when you reheat it.*

❋ *Use any firm, meaty fish in place of the salmon. Trout, haddock, or cod would all work well.*

❋ *If you don't want to use the bacon, cook the vegetables in 2 Tbsp of butter instead.*

Smoked Salmon and Cream Cheese Corn Cakes

These corn cakes are why I started a food blog. After I posted a photo of them on Facebook in the summer of 2010, a hullabaloo ensued. Comments from friends urging me to start writing a blog were noted and appreciated, but I claimed I was too busy or too technologically challenged to start one. But those friends did not rest. They kept vocalizing their wishes to see me write about all of the cool stuff I was cooking and baking, and finally I gave in. During the winter of 2011, I brushed up on a little computer lingo, and the rest is history. To those friends, thank you for being so bossy. Without a food blog there would be no cookbooks, and here we are. The corn cakes have crispy edges with a light cakey middle, and when you get a bite of all of the tasty garnishes, well, that's a little bit of heaven. Serve these for a light lunch or dinner, or make mini versions as an appetizer. They're also quite delicious as a fancy brunch item with poached eggs nestled on top.

MAKES 10–12 CAKES

Corn Cakes

¾ cup cornmeal

6 Tbsp all-purpose flour

½ tsp baking soda

½ tsp salt

2 large eggs, lightly beaten

¾ cup buttermilk, shaken before measuring

½ cup cream cheese, softened

1 cup corn, divided (see note)

1 tsp your favourite hot sauce

2 Tbsp finely chopped fresh chives (or green onions)

2 Tbsp finely chopped fresh dill

4 oz smoked salmon, finely chopped, about ¾ cup (see note)

¼ cup canola oil, divided

Flaky salt

Garnishes

Sour cream

Lemon wedges

Sliced cherry tomatoes

Fresh herbs

Diced red onion (optional)

Prepare the corn cakes: In a small bowl, whisk together the cornmeal, flour, baking soda, and salt. In a larger bowl, whisk together the eggs and buttermilk, then break apart the cream cheese into small bits (each piece about half a teaspoon) and stir it in. Add ½ cup of the corn and the hot sauce to this. Mix well. Stir the wet ingredients into the dry, just until combined. Add the remaining ½ cup of corn, the chives, dill, and smoked salmon. Stir just until combined.

In a large cast-iron skillet or non-stick pan, warm 2 Tbsp of the oil over medium heat. Working in batches, drop the batter by a heaping ¼-cup measure into the skillet. Spread the batter evenly to form 3½-inch cakes. Cook until golden brown, 3 minutes per side. If the cakes get too dark, turn down the heat.

Transfer the cooked cakes to a baking sheet and keep them warm in a 225°F oven while you cook the rest, using more oil as needed. Sprinkle the corn cakes with flaky salt and serve warm with sour cream, a squeeze of lemon, sliced tomatoes, a smattering of fresh herbs, and diced red onion, if you like.

✴ *You can roast the corn (page 99), use canned and rinsed corn, frozen and thawed corn, or fresh corn, shaved off the cobs.*

✴ *You can use cold-smoked salmon, such as lox, or hot-smoked salmon for this recipe.*

There's nothing like a summer-fresh cucumber, sprinkled with salt and eaten as is. I will eat them like this one after another, day in day out, until Dixon brings me no more. I also love fresh cucumber salads with tomatoes, dill, and feta cheese, along for the ride. It's dreamy stuff. But the salad I love best is one my mom makes by simply tossing sliced fresh cucumbers in a dressing of mayonnaise, vinegar, chopped dill, and pinches of sugar, salt, and pepper. Glory be, it's so light and refreshing and just what you want a summer salad to be. I especially like this salad with grilled chicken or pan-fried fish. It's a summer feast!

I also love cucumbers in pickle form, but I don't really like making pickles. For typical dills, you have to find the canner, wash the jars and lids, slice the cucumbers, make a brine, fill the jars, then boil them like crazy in a hot water bath. This method takes time and effort and a willingness to heat up the kitchen when you're already a hot, sweaty mess. No, I won't be making pickles this way, but hats off to those who do. I admire your work ethic! Refrigerator dill pickles are more my style. Got vinegar? Got salt? You can so do this. The main thing is to use thin-skinned cucumbers like Kirby or Manny. The cucumbers should be firm and crunchy; no soft and squishy cukes allowed. Slice them very thin. If you have a mandolin at home, go to town. I personally consider mandolins death traps, so I use my knife skills and slice the cukes ⅛-inch thick. Pile them into a clean 4-cup jar. You can't have dill pickles without the dill, of course, so finely chop about 1–2 Tbsp of the stuff and add it to the pickles. Sprinkle in 1 Tbsp of pickling salt and pour ½ cup of white vinegar over the whole thing. With the lid on, shake the pickles until the ingredients have been evenly distributed. You may be slightly alarmed at the small amount of liquid. I was too. Don't be. The salt will draw out the moisture from the cucumbers, which are pretty much all water anyway. In about 2 hours, you'll have a healthy amount of liquid. This is also a good time to try them, but they'll be tastier at the 8-hour mark. To tweak the recipe, you can add a few cloves of slightly crushed garlic, 1 Tbsp pickling spice, a bay leaf, or slivers of white onion. But I like that this recipe only has four ingredients. It doesn't get easier than that. And the really neat thing about this recipe is that these pickles will keep in the refrigerator for up to 3 weeks. They make great snacking material and add a decent crunch to sandwiches. They're also a tasty addition to salads and charcuterie platters. Or you can eat them out of the jar, like I do.

Dixon Says: Cucumbers don't require a lot of special effort to grow, but they do require space and regular attention. They can be planted two or three to a hill (small mound of dirt) with hills about 2 feet apart. As they vine out, they take up considerably more room. The roots spread with the vines too, so try not to disturb the soil, especially when they start flowering. It's a great idea to plant lots of flowers nearby to attract pollinating insects. If the cukes turn yellow and start to ripen, the plant will stop producing, so keep them picked off.

CUCUMBERS

Anything Goes Cucumber and Chickpea Salad

This is one of my favourite salads to make when cucumbers and tomatoes are at their tastiest. I keep canned chickpeas in my pantry for this very salad alone. They mingle so well with the freshness of the veg and herbs, all while providing a hefty dose of fibre and protein. I often don't measure the amount of veg and herbs I'm using, but I understand that this is a recipe book and y'all like exact measurements, so I followed suit. Sometimes I omit the red pepper and onion, and sometimes I don't. Sometimes I use cold-pressed canola oil or camelina oil (two fabulous Saskatchewan-based products) instead of the olive oil, and often I'll swap mini bocconcini for the feta. Just like the recipe title says, anything goes!

In a large bowl, combine the chickpeas, cucumbers, tomatoes, red pepper, garlic, and red onion (if using). Stir in the feta and herbs. Drizzle in the oil and vinegar. Season with the salt and pepper. Toss well. You might want to adjust the seasoning to your liking. Divide into bowls and eat. This is best eaten the day it's made, but leftovers will be okay in the refrigerator for a day.

SERVES 2–4

1 can (19 oz/540 mL) chickpeas, rinsed and drained

4 mini cucumbers, chopped

1½ cups halved cherry tomatoes

½ red bell pepper, diced

2 garlic cloves, minced

2 Tbsp finely chopped red onion (optional)

1 cup crumbled feta cheese

½ cup chopped parsley (flat-leaf or curly)

2 Tbsp chopped dill (or basil or mint)

3 Tbsp extra-virgin olive oil

1½ Tbsp apple cider vinegar (or red wine vinegar)

½ tsp salt

¼ tsp pepper

* *Try using white beans or cooked green lentils instead of the chickpeas.*

* *The type of cucumber I use depends on the season. In summer, they are from the garden and I peel them. For the rest of the year, they are the greenhouse mini cucumbers, and I leave the peel on. You can also use long English and peel them, if you like.*

High Tea Cucumber and Cream Cheese Sandwiches

Once upon a time I was the chef at a tea room, and I busted out hundreds of dainty cucumber sandwiches every week for our high tea menu. Served in the afternoon, they made a lovely snack alongside pretty scones with raspberry butter and other sweet treats. The cucumber sandwich is nothing fancy, and yet it's so darn satisfying when done right. You won't find any squishy white bread with wilted cucumbers here. Instead, I've whipped the cream cheese with lemon and dill. When it's slathered on the fresh baguette slices, this barrier will prevent any soggy sammies. The fresh, crunchy slices of cucumber go for a quick swim in white wine vinegar. The dip is long enough to render them assertive yet refined and tasteful—not unlike some members of the royal clan themselves. (Hi, Meghan!) Whether you're hosting a baby shower or a ladies' lunch, or you just want to have a tea party with your littles, a simple cucumber sandwich is a winner every time.

In a small food processor fitted with a metal blade, blend the cream cheese, dill, lemon zest and juice, salt, and pepper until smooth. Season to taste with more salt and pepper, if desired. The cream cheese spread can be made up to a day ahead. Just bring it to room temperature 1 hour before assembling your sandwiches.

Toss the cucumber slices and vinegar together in a small bowl. Let the cucumber marinate while you spread the lemony dill cream cheese onto the baguette slices. The vinegar won't cover the cucumber slices entirely, so give them a toss now and then. Arrange the cucumber slices (about 3 per slice of bread) on top of the bread, then sprinkle with flaky salt and garnish with fresh dill. Serve immediately.

MAKES 20–22 SANDWICHES

8 oz cream cheese, cubed, at room temperature

¼ cup torn fresh dill sprigs

Grated zest and juice of 1 lemon

¼ tsp salt

⅛ tsp pepper

1 seedless long English cucumber, thinly sliced

½ cup white wine vinegar or sherry vinegar

1 fresh baguette, cut into 20–22 (½-inch-thick) slices

Garnish

Flaky salt, for sprinkling

Fresh dill sprigs, for garnish

✳ *The lemony dill cream cheese also makes a terrific dip for fresh vegetables or cold seafood.*

✳ *For smaller gatherings, the recipe can be easily halved.*

✳ *Instead of a baguette, try using a fresh sandwich loaf. Cut the crusts off, if you like.*

✳ *Refrigerate the leftover vinegar marinade for future salad dressings.*

Herby Couscous and Cucumbers
with Pan-Seared Halloumi

I admit that before this salad was in my repertoire, I didn't cook couscous all that often. The jar of tiny pasta grains would just stare back at me when I asked, "What am I going to do with you?" Happy to report it never answered me back, but I did eventually garner inspiration from a bounty of summer herbs and fresh cucumbers from my kitchen garden. I added heaps of Mediterranean flavour with sun-dried tomatoes and olives, but the pan-seared halloumi is what makes me giddy with joy. I love it when I get a little bite of melty, squeaky cheese with the herbaceous couscous salad. This is something that comes together super quick for a light summertime meal, and I like to pack up the leftovers for Dixon's lunch in the field the next day.

Place the broth in a medium saucepan and bring it to a boil over medium-high heat. Turn off the heat and stir in the couscous. Cover with a lid and let it stand for 6–7 minutes to cook. Fluff with a fork and transfer to a large bowl. If the couscous is clumpy, you can break it up with your hands. While the couscous is warm, stir in the lemon zest, juice of 1 lemon (about ¼ cup of juice), and 4 Tbsp of the oil. Season with generous pinches of salt and pepper.

When the couscous has cooled to room temperature, stir in the chopped cucumbers, herbs, sun-dried tomatoes, olives, chives, and remaining 2 Tbsp of lemon juice. Season to taste with salt and pepper. Refrigerate the salad, uncovered, for 30 minutes so the flavours have a chance to mingle.

Place a non-stick skillet over medium heat. Pour in the remaining 2 Tbsp oil. When it has warmed, add the slices of halloumi to the skillet and cook on each side until golden brown, about 2 minutes per side.

Divide the salad into bowls and top each with golden brown halloumi. Eat immediately.

Makes enough for 3 to 4 main dishes or 6 to 8 sides.

SERVES 3–4

1¾ cups vegetable broth

1½ cups couscous

Grated zest and juice of 1½ lemons, divided (you need 6 Tbsp total of juice)

6 Tbsp extra-virgin olive oil (or oil from sun-dried tomatoes jar), divided

Salt and pepper

5 mini cucumbers, chopped (see note on page 109)

⅓ cup chopped basil

⅓ cup chopped mint

⅓ cup chopped parsley (flat-leaf or curly)

⅓ cup oil-packed sun-dried tomatoes, sliced

⅓ cup whole green olives

2 Tbsp chopped chives or green onions

1 package (8 oz/250 g) halloumi cheese, sliced into ¼-inch pieces

✳ *I always save the oil from my sun-dried tomatoes! Packed with flavour, it's great in place of olive oil in a salad like this, or as a base for pesto (page 85) or salad dressing (page 136).*

✳ *Feel free to add cooked chicken, shrimp, or chickpeas for extra protein. If you don't want to use halloumi, crumbled feta cheese or goat cheese works great, too.*

've been writing my blog *Sweetsugarbean* for over ten years. Ten whole years! The header at the top of the landing page is a photograph I snapped of some pretty leaves belonging to green beans. They were particularly prolific in my garden that summer of 2011, and I recall being out there quite a bit, picking almost every day, which meant eating them almost every day. I really do love beans—so much so that I put them in the name of my food blog.

Beans, like most vegetables when they're just picked and super fresh, don't really need much more than a quick simmer in the saucepan or a turn in a hot skillet to take off some of the crunch. For all that is good and holy, do not boil your beans to the point where they lose their colour and their snap. Not only do the nutrients leak out into the water but so does all of that flavour and texture. Repeat after me: Mushy veg are bad. A few minutes in simmering water is really all fresh beans require. They should be dark emerald green and bend a little. After I've drained them, I like to swirl in some butter and season to taste with salt and pepper. Vegetables need salt to enhance their flavour, while pepper adds depth and spice to the dish. When they taste delicious (not bland or boring), you've seasoned correctly. In the summer, there's no shortage of dill where I live, so I'll add a good amount to these beans, which are Dixon's absolute favourite. We like to call them Moonbeans. Okay, here's a dorky story for you: One night years ago, Dix and I were talking on the phone until the wee hours, like we always do when we can't be together. As I was saying goodbye, I wished him sweet dreams and moonbeams. He thought I said moonbeans, and so we had a good laugh and talked about how those delicious dilly summer green beans are the perfect moonbeans. And forevermore, when we say goodnight, it's now sweet dreams and moonbeans. We really are the two biggest cheeseballs ever.

❋❋❋❋❋❋❋❋❋❋❋❋❋❋❋❋❋❋❋❋❋❋❋❋❋❋❋❋❋❋❋❋❋❋

Dixon Says: I don't really have a lot to say about beans, and, at the same time, I have everything to say about them. Let me explain. I don't really do much with beans in the garden. My brother often plants them and my sister usually picks them. (And how!! On a good day, I'm half as fast as her!) My involvement is usually weeding and wheel hoeing them. We sow beans in a row, with 1-inch spacing between plants. They're a low-maintenance vegetable, as they seem to grow without much effort or worry on my part. As long as they receive regular watering and the beans are picked off when ready, we'll get as many as five pickings per plant.

One of my favourite meals ever was one made by my dear Ren. It was a Saturday, after the market. I had picked up some fish from the market and brought fresh potatoes, corn on the cob, and green beans to her place. Renée makes the best beans! Cooked just enough so they have that slight crunch yet and slathered in butter and dill. They were amazing!! I still think about them almost four years later! I came to a profound realization that day. Ren is more than just amazing and wonderful; she makes the ordinary extraordinary.

GREEN

BEANS

Miso and Maple Blistered Green Beans

There are some vegetables that are so good they'll have a hard time making their way out of the skillet and onto a serving platter. These sweet, salty, spicy beans are one of them. You'll pluck one bean from the pan, and then another, and, believe me, I know the urge is strong to just keep going. The umami is flying high here! I love how the little bit of blistering can elevate ordinary green beans, with punchy flavours taking them even higher. These beans are somewhat sticky, and, for that reason, I like to serve them with plenty of basmati rice and grilled chicken or fish. Or you can be like me and just eat them out of the skillet.

Whisk together the garlic, ginger, miso, vinegar, maple syrup, and Sriracha in a medium bowl.

Warm a 12-inch skillet over medium-high heat. Add the oil. When it's hot but not smoking, add the beans and cook, undisturbed, until they begin to blister, about 2 minutes. Toss and continue to cook, stirring often, until the beans are tender, yet still a little crisp, and blistered in spots, about 5 minutes.

Pour in the miso mixture and a pinch of red pepper flakes. Toss to coat evenly and cook for 1 more minute. Season to taste with salt and pepper. Serve immediately.

SERVES 4

2 garlic cloves, minced

2 tsp minced fresh ginger

2 Tbsp light miso paste

2 Tbsp rice vinegar

1 Tbsp maple syrup

1 tsp Sriracha

2 Tbsp canola oil

1 lb fresh green beans, trimmed

Red pepper flakes

Salt and pepper

Green Beans with Browned Butter and Sage

Browned butter makes everything better, including green beans. I could have just stirred the beans in the butter and that would have been fine, but I took it one step further and added sliced almonds to the skillet, as well as fresh sage leaves. The smell radiating from the stove is pretty terrific. Everything gets tossed together, and that's it really. You'll want to watch the skillet once the almonds join the party, as they can go from golden brown to burnt very quickly. I like this recipe because it works really well with both frozen and fresh green beans. Fresh is optimal, of course, but, in the dead of winter, when only frozen are available, this is a tasty way to get your green bean fix.

If you're using fresh green beans, trim the ends. If you're using frozen, don't bother thawing. Place the beans in a large saucepan along with 1½ cups of water. Cover and bring to a boil over medium-high heat. Once the beans have come to a boil, uncover, and cook them until they're fork-tender but still a little crisp, about 1–2 minutes. Drain and rinse under cool running water for 1 minute. It's okay if they're still warm. They don't have to be completely cooled down.

Place a large non-stick skillet over medium heat. Add the butter. Once you see some brown bits starting to form and the butter is getting foamy, add the almonds and cook, stirring constantly, for 1 minute, until they're beginning to turn golden. Be careful not to burn the almonds. If they get too dark, turn the heat down. Stir in the sage leaves (you'll hear an excellent hissing sound) and cook, stirring constantly for 1 minute, until they're crisp.

Add the cooked green beans to the skillet, gently toss to marry everything together, and heat the beans through. Season to taste with salt and pepper. Serve immediately.

SERVES 4–6

1 lb green beans, fresh or frozen

3 Tbsp unsalted butter

½ cup sliced almonds

12 medium sage leaves

Salt and pepper

Roasted Green Beans with Chili Bread Crumbs and Mozzarella

I know sometimes green beans can be a tough sell, especially to selective eaters. That's where melty cheese comes to the rescue. These beans have delectable crispy bits and heaps of flavour from the garlic and bread crumbs. But the cheese—oh, the cheese—really makes you want to pick them up and eat them with your hands. Totally guilty of it, myself. Sometimes playing with your food is the only way to go, especially if it means more vegetables get eaten. Dix and I love eating these green beans in the summer when they're bursting with fantastic flavour. Forks are optional. Napkins are essential.

Preheat the oven to 425°F.

In a large bowl, whisk together the oil, garlic, chili powder, salt, and pepper. Add the beans and toss until they're evenly coated.

Spread the beans (be sure to scrape all of the oil out of the bowl, too) onto a rimmed baking sheet (no parchment paper) in a single layer. Roast for 10 minutes. Remove from the oven, add the bread crumbs, and stir to combine. Return the baking sheet to the oven and roast for another 5 minutes. Remove from the oven and stir (we don't want the bread crumbs to burn). Return to the oven until the bread crumbs are a deep golden brown and the beans have some blistered spots, about 3–4 minutes. Remove the beans from the oven and sprinkle on the mozzarella.

Preheat the broiler. Put the baking sheet under the broiler and keep it there until the cheese is melted and browned, about 2–3 minutes. Serve immediately.

SERVES 4-6

¼ cup extra-virgin olive oil

2 garlic cloves, thinly sliced

1 tsp chili powder

1 tsp salt

¼ tsp pepper

1 lb fresh green beans, trimmed

½ cup panko bread crumbs

1½ cups shredded mozzarella cheese

✳ *For a variation, omit the mozzarella and add 1 cup of crumbled feta cheese to the beans. Instead of putting them under the broiler, simply roast a few minutes longer until the cheese is melted and lightly browned.*

Worth the Wait

Summer 2011: I've owned my little house in Saskatoon for three years. I worked hard to save up the down payment (it took years!), and I'm super proud that my name is on the property title, especially since I required no financial help from anyone else (except the bank, obviously). Single, strong-willed, and independent, I live here with two cats. I'm alone, but not lonely. And I love my garden. I love the feeling of cool grass underfoot as I pad my way to the back of the garden where I check in on the latest growth spurt. Along the way, I stop to smell the sweet peas and take in the ferocious beauty of the purple coneflower. I don't even stop to put shoes on as I enter the dirt path. There's something almost rebellious about a grown woman going barefoot in her own garden, but if this is the full extent of my rebellion, I don't think any of us need to worry. I open the gate, which has been carefully rigged so the cats can't climb over and do their own digging, and I carefully step along the rows of beets, carrots, Swiss chard, and tomatoes. The peas have tangled their way up the woven wires of the fencing, and some of the zucchini blossoms, the yellow beauties, are bursting out into star shapes, while others are softly enclosed. I stop and admire them, for squash flowers really are worthy of

admiration. Every now and again I think back to how all of this garden gorgeousness started with just a few seeds. And water and sun and careful attention. I can't help but think about how that truckload of manure that was dumped on the plot in early May is now working its magic. The garden is truly bursting with goodness. I pick the green beans, some of which like to play hide-and-seek behind the emerald leaves, and so I've really got to search them out. As I make my way back to the house, feeling the warm dirt, then the cool grass on my feet, the cats following closely behind, I think how lucky am I to have this little urban oasis. The garden is work, lots of it, but there's no better place to get food than your own backyard. Inside my little green kitchen, I package up some of the green beans in a plastic bag, and the others get transferred to the refrigerator. I've got a date later that day, and I want to bring him some beans. It's a first date, and I'm so nervous I think I'll barf before I get there. I've not dated anyone since a break up in 2008, and I really want it to go well. What grown man wouldn't want a bag of just-picked beans? Or the woman who tended to those beans?

Me and this fella have a grand time walking and talking, but I never hear from him again. I peel apart every bit of the conversation, looking for clues as to why he wouldn't want to see me again. Was it because I was older than him? Or that I owned my house and he lived in his mom's basement? Or was I trying too hard with the offering of beans? As women, we tend to put all of the blame on ourselves when things don't work out, but, honestly, nothing was meant to happen with this dude. And I'm sure I'm better off for it. One day, I tell myself, I'll find someone who is worthy of my vegetables. And my love.

Spring 2016: My garden spot grows no vegetables, and the chickweed has crept in and staked its claim to the dirt. There is a small patch of raspberry bushes, and, in the far corner, two rhubarb plants take up residence. Watching them slowly unfurl from the ground is one of my favourite harbingers of spring. As soon as the rhubarb is ready, I'm out there plucking it from the ground and rinsing it off with the garden hose.

vegetable growing has been downsized to pots of tomatoes, lettuce, cucumbers, and herbs. I've still got plenty of light near the house, and so these pots will have to do. But I've just met a handsome man, and he grows all the vegetables I could ever want. On our first date he brought me a bundle of asparagus, and it was like a meeting of kindred spirits. Instead of me giving him green beans, it was he offering the first spears of his own garden bounty. Rather than shy away from such a romantic overture, I'm so into it. And into him. He was worth the wait.

Summer 2020: The garden spot has been taken over with thick and hardy raspberry bushes, which are a joy to pick from in the summer, and the cats, now totalling four, love to catch a nap in their shade, or hide from me when I tell them it's time to come inside the house. Dixon, the love of my life, continues to bring me all of the vegetables I could ever want, and while the

ON OUR FIRST DATE HE BROUGHT ME
A BUNDLE OF ASPARAGUS, AND IT WAS
LIKE A MEETING OF KINDRED SPIRITS.

The poisonous leaves get discarded, and the stalks are chopped for scones, compotes, cakes, and pies. It's the plant that keeps on giving, and I'm fortunate to have two so generous. They even withstand the high-traffic antics of my three cats (yes, three now), who think that this part of the yard is their jungle playground. So far no rhubarb stalks have been damaged due to their hi-jinks, but I can't say the same for the bleeding heart. The trees, oh the trees, have grown taller and wider and their leaves have crowded out most of the sunlight that used to fall down on the soil. I've not planted a garden in a year, and I miss it so. Everyone knows you need light to grow food, and now my

trees have continued to grow wider and taller in this old neighbourhood, there is still enough light near my house for a few pots of tomatoes and herbs. Time has altered some things, but ten years on, my love for the earth and all of the good things that come from it has changed only in that it has deepened even more. And if you were to peek over my fence, you would still see me walking barefoot in the grass, taking in the ferocious beauty of the purple coneflower and inhaling the intoxicating scent of the sweet peas, a cat or two trailing behind me.

I can hear your collective sighs and detect possible eye-rolling at the thought of yet another kale recipe coming at you, but, please, hear me out. These are kale recipes you are actually going to want to eat. Kale cannot be eaten as is, straight from the store or the garden. For those of you who aren't fans, it's likely because it was served raw and unruly and now you're scarred for life. I agree that raw kale can be tough like cardboard, and you have to chew it for a million years to swallow it down, but that doesn't mean you can't eat it raw. I've said it once and I'll say it again: Kale needs some good lovin'. When you're serving kale raw in a salad or in the Supersonic Power Bowls (page 229), you NEED to massage it with olive oil and a bit of salt for a few minutes so those tough fibres break down. The effect of the massaging is obvious within mere minutes: the leaves are no longer dull and tough and instead are forest green and buttery soft. It's almost like a different vegetable. You can then add more olive oil, lemon juice, Dijon, minced garlic, toasted croutons, and heaps of Parmesan for a quick Caesar. Or add toasted nuts, dried fruit, crumbled feta, and cooked grains, such as barley or quinoa, for a satisfying salad. Add the massaged kale to a sheet pan supper and roast it until it becomes crispy, for a twist.

I also love kale in warm and cozy dishes like chili, shepherd's pie, soups, and pastas. There's no need to massage it before stirring it into saucy things, as the leaves soften up in the liquid and absorb all of the gorgeous flavours in the dish. My mom gives me a hard time because she thinks I put kale into everything—and she's not wrong. I could have had 10 more kale recipes in this book, but space is at a premium!

Not only am I fond of its bold flavour and high-maintenance nature, I also eat it because it is a superfood. And I mean SUPERFOOD. It is bursting with all sorts of vitamins, minerals, phytonutrients, antioxidants, carotenoids, and other good things your body loves. It's one of the most nutrient-dense vegetables out there— they don't call it the Queen of Greens for nothing. Just remember to remove the tough centre ribs when chopping it up for recipes. I usually compost these stems, but I've heard of people pickling them, too. I'm not so sure about that. I love me some kale but probably not to that extent.

After all of my coercing, if kale is still not your style, you can substitute spinach or Swiss chard for the recipes in this cookbook.

✳︎

Dixon Says: Kale grows well in a sheltered spot in any kind of soil. The plants should be covered with a screen to protect them from cabbage butterflies. Water the plants generously, about an inch or two a week. When harvesting, choose the biggest leaves and pick off any that are old and weathered looking to ensure that the plant continues to produce new leaves.

KALE

Hearty Kale and Sausage Soup

Everyone needs a quick and delicious soup teeming with sausage, pasta, and greens. It's a full-meal deal, right from your own kitchen. I love using good sausage in soup as it comes already loaded with garlic and spices, which saves me from having to rummage around in my spice cupboard. Of course, where you buy your sausage from will affect the flavour, so make friends with a local butcher, if you can. (Shout-out to Jordan at the Pig and Pantry in Saskatoon. He makes really great sausage!) This soup is a tasty way to become a kale convert. The assertiveness of the green softens in the broth and makes fast friends with all of the Parmesan you're going to grate on top of each bowl. Dixon likes to tell me this is one of the best soups I make for him. How's that for a recommendation?

Warm a Dutch oven over medium-high heat. Squeeze the sausage out of its casings directly into the pot. Break it up with the back of a wooden spoon. Cook until it's no longer pink inside.

Depending on how much fat is in your sausage, you may need to add a bit of canola oil to slick the pot. Stir in the onion and carrots. Add generous pinches of salt and pepper. Cook just until the vegetables are softened, about 5 minutes. Scrape up any browned bits from the bottom of the pot.

Stir in the broth and bring to a boil over medium-high heat. Stir in the pasta and tomatoes with their juice. You can use your hands to squeeze the tomatoes into the soup, or be more civilized and cut them with kitchen scissors. Your call. Rinse out the tomato can with about 1 cup water and add this tomatoey water as well.

Turn down the heat to medium-low, cover the pot, and simmer the soup until the pasta is cooked, about 15–20 minutes. Stir in the chopped kale and 1 cup of water. Cook until the kale is softened, about 3–4 minutes. Stir in the vinegar and season to taste with more salt and pepper.

Divide the soup into bowls and garnish with the Parmesan and parsley.

SERVES 4–6

1 lb fresh chorizo or Italian sausage

Canola oil, if needed

1 medium yellow onion, diced

2 medium carrots, diced (about 1½ cups)

Salt and pepper

6 cups low-sodium chicken broth

1 cup uncooked ditali or orzo pasta

1 can (28 oz/798 mL) whole tomatoes

3 cups chopped kale, centre ribs removed

2 Tbsp balsamic vinegar

½ cup shaved Parmesan, for garnish

2 Tbsp chopped parsley (flat-leaf or curly), for garnish

＊ *This recipe can also be made with barley instead of pasta. Just add ⅔ cup of barley in place of the pasta and simmer for 30–35 minutes until tender.*

A Very Veggie Shepherd's Pie

Back in the day, I clipped recipes out of newspapers and magazines and taped them into notebooks. Yellowed and stained, these pages tell stories of where I was and what was happening in my life. In 1997, I had just entered culinary school in Edmonton, and this budget-friendly shepherd's pie recipe was taped into my notebook around then, too. I've tweaked the recipe a lot since those student days, adding more veg to the filling, and I've gussied up the mashed potatoes with roasted garlic and cheese. This is one of those cozy, affordable dishes that comes together with whatever you have on hand and makes awesome leftovers.

Prepare the potatoes: Place the potatoes in a large saucepan and cover with plenty of cold water. Add a generous pinch of salt. Cover, bring to a boil over high heat, then turn down the heat to medium-low and simmer until tender, about 10–14 minutes.

Drain the potatoes, then dump them back into the pot. Add the butter, cream, and cheese (in that order). Mash until smooth. Squeeze in the roasted garlic pulp, mash again, and season to taste with salt and pepper. Add more milk if needed.

Prepare the filling: Preheat the oven to 375°F. In a 12-inch cast-iron skillet, warm the canola oil over medium-high heat. Sauté the onion until soft and translucent, about 5 minutes, then stir in the mushrooms, carrots, garlic, and herbs, cooking for 5 more minutes. Season with generous pinches of salt and pepper. Stir in the kale, tomatoes with their juice, broth, parsley, Worcestershire sauce, and hot sauce. Cook over medium heat until the kale is soft, about 3 minutes, then stir in the cooked lentils. Cook for 2 minutes. Season with more salt and pepper.

If you plan on baking the shepherd's pie in the cast-iron skillet like I do, place the mashed potatoes over the filling, smoothing the top and using the tines of a fork to create ridges in the potatoes. Drizzle with the olive oil. If you don't have a cast-iron skillet, just spoon the filling into a 9- × 13-inch baking dish and proceed with the recipe. Bake until the potato topping is golden, about 35 minutes. Place a foil-lined baking sheet on the bottom rack to catch any juices, should the pie run over.

---

* *To roast garlic, slice the top off of the garlic bulb. Place it on a small sheet of aluminum foil. Drizzle with olive oil. Wrap up tightly and place in a preheated 375°F oven until softened, golden, and fragrant, 35–40 minutes.*

* *Instead of kale, use spinach or Swiss chard. Instead of mushrooms, use 1 cup peas (fresh or frozen) or corn.*

SERVES 6

Potatoes

2 lb Yukon Gold potatoes, cut into 1½-inch chunks

Salt and pepper

¼ cup butter

⅓ cup coffee cream (or sour cream)

1 cup shredded extra-old white cheddar cheese

1 head roasted garlic (see note)

Filling

2 Tbsp canola oil

1 large yellow onion, diced

2 cups thinly sliced button mushrooms

2 medium carrots, grated

2 garlic cloves, minced

2 tsp finely chopped fresh rosemary (or 1 tsp dried)

2 tsp finely chopped fresh thyme (or 1 tsp dried)

3 cups packed, chopped kale, centre ribs removed

1 can (19 oz/540 mL) diced tomatoes

⅔ cup vegetable broth

¼ cup chopped fresh parsley

2 tsp Worcestershire sauce

2 tsp your favourite hot sauce (or more!)

2¼ cups cooked whole green lentils (see page 165)

1 Tbsp olive oil, for drizzling

Tortellini with Kale and Buttered Bread Crumbs

There are a few things that I remember about Dixon's and my second date: 1) The deep blue of his sweater and how well it complemented his chestnut hair. 2) How we couldn't keep our eyes off each other. 3) How fantastic the food was. We were dining at Primal—one of the best restaurants in Saskatoon—and it has come to be the place we return to over and over again for excellent pasta and sexy date-night vibes. This is my version of the agnolotti we ate that night, but instead of making my own stuffed pasta, I use packaged tortellini—I love a good shortcut when I see one! The flavourful broth just kisses the pasta, inching oh so close to making this dish a soup, but not quite. The simple garnish of buttered bread crumbs makes me swoon for this pasta—almost as much as I swooned for Dixon on that second date.

Prepare the bread crumbs: Melt the butter in a large non-stick skillet over medium heat. Stir in the bread crumbs and toast, stirring occasionally, until golden brown, 4–6 minutes. Remove from the heat, transfer to a small bowl, and stir in the lemon zest. Wipe out the skillet.

Prepare the pasta: Bring a pot of salted water to a boil over high heat. Add the tortellini and cook according to the package directions. Drain, return to pot, stir in 1 Tbsp of butter, and set aside.

Meanwhile, in the skillet you used for the bread crumbs, melt the remaining butter over medium-high heat. Stir in the onion and carrot. Sauté for a few minutes, then add the garlic. Cook for another minute or two, then stir in the kale, cherry tomatoes, and sun-dried tomatoes. Give it a good stir, then add the broth, salt, and pepper. Bring to a boil, then turn down the heat to medium-low and simmer for 5 minutes. Season to taste with more salt and pepper, if needed.

Divide the pasta into bowls and add the brothy kale mixture. Be sure each bowl has some broth. Top with Parmesan cheese, a heaping spoonful of buttered bread crumbs, and chopped herbs, if using. Serve immediately.

SERVES 3–4

Bread crumbs

1 Tbsp butter

⅓ cup panko bread crumbs

Grated zest of ½ lemon

Pasta

1 package (12 oz/350 g) cheese or beef tortellini

3 Tbsp butter, divided

1 small onion, diced

½ cup diced carrot

2 garlic cloves, minced

2 cups packed, chopped kale, centre ribs removed

1 cup halved cherry tomatoes

⅓ cup oil-packed sun-dried tomatoes, sliced

2¾ cups low-sodium chicken (or vegetable) broth

½ tsp salt

¼ tsp pepper

½ cup grated Parmesan cheese

2 Tbsp chopped herbs such as basil, parsley, dill (optional)

✳ *For a little meat action, add some chopped dry cured chorizo, cooked bacon, or ham when you add the kale.*

✳ *If you have ¾ cup of canned white beans or cooked lentils in the refrigerator, toss them in when you add the kale for a little protein boost.*

White Bean and Kale Chicken Chili

One can never have enough delicious chili recipes. While I love a good tomato-based chili, like the one on page 195, there's something quite special about this brothy version with ground chicken and white beans. I developed this recipe in the midst of COVID-19 when I had to rustle up dinner with whatever was lurking in my pantry, refrigerator, and freezer. It's also a good way to eat more kale. This hardy green loves to absorb the spicy and bright flavours happening here, while the sweet potato tames the heat of the jalapeño and the lime juice tingles with tang. And to really make the flavours dance, be sure to garnish with the toppings I've listed.

In a Dutch oven, warm the oil over medium-high heat. Add the onion and jalapeño. Cook, stirring occasionally, until the onion has softened, about 4–5 minutes.

Add the chicken and cook, stirring occasionally, until it's lightly browned on the outside and no longer pink, about 5 minutes.

Toss in the garlic, dried spices, salt, and sugar. Cook for a few minutes, just to toast the spices. Add the sweet potatoes, bell pepper, and corn. Stir to combine. Add the beans, broth, and hot sauce. Cover and bring to a simmer. Turn down the heat to medium-low and cook, stirring occasionally, for 20 minutes.

Stir in the kale and cilantro. Cover and cook for about 5 more minutes. Stir in the lime juice. Remove from the heat and add more salt, pepper, and hot sauce, if you like.

Divide into bowls. Garnish with toppings to taste.

* For more heat, use the whole jalapeño.

* Use ground turkey or chorizo sausage instead of the ground chicken. Use cooked green lentils, black beans, kidney beans, or chickpeas instead of the white beans. Omit the meat and use additional vegetables to keep it vegetarian. Swap the chicken broth for vegetable broth.

* The chili will thicken up as it cools. Thin out any leftovers with more broth.

* I like the flavour of a mild jalapeño hot sauce in this recipe.

SERVES 6

Chili

1 Tbsp canola oil

1 large yellow onion, diced

½ jalapeño pepper, minced

1 lb ground chicken

2 garlic cloves, minced

1 Tbsp chili powder

1 Tbsp ground cumin

½ Tbsp dried oregano

1¼ tsp salt

1 tsp granulated sugar

2 cups peeled and chopped (½-inch pieces) sweet potatoes

1 red bell pepper, chopped

1 cup frozen corn kernels

2 cans (each 19 oz/540 mL) white beans, rinsed and drained

3 cups low-sodium chicken broth

1–2 Tbsp your favourite hot sauce

3 cups chopped kale, centre ribs removed

¼ cup chopped fresh cilantro

Juice of 1 lime

Toppings

Pickled red onions (page 165)

Chopped cilantro

Sour cream

Shredded cheddar

Lime wedges

Sliced avocado

Corn tortilla chips

Hot sauce

Life's Rich Pageant

Oh, All Hallows Eve. The night of ghouls and goblins; princesses and pirates; tricksters and treaters. The jack-o'-lanterns are all aglow on my front porch as the candy seekers climb up the steps, belting out "Trick or treat!" just about loud enough to wake the dead. The cats, rustled from their slumber, scamper away to The Safe Spot Under the Bed until the treating ends. I've got a pot of chili on the stove, slowly burbling away with beans and vegetables, filling the house with a cozy wholesomeness that I crave on brisk autumn nights. Dixon and I take turns dishing out the candy, and once we've heard the last of the witches and warlocks, we turn off the lights, settle in with our spicy beans, and watch a scary movie. Dessert is whatever remains in the candy bowl. I call dibs on the mini Jersey Milks.

When I think of the Halloweens of long ago, I remember some years my siblings and I had to trudge through what felt like knee-deep snow to get the sweet stuff. We had to wear our snowsuits under our costumes, but we didn't care. There was *candy* to be had at the end of our snowy trek. When we were lucky enough to get *full-size chocolate bars* in our pillowcases, I made a mental note to return to that address the following year. Bless those most generous people! Then, of

course, we'd get the Homemade Popcorn Ball People, and no one ever ate the popcorn balls, did they? They were almost as bad as the Apple People, or God forbid, the Toothbrush People.

After we'd tricked and treated our little hearts out, our pillowcases sagging from the weight of all of that candy, I remember coming into a warm, cozy house and my mom having a pot of chili on the stove. The snowsuits were quickly shrugged off, and, while we may have already had a belly full of sugar, we still sat down together, tucking into bowls of hearty chili and dishing the deets on whose house gave the best/most/worst candy, and who made us sing for it. Mom's chili was a pretty standard ground beef and beans type, nothing too wild and crazy, but comforting and delicious all the same.

Sometimes I wish I'd met Dixon when I was 33 instead of 43, before I knew what endometriosis was and what complete and utter havoc it would wreak on my uterus. Sometimes I wonder if we would have been blessed with a wee one to dress up as a tomato or a carrot on Halloween, who'd sit with us at our own kitchen table and scoop up delicious chili as we giggled about who gave out the whole bars of chocolate and how we'd have to avoid the house where the Homemade Popcorn Ball People live next year. Sometimes I have a small pang in my heart that there won't be a little face that looks up at me with the same blue-green eyes as I have or watches as I show her how to shell peas and stuff cabbage rolls. She'll never grow up and go away to university, and I won't have the chance to put together carefully curated care packages full of recipes and brownies. There'll never be a little boy who rides around on Dixon's shoulder, giggling with delight exactly like his daddy. He'll never work alongside his dad in the field, slipping over to the pea patch to have a snack. It's a slippery slope down this childless rabbit hole, and I don't like to stay down there too long. Blessings come in all shapes and sizes, and for me it didn't come in the way of a baby, and that's okay. Life's rich pageant continues, full and glorious, shining on, shining on.

Whenever we go out for dinner, Dixon will order a green salad. He's fairly particular about his lettuce/dressing/accoutrements, and he thinks it's a great indicator of what else the kitchen can do. I've realized over the years he's not wrong. Great salad = great meal.

Given Dixon's penchant for a tasty bowl of greens, I'll often whip us up a bowl of baby kale or arugula, with other leafy greens added to the mix depending on the season. He thinks my dressing is off the charts, but it's often just a jam jar of apple cider vinegar, good olive oil or cold-pressed canola oil, a spoonful of Dijon, and a smidge of sugar or honey, salt, and pepper, all shaken up. Real simple, right there. I learned this simple yet delicious way of dressing greens from my mom, who makes the best summertime salad of fresh lettuce and an uber-light dressing of olive oil and lemon juice. When I moved away from home for the first time I asked her about this dressing, and, of course, she never really measured anything, but eventually it went into my coil-bound recipe book as Mom's Best Salad Dressing: 3 Tbsp olive oil, 1 Tbsp fresh lemon juice, 2 tsp finely chopped dill, ½ tsp garlic powder, 2 pinches dry mustard powder, and sugar, salt, and pepper to taste. If she had lemon pepper in the house, she

would add a few shakes of that, too. Tossed with fresh lettuce from the garden, this was the salad dressing of my youth.

I'm a giant fan of big salads. The bigger, the better. I'll never say no to a Cobb loaded with grilled chicken, roasted corn, chopped egg, creamy avocado, crumbled blue cheese, and plenty of bacon. Drizzled with a honey mustard buttermilk dressing, it's one of the best reasons ever to eat iceberg lettuce. Romaine lettuce takes on a whole new life when it's sliced in half, brushed with olive oil, and grilled for a minute or two until the leaves have lovely charred bits. This short time on the grill gives the lettuce a lush smokiness, and, while the leaves are a little blackened, there is the pleasant textural contrast of crisp and tender playing about on the plate.

Another fun fact about Dix: he likes a lot of lettuce in his sandwiches. When I think I've added enough, he'll ask for just another leaf. Or two. We both grew up eating fresh lettuce sandwiches in the summer, on soft, squidgy white bread with nothing else but a slick of mayonnaise and a dusting of salt and pepper. The lettuce was picked just that morning, and you could tell. Earthy and fresh, it was so buttery soft, it sunk into the bread and into one perfect bite. And another.

✳✳✳✳✳✳✳✳✳✳✳✳✳✳✳✳✳✳✳✳✳✳✳✳✳✳✳✳✳✳✳✳✳✳✳✳✳✳

Dixon Says: Lettuce and spinach are two of my favourite vegetables. (I love fresh salad, and no one makes a dressing like my sweetheart.) And they're so easy to grow, too! They're not fussy when it comes to soil and really only need a shot of fertilizer and regular watering. They're very container-friendly if you don't have room for a garden; just make sure they are placed where they can get some light. Honestly, who doesn't like a fresh-picked leaf (or five) of lettuce in their sandwich?

LEAFY

GREENS

Winter Salad with Candied Pecans
in Balsamic Vinaigrette

Winter salads need to impress. Unlike their summer sisters, the greens have to travel a fair distance, as opposed to just down the garden path. For this reason alone, grocery store greens need to be accented with really great toppings such as slices of blood oranges, the flavour of which reminds me of raspberries, and the colour a stunning sunset. Pomegranates are like the precious jewels of the fruit world, and the pretty arils really make this salad sing. But the topping you are most going to love is the candied pecans. They are a little spicy and highly snackable. Not all will go on the salad, that's for sure, and that's okay! I serve a platter of this gorgeous salad on Christmas Day, as Dixon loves a good salad *almost* as much as he loves turkey, stuffing, mashed potatoes, and gravy. Almost.

Prepare the pecans: Preheat the oven to 375°F. Line a rimmed baking sheet with parchment paper.

In a small bowl, toss together the nuts, maple syrup, cinnamon, and cayenne. Spread onto the baking sheet in a single layer. Roast for about 13–15 minutes, stirring every 5 minutes so they don't burn. The nuts are done when they are more dry than sticky. Remove from the oven, sprinkle with flaky salt, and let cool while you prepare the rest of the salad.

Prepare the dressing: Place all of the dressing ingredients in a jam jar. Shake vigorously until the dressing has emulsified. Season with more jam, salt, and pepper, if you like.

You can assemble the salad on either individual plates or on a large platter. Heap the greens, layer in the cabbage, top with the fruit, scatter the cheese and nuts, drizzle with the dressing.

SERVES 4

Candied Pecans
1 cup raw pecan halves

¼ cup maple syrup

⅛ tsp ground cinnamon

Cayenne pepper

Flaky salt

Dressing
⅓ cup canola oil

¼ cup balsamic vinegar

1 Tbsp apricot jam

1 Tbsp Dijon mustard

½ tsp salt

¼ tsp pepper

Salad
8 cups mixed salad greens, such as baby kale, arugula, spinach, lettuce, etc.

1 cup shredded red cabbage

2 blood oranges, peeled and sliced into rounds

½ cup pomegranate arils

¾ cup crumbled goat cheese

✳ *Try navel orange or grapefruit segments instead of the blood orange, or use feta cheese as the goat cheese. Use fig jam instead of apricot. Layer in thin slices of cooked beets or even slivers of red onion. Go wild.*

✳ *To switch things up for summer, use fresh strawberries and slices of peaches or nectarines instead of the citrus and pomegranate. Add some torn fresh herbs such as basil or mint. Add torn bocconcini cheese instead of goat cheese.*

Grapefruit and Avocado Salad with Lemony Shrimp

This is my go-to salad in January, when the holiday buzz has burned off and any resolutions, if they were even made, have already burned out. Swimming with buttery avocado, lemony shrimp, and just the perfect amount of tangy grapefruit segments, this salad brings a welcome lightness in a month of full-on Christmas Recovery. You'll feel like you are on a cleanse at some posh oceanside spa, and Ryan Gosling is your waiter, and he brings you glasses of sparkling water with lime, and brushes the sand out of your hair, and laughs at all your jokes, and . . . Errr, sorry about that. Daydream, interrupted. Back to the salad! This recipe is simply a guide. Make it as you like it. Sub in some spinach for the greens or blood oranges for the grapefruit. I know you'll eat a few shrimp out of the bowl before assembling the salad. That's okay. Quality control is important!

Prepare the shrimp: In a medium, non-reactive bowl, combine the marinade ingredients, using just a pinch of red pepper flakes. Add the shrimp. Toss thoroughly so all of the shrimp are evenly coated. Cover and refrigerate for 15 minutes.

Remove the shrimp from the marinade, discard the marinade, and place the shrimp in a large non-stick skillet over medium-high heat. Cook the shrimp until they're pink and opaque on each side, about 4 minutes in total. Let the shrimp cool in the skillet to room temperature, then place them in a clean bowl, as well as any juices left behind in the skillet. Cover and refrigerate for 2 hours.

Prepare the salad: Slice the peel from the top and bottom of the grapefruit. Peel the sides so all the flesh is showing. Cut out segments over a bowl to catch the juice. Reserve 1 Tbsp of the juice for the dressing. Use the rest up in a cocktail or some sparkling water.

In a small bowl, whisk together the reserved grapefruit juice, the oil, vinegar, mustard, maple syrup, salt, and pepper. Adjust the seasonings to taste.

Divide the greens among four plates or on a large platter. Top with the grapefruit, avocado, cucumber, shrimp, and fresh dill (in that order). Drizzle with the vinaigrette.

SERVES 4

Shrimp and Marinade

Grated zest of 1 lemon

¼ cup fresh lemon juice (from about 2 lemons)

3 Tbsp extra-virgin olive oil

2 garlic cloves, minced

1 tsp Dijon mustard

1 tsp maple syrup

½ tsp salt

¼ tsp pepper

Red pepper flakes

1 lb large raw shrimp, peeled and deveined

Salad

2 large Ruby Red grapefruits

¼ cup extra-virgin olive oil

2 Tbsp sherry vinegar or red wine vinegar

1½ tsp Dijon mustard

1 tsp maple syrup

½ tsp salt

¼ tsp pepper

8 cups mixed salad greens, such as baby kale, arugula, spinach, lettuce, etc.

1 ripe avocado, sliced

½ English cucumber, thinly sliced

2 Tbsp fresh dill sprigs

Aunt Helen's Caesar Salad

My aunt Helen made a terrific Caesar salad. Whenever I was invited over to dinner at her Edmonton kitchen table, this salad was always there, front and centre. I'm sure she cooked many other things to go with it, but I only remember the Caesar salad. When I called up my 85-year-old aunt to ask for her recipe, she rattled off the ingredients and the amounts without hesitation. This salad is engraved in her memory—and her taste buds, too. The dressing is rich in flavour with garlic and Parmesan, and while I know anchovies will not appeal to some of you, a spoonful of paste really makes this salad the success that it is. Aunt H was quite adamant that the chopped romaine be bone dry, and when I asked her about bacon, she was like, "Heavens, no." She thinks it takes away from the flavour of the fresh lettuce and the rich, savoury dressing. Being the bacon fiend that I am, I've tossed some in on occasion. Just don't tell her, okay?

Prepare the dressing: In a large salad bowl, whisk together the garlic, anchovy paste, and mustard until smooth (though you'll spot some bits of garlic in it). Whisk in the lemon juice, then 1/3 cup of the Parmesan cheese. Gradually whisk in the oil. Season to taste with salt and pepper.

Prepare the salad: Add the dry lettuce to the dressing and toss to evenly coat the leaves. Add the remaining Parmesan cheese, croutons, and bacon (if using). Serve with lemon wedges on the side.

SERVES 4–6

Dressing

2–3 garlic cloves, minced

1 Tbsp anchovy paste

1 tsp Dijon mustard

2 Tbsp fresh lemon juice

⅔ cup freshly grated Parmesan cheese, divided

⅓ cup extra-virgin olive oil

Salt and pepper

Salad

1 large head romaine lettuce, leaves chopped and thoroughly dried

2 cups croutons (see note)

Chopped cooked bacon (optional, and volume is according to taste, or, in my case, gimme all the bacon)

Lemon wedges, for serving

* Look for anchovy paste in the seafood section of the supermarket.

* Use 2 bunches of romaine hearts instead of 1 large head of romaine lettuce.

* If you use my croutons recipe from the Tomato Bread Salad on page 257, omit the sliced garlic, as there is already plenty of garlic in the dressing.

Mushrooms are great to cook with year-round, but I use them more often in winter as they're the only vegetable that contains vitamin D. Bursting with antioxidants, not to mention being low in calories, mushrooms always find their way into my shopping cart, and I adore them in a multitude of ways. The big cremini love to be stuffed with sausage and cream cheese for an awesome appetizer. I like to roast them first with olive oil and balsamic vinegar, so they don't get soggy like some other stuffed mushrooms you've likely had. Roasting mushrooms before adding them to pizza and quiche does the same thing. You want them to release their juices on the baking sheet, not on your dough or pastry.

Shiitake mushrooms are great for soups, especially those teeming with noodles in a spicy, gingery broth. Mild-tasting yet meaty, oyster mushrooms are great for stir-fries, tacos, and quesadillas. Porcini mushrooms are prized in French and Italian cuisine; their stronger, nuttier flavour makes them a natural fit for pastas and risotto, or they are delicious simply sautéed in butter and served alongside a juicy steak and a glass of Cabernet. Portabella, or portobello, is really just a giant cremini mushroom that's harvested once it reaches between 4 and 6 inches in diameter. These guys love to be grilled or stuffed, and are often used as a vegetarian main course. Rich and earthy-tasting morel and chanterelle grow wild in the boreal forest of my beloved province of Saskatchewan, and, while I don't often cook with them when they're fresh, I'll go out to my favourite restaurants to taste what magic their chefs weave with them. Each variety of mushroom brings different flavours and textures to the plate, but, more often than not, the ever-so-common button mushroom is what I use in my kitchen. Well-balanced and affordable, this mushroom works well in all of the recipes in this book.

There is a myth in the cooking world that says you should never wash mushrooms, and that wiping them clean with a damp paper towel is the way to go. I don't know about you, but I have better things to do than stand at my kitchen counter and wipe every. single. mushroom. clean. Mushrooms are mostly water to begin with, and any moisture that's retained will be beaded on the surface and won't affect texture or taste. My favourite method (Martha Stewart is with me on this one) is to put the mushrooms in a bowl of cool water. Swirl it with your hands so any debris comes away from the mushrooms. Drain the 'shrooms, place them on clean kitchen towels, and thoroughly pat them dry. It is best to clean the mushrooms right before you want to cook them, though. Rinsed mushrooms won't last long in the refrigerator.

✳✳✳✳✳✳✳✳✳✳✳✳✳✳✳✳✳✳✳✳✳✳✳✳✳✳✳✳✳✳✳✳✳✳✳✳✳✳✳

Dixon Says: Mushrooms are a specialized crop grown indoors under specific conditions. They can't grow in an open field like ours. I mean, a few will pop up after a rain, but I don't think I would want to eat them. That's the thing with foraging for wild mushrooms—you have to be very certain that what you are picking isn't poisonous. That's why I leave foraging to the professionals!

MUSHROOMS

Skillet Mushroom Lasagna

Everyone loves a good lasagna, and this one is definitely for the mushroom lovers. I love how this pretty pasta bakes up in no time, and don't get me started on the crispy bits near the edge of the skillet. The mushroom cream sauce has whispers of white wine, garlic, Dijon mustard, and thyme, so you know it's going to be good. And I haven't even mentioned the ricotta and mozzarella yet! To be sneaky like me, stir in your favourite baby greens (nutritional bonus points). There are layers of creamy mushroom goodness in this lasagna, and, thanks to a short stint under the broiler, that ooey-gooey cheesy crust tastes even better than it looks. Served with a side salad, this pasta is fancy enough for company and quick and simple enough for a weeknight family meal.

In a large saucepan of boiling salted water, cook the noodles for 2 minutes less than the package instructions. Drain and lay them in a single layer on clean kitchen towels.

While the noodles are cooking, in a 10-inch cast-iron skillet, heat 1 Tbsp of the butter over medium-high heat. Sauté the mushrooms, stirring occasionally, until softened and almost no liquid remains, about 9 minutes. Stir in the garlic and thyme. Cook until the skillet is dry, about 2 minutes. Stir in the white wine. Cook until all of the liquid has been absorbed. Add the baby greens, and cook, stirring occasionally, until they begin to wilt, about 2 minutes. Scrape the mixture into a bowl. Stir in ¼ tsp of the salt and the pepper.

In the same saucepan you cooked the pasta in (no need to wash it first), melt the remaining 3 Tbsp butter over medium heat. Stir in the flour and cook, stirring constantly, for 2 minutes. Gradually whisk in the milk. Cook over medium heat, whisking constantly, until thickened, about 5–6 minutes. Add ¾ cup of the mozzarella, the ricotta, and mustard, then the remaining ¼ tsp salt, a pinch of cayenne pepper, and a pinch of nutmeg. Stir constantly until the cheese is melted. Remove from the heat. Season to taste.

Preheat the oven to 400°F. Wipe out the cast-iron skillet you used for the mushrooms and greens and add the oil, tipping the pan so it's evenly coated. Pour ½ cup of the sauce into the skillet. Arrange 3 of the noodles over top. It's ok if they go up the sides but not if they peek over the top. Top with half of the mushroom mixture. Spoon half of the remaining sauce over top. Arrange the remaining noodles, perpendicular to the bottom ones, over top. Finish layering with the remaining mushroom mixture, sauce, and ¾ cup mozzarella. Sprinkle with the Parmesan.

Bake the lasagna until the mozzarella is melted and the sauce is bubbly, about 15 minutes. Turn on the broiler and broil until the top is golden brown, 2–3 minutes. Let stand for 5 minutes before serving.

SERVES 4–6

6 lasagna noodles

4 Tbsp butter, divided

1 lb cremini mushrooms, sliced

1 garlic clove, minced

1 tsp chopped fresh thyme leaves

½ cup white wine

5 cups baby greens, such as kale, spinach, or chard

½ tsp salt, divided

¼ tsp pepper

3 Tbsp all-purpose flour

2 cups milk

1¼ cups shredded mozzarella cheese, divided

½ cup ricotta cheese

1 Tbsp Dijon mustard

Cayenne pepper

Ground nutmeg

1 Tbsp canola oil

¼ cup grated Parmesan cheese

✳ *Prepare the filling and the sauce a day or two ahead of time, then assemble as noted above. If the sauce is too thick, warm it in the microwave for a minute.*

Creamy Mushroom Soup

Homemade mushroom soup is a real treat. The beige gloop in a can doesn't even come close to the stuff made with fresh ingredients—and spoiler alert! There's booze! I stirred in just a wee bit of sherry because it really adds another layer of flavour to the soup. I learned the trick of tossing sliced mushrooms in fresh lemon juice at culinary school. The acidity helps balance out the richness of the butter and cream. I like to purée half of the soup just to make it extra creamy, but if you want to keep it chunky, that's fine too. Have ample toasty bread on hand so the dunkers (like Dixon) can dunk and the spooners (like me) can spoon creamy mushroom bits onto the toast.

Wash the mushrooms, pat them dry, and trim off any tough stems. Cut the mushrooms into ¼-inch-thick slices. Place them in a large bowl and toss with the lemon juice.

In a Dutch oven, melt the butter over medium-high heat. Stir in the diced onion and cook until softened and translucent, about 5 minutes. Add the mushrooms, garlic, salt, and pepper. Turn down the heat to medium and cook until the mushrooms release most of their liquid, about 10 minutes.

Add the flour and stir to coat the mushroom mixture. Cook for 1 minute, then stir in the sherry and cook for another minute. Scrape up any browned bits from the bottom of the pot. Stir in the broth, mustard, and thyme leaves. Cover, increase the heat to medium-high, and bring to a boil. Turn down the heat to medium-low and simmer, uncovered, for 20 minutes, stirring occasionally.

Remove the soup from the heat. Purée 2 cups of soup in a blender. This is hot liquid, so be careful! Return the purée to the soup and stir in the cream and milk. If the soup cools down too much, place it over low heat to warm through for a few minutes. Stir in the parsley and season to taste with salt and pepper.

If you'd like to garnish your soup, melt the butter in a small pan. Add the sliced mushrooms and cook on both sides until browned. Garnish the soup with the fried mushrooms.

SERVES 4

1 lb assorted fresh mushrooms, such as cremini, oyster, button, or shiitake

Juice of 1 lemon

6 Tbsp butter

1 large yellow onion, diced

2 garlic cloves, minced

½ tsp salt

¼ tsp pepper

⅓ cup all-purpose flour

¼ cup sherry

4 cups low-sodium chicken (or vegetable) broth

2 tsp Dijon mustard

2 tsp chopped fresh thyme leaves

½ cup whipping (35%) cream

½ cup milk

2 Tbsp chopped parsley (flat-leaf or curly)

Garnish

1 Tbsp butter (optional)

½ cup sliced mushrooms (optional)

Tourtière

Tourtière is a classic French-Canadian dish that's enjoyed around many dining room tables at Christmas. Generally, it's a savoury meat pie composed of ground pork and/or beef and potatoes under a dome of flaky crust. There has got to be at least a million recipes out there, all slightly different from each other in some way, some handed down from generation to generation. Every year, for as long as I can remember, my mom takes a day in the middle of December to assemble her meat pies. Her kitchen countertop is an assembly line of the best kind. And, of course, the house smells wonderful. Sage, cinnamon, and cloves mingle in the air, and I know that soon it will be Christmas. The pastry is buttery and tender; the filling absolutely delicious and hearty. Together, it is pie perfection. I've tweaked my mom's recipe by adding earthy mushrooms to the filling, and, while I realize it's a bit unconventional, I'm willing to bet that even traditionalists will be most happy with the result.

Prepare the pastry: In a large bowl, mix together the flour and salt. Cut in the lard with a pastry blender until the mixture resembles coarse oatmeal. Cut in the butter and leave a few pea-sized pieces of fat. In a 1-cup liquid measure, beat the egg, add the vinegar, and fill to the 1-cup mark with ice-cold water. Using a wooden spoon, gradually stir this into the flour mixture. Stir only until the mixture clings together, being careful not to overwork the dough.

Gather the dough into a ball and divide it into five equal portions. Wrap each piece separately in plastic and chill for at least 1 hour. For this tourtière recipe, you will need two portions of dough. You can either freeze the remaining portions of dough, or double the tourtière recipe, with one disc of dough remaining. The choice is yours!

Prepare the filling: In a large skillet, warm the oil over medium-high heat. Add the beef, pork, mushrooms, onion, garlic, salt, and spices. Cook until the meat is browned and most of the liquid has been cooked out of the mushrooms, about 10 minutes. Turn down the heat to low and stir in the mashed potatoes. Season to taste with more salt and pepper. Let the mixture cool before you start to assemble the tourtière. This process can be sped up by putting the meat mixture in the refrigerator or preparing it a day ahead.

Half an hour before you plan to bake the pie, bring the pastry out of the refrigerator to sit at room temperature. When you're ready to bake, preheat the oven to 350°F.

On a lightly floured surface, roll out one disc of pastry to about 10 inches in diameter. Place it in a 9-inch pie plate, being sure to let some dough overhang the edges of the dish. Place the cooked meat filling inside the pastry.

Roll out another disc of dough to 9 inches in diameter and place it on top of the meat. Trim the edges of the pastry and pinch them shut. Then, using a sharp knife, slice a few steam vents on top of the tourtière. Add decorative touches cut

SERVES 6

Pastry
5½ cups all-purpose flour

2 tsp salt

1 cup lard, cubed

1 cup cold butter, cubed

1 large egg

1 Tbsp white vinegar

Ice-cold water

Filling
2 Tbsp canola oil

½ lb lean ground beef

½ lb ground pork

½ lb cremini mushrooms, sliced

1 large onion, finely diced

3 garlic cloves, minced

1 tsp salt

1 tsp ground sage

¾ tsp ground cinnamon

¾ tsp ground cloves

¼ tsp allspice

¼ tsp pepper

2 cups plain mashed potatoes, room temperature

1 large egg beaten with a bit of milk, for egg wash

from the remaining pastry scraps, such as mushrooms, leaves, etc. Or you can use tree and star cookie cutters to cut out decorative toppings instead of laying the full disc of pastry on top of the tourtière (in which case, you won't need to cut any steam vents).

Brush the egg wash over the pastry. Bake until the tourtière is golden brown, 1 hour. Let it rest on a cooling rack for 10 minutes before cutting.

---

* *Having discs of pastry in the freezer is never a bad thing. I highly recommend doubling the tourtière filling to make two meat pies, but that's just me. Use the remaining discs of dough for pies, quiches, or galettes.*

* *Tourtières freeze very well. After they are assembled, do not brush on egg wash. Wrap tightly in plastic wrap, cover with aluminum foil, and freeze for up to 2 months. Thaw in the refrigerator overnight, then brush with egg wash and bake as above.*

* *Try serving with pickled beets, relish, cranberry compote, rhubarb chutney, or sour cherry preserves.*

Mushroom Risotto Cakes

Risotto is one of those dishes that has a reputation for being fussy and time-consuming. While there is a fair bit of stirring involved, the end result is well worth it. And is it just me, or is the motion of ladling and stirring quite therapeutic? Having a glass of wine to keep you company helps, too. Leftover risotto doesn't reheat to its former glory super well, but when it's cold, it's absolutely perfect for shaping into cakes. You'll be making a batch of risotto for this reason alone! (I've separated out the risotto part of this recipe in case you want to eat it as is.) With a crispy crumb coating, these pan-fried mushroom risotto cakes make an excellent appetizer and side dish. Serving them at brunch would also be a smart idea. I usually use button and shiitake mushrooms here, but any combination of 'shrooms will do.

Prepare the risotto: In a large saucepan, warm the oil over medium heat. Stir in the mushrooms and sauté until they've released most of their juices, about 5–7 minutes. Season generously with some salt and pepper. Transfer the mushrooms to a small bowl.

In a medium saucepan, warm the broth over medium heat. When it starts to simmer, cover, turn down the heat to low, and keep the broth warm.

In a large saucepan, melt the butter over medium heat. Stir the onion into the butter and cook until it's softened, about 5 minutes. Stir in the garlic and cook until it's golden and fragrant, about 2 minutes. Add the rice, and, using a wooden spoon, stir until it's evenly coated in butter.

Stir the wine, thyme, and generous pinches of salt and pepper into the rice. Continue to stir until the rice has absorbed the liquid. Add a ladleful of hot broth and continue to stir until the rice has absorbed all of the liquid again. Continue like this until the rice is softened and tender but still has a bit of a bite. It should have absorbed all of the liquid and have a creamy consistency. This takes about 25–30 minutes.

Stir in the cheese and mushrooms (and any accumulated juices). Cook for 1 minute. Season to taste with more salt and pepper. Transfer the risotto to a shallow bowl, let it cool down to room temperature, then cover and refrigerate. You need about 3½ cups of risotto for the cakes, so feel free to snack on the rest!

Prepare the risotto cakes: Preheat the oven to 350°F. Stir ½ cup of the panko, the egg yolk, chives, and salt into the cold risotto. I like to use my hands to mix this. Shape the risotto into 2-inch balls and flatten the tops a little bit. Place these balls on a small tray or baking sheet.

Place the remaining 1 cup of panko in one shallow bowl and the beaten eggs in another. Dip each ball into the beaten egg, then the panko, shaking off any excess, and set on another tray.

Warm 2 Tbsp of the oil in a large non-stick skillet over medium-high

MAKES 12 CAKES

Risotto

2 Tbsp extra-virgin olive oil

3 cups sliced assorted mushrooms such as button, cremini, shiitake, or oyster

Salt and pepper

4½ cups low-sodium chicken broth

3 Tbsp butter

1 small yellow onion, finely diced

2 garlic cloves, minced

1¼ cups Arborio rice

½ cup white wine

1 tsp chopped fresh thyme leaves (or ½ tsp dried thyme)

1 cup grated Asiago (or Parmesan) cheese

Risotto Cakes

1½ cups panko bread crumbs, divided

1 large egg yolk

2 Tbsp finely chopped fresh chives

Pinch of salt

3½ cups cold mushroom risotto

2 large eggs, beaten

4 Tbsp canola oil, divided

heat. Fry each risotto cake until golden brown on both sides, about 2 minutes per side. Do this in two batches. You may have to remove any browned crumbs from the skillet between batches and you may need to add another 2 Tbsp of oil for the second batch of frying. Place the cooked risotto cakes on a baking sheet. When they're all fried, place them in the oven for 5 minutes, to ensure they're cooked through.

If you want to garnish the risotto cakes with fried mushrooms, wipe out the skillet, then warm 1 Tbsp canola oil over medium heat. Cook the sliced mushrooms until golden.

Garnish the risotto cakes with the fried mushrooms and shaved Parmesan.

Garnish

1 Tbsp canola oil

1 cup sliced mushrooms (optional)

¼ cup shaved Parmesan cheese

Me and the onion. We're pretty tight. There were times over my 20+ years of professional cooking when I sliced and diced anywhere from 5 to 15 onions *every day*. Good thing I wear contact lenses or I would have been a runny-nosed, tear-stained-face cook. Onions are a staple in every pantry. They complement rather than overwhelm most of the ingredients they're paired with and are the base for oh-so-many savoury dishes. I particularly love it when a couple of pounds of onions are cooked down in a knob of butter until they are a deep golden brown and almost jammy. This takes about an hour, but that time is largely hands-off. Just give them a nudge once in a while as you walk by the stove. If you're so inclined, add a splash of white wine near the end. Dix and I never seem to finish a bottle of wine, so there are always a few glugs left in the refrigerator for me to cook with. These buttery, glistening onions are so good when served over pappardelle with plenty of Parmesan cheese. Talk about a fancy pantry meal!

My fondness for onion rings is fairly legendary, and I'll choose them over fries any day. I especially love it when they come already tucked inside my hamburger, but if they don't, I make sure to order onion rings on the side so I can slide one or two between the meat and bun myself. So dreamy.

Raw onions are a different beast compared to their cooked counterparts. Sharp and biting, there's nowhere to hide once you've eaten an uncooked onion. This is where breath mints are your friend.

Some interesting things about onions: 1) Worldwide, more onions are consumed than any other vegetable. 2) The onion is an ancient vegetable thought to have come from Central Asia and has been grown for over 5,000 years in Egypt and 2,000 years in Italy and in Europe more broadly since the Middle Ages. That's a really long time! Because relatives of the onion are found all over the world, it's likely that it's been a common ingredient of the cuisines of the world since prehistoric times. 3) In its long and robust life, the onion has found many champions. Greek physicians around AD 60 prescribed onions for eating, as well as for medicinal reasons. The Romans considered the concentric rings of cut onions and the globe shape of uncut ones symbolic of eternity. The Egyptians painted or carved onion shapes on monuments and in tombs to depict their use as funeral offerings. And lastly, Greek and Phoenician sailors carried onions on board their ships—the high vitamin C content came in handy for preventing scurvy. Onion talk! It's the best!

Dixon Says: Onions are perhaps the easiest thing to grow when starting from sets. (They resemble a small dried onion.) Onions like long days, so pick a sunny part of the garden. We plant them about 2 or 3 inches apart, which is a little close together, but then we thin them out for green onions during the season. Once thinned, they size up nicely. Around late August, when the nights become cool and dewy, go out and knock all the tops over. This will spur them into curing off and help prevent disease, as the moisture can carry and promote mould, starting in the stems of the onions. Harvest them when the tops start to dry before the frost, and they should keep well into winter.

ONIONS

Epicurean Epiphanies

Tucking into my first bowl of French onion soup was a revelation. I was 10 years old and my family was out for dinner, something we typically did not do unless there was a birthday to celebrate. The first time this bowl of steaming cheesy goodness was placed before me, I was like, "Hello, gorgeous." Maybe the cook was having a good night, or maybe my taste buds were thrilled with the encounter of something new, but I fell in love. While my siblings were dunking chicken fingers into honey mustard, or beef dip into jus, I had an epicurean epiphany: *melted cheese on top of onion soup is very, very good*. I loved breaking through that lid of browned and bubbling cheese only to discover there was bread underneath. What the whaaaa?! I was impressed with how strings of cheese would tether the soup to my mouth via the spoon. Even a child on their best behaviour is going to act a little obnoxious when that happens. The onions were so soft and so fragrant as they swam in a dark and dreamy broth. When the last bit of cheese and onions were gone, I certainly thought about licking the bowl, but my mom didn't raise a heathen. I'm still prone to ordering French onion soup if I see it on a menu—if only to take me back to when I was 10, sitting in an upholstered booth with my mom and siblings, broth running down my chin and sheer gastronomic joy coursing through my veins.

In the early to mid-'90s, there was a Lebanese restaurant on Le Plateau-Mont-Royal called Sara. Being that it was on the corner of Rues Saint-Laurent and Mont Royal, my friends and I often ended up here after a night of pub beers or club dancing. When you're 20 years old and away from home for the first time, these are the things you do. *Je ne regrette rien*. The gentlemen behind the counter were always very handsome and would flash big grins at me when I said "Yes, please" to the ultraviolet pickled turnip tucked inside my pita sandwich, alongside crispy falafel balls, chopped lettuce, tomato slices, and garlicky tahini sauce. Wrapped snugly in white waxed paper, the sandwich was quickly devoured as I took one bite and then another. The textures! The flavours! I didn't know what the heck that thick baton of bright purple turnip was all about, but I did know that my sandwich was better for it. This was the perfect food to eat late at night with good friends, as we hunched over small tables and dissected the evening's activities. When the paper wrappers were emptied of their delicious contents, we said goodbye to the handsome Lebanese men behind the counter, hugged each other goodnight, and walked off in different directions into the Montreal night. The sandwich cost only a handful of dollars, but the memories of those falafel sandwiches eaten with those good friends are pretty priceless.

There is one vegetable dish in my city that is so good it gives me the shimmies and the shakes every time I eat it. I'm talking about the Mushrooms served at Hearth Restaurant, one of Saskatoon's best farm-to-table dining spots, and where Dixon and I go to celebrate big and small moments. The mushrooms are prepared by chefs/owners Beth Rogers and Thayne Robstad, who every summer go up to their secret spot in the northern Saskatchewan boreal forest and forage some of the wild chanterelle mushrooms that go into this delicious appetizer. Served in a cast-iron skillet on top of the prettiest vintage plate, the mushrooms sink into a lava of hot melted cheese; the golden chanterelles and earthy reindeer moss render the dish so photogenic, I get my camera out, every single time—if only to remember how dreamy these mushrooms, this moment can be. When I heap them onto slices of fresh bread, Dixon is resigned to the fact that I'll be pretty much rendered speechless for several minutes. I'm in my happy place. I've got the shimmies and the shakes. I'm having an epicurean epiphany.

I'M IN MY HAPPY PLACE. I'VE GOT THE SHIMMIES AND THE SHAKES. I'M HAVING AN EPICUREAN EPIPHANY.

French Onion Soup

Any vessel for melted cheese always gets bonus points from me, and French onion soup is one of the best there is. There are heaps of onions involved, but they cook down quite a lot in a good glob of butter. Be sure to get them nice and brown too, scraping up all of those lovely bits from the bottom of the pot. This is a time-consuming affair, but the onions only need a nudge here and there with a spoon, so you can multi-task, if you like, or you can sit at the counter and drink some wine and read a book. Won't tell which camp I'm in—you'll have to guess. I like serving this soup in classic French onion soup bowls. You know the ones. Maybe you received them as a wedding present in 1985 and have them tucked away in a cupboard. French onion is a very physical soup. You have to break through that lid of crusty cheesy goodness to get to the onions and broth. Cheese strings are pulled up and out and into the mouth while onion broth runs down the chin. Having napkins close at hand is a must.

In a Dutch oven, melt the butter over medium-high heat. Add the onions, stirring well to evenly coat. Cover with a lid and cook, stirring often, until the onions are soft and quite juicy, about 10–12 minutes. Remove the lid, stir in the sugar and ½ tsp salt, and continue to cook until most of the liquid has evaporated, another 5–7 minutes.

Turn down the heat to medium-low and allow the onions to slowly, deeply caramelize, uncovered, stirring once in a while so they don't stick. This will take about 1 hour. If they do show signs of sticking, lower the heat a little. If they are starting to burn, turn down the heat even lower.

After the onions are caramelized, increase the heat to medium-high, add the garlic, and cook for a minute or two, then stir in the wine. Cook for another minute or two, until most of the liquid has evaporated. Stir in the mustard, thyme, 1 tsp salt, and pepper. Stir in the broth, then cover and bring to a boil. Turn down the heat to low, uncover, and simmer for 15 minutes.

Preheat the broiler. Ladle the soup into four to six oven-proof bowls and top with toasted bread that fits snugly into each bowl. Mound the cheese on top of the bread and broil until the cheese is melted, browned, and gorgeous.

SERVES 4–6

¼ cup butter

4 large white onions, thinly sliced

½ tsp sugar

1½ tsp salt, divided

2 garlic cloves, minced

½ cup dry white wine

2 tsp Dijon mustard

1 tsp chopped fresh thyme leaves (or ½ tsp dried thyme)

¼ tsp pepper

5–6 cups low-sodium chicken (or beef or vegetable) broth

Crusty sourdough (or hearty whole grain) loaf, sliced to fit your bowls and toasted

2 cups grated Gruyère cheese

✱ *If you don't have oven-proof bowls, simply make some slices of cheese toast and set these atop your bowls of soup.*

Not Your Average Onion Dip

Who else has fond memories of Lipton onion soup dip? You know the one. Just empty a packet of the dehydrated onion soup mix into a vat of sour cream and stir. Yes, I see you nodding. It was a good one, all right, hitting all of the right notes of tangy, creamy, and salty. It was also an excellent vehicle for consuming copious amounts of potato chips. Now, let me introduce you to my dip. It has rich, deep *real* onion flavour, with nary a dehydrated onion flake in sight. Roasting not one but two kinds of onion ensures a mellow sweetness, while balsamic vinegar and Dijon mustard bring a bit of acidity. I haven't done away completely with the sour cream (why would I do that?), but I've cut it with some plain Greek yogurt, and no one has ever complained. While potato chips are obvious companions to this dip, be sure to try it with crudités as well.

Preheat the oven to 425°F. Line a rimmed baking sheet with parchment paper.

Trim off the very dark green tops of the green onions and discard. Slice the white and light green parts into 1½-inch pieces. Place the green onions on the baking sheet along with the red onion. Using your hands, toss the onions with the oil and salt. Rub everything together so the onions are well coated. Spread them out into an even layer and roast, stirring once, until tender and browned in some spots, about 22–27 minutes. Let cool to room temperature.

Transfer the roasted onions to a food processor fitted with a metal blade, and add the sour cream, mayonnaise, yogurt, vinegar, mustard, parsley, and pepper. Process until relatively, but not completely, smooth. A little texture is a good thing. Season to taste with more salt, pepper, and vinegar, as needed.

Scrape the dip into a bowl and chill for at least 1 hour. Garnish with the chopped green onion before serving with your desired potato chips and/or vegetables. The dip keeps well, covered, in the refrigerator for up to 3 days.

MAKES 1½ CUPS

2 bunches of green onions, reserving 1 green onion for garnish

1 large red onion, cut into ¼-inch-thick wedges.

2 Tbsp canola oil

1 tsp salt

½ cup sour cream

⅓ cup mayonnaise

¼ cup plain Greek yogurt (or sour cream)

1 Tbsp balsamic vinegar

1½ tsp Dijon mustard

2 Tbsp roughly chopped parsley (flat-leaf or curly)

¼ tsp pepper

Potato chips, preferably plain, salt and pepper, or ripple, for serving

Fresh cut-up vegetables, for serving

✳ *This is a delicious condiment for hamburgers and other grilled sandwiches, too.*

Ren and Dix's Loaded Lentil Nachos with Pickled Red Onions

Of all the things I make for Dixon, I think he honestly loves these nachos the best. He's sitting beside me, nodding his head in agreement, so there you go. I sing "Macho Man" to him but swap Nacho for Macho. It never gets old. The first time I put the spiced lentils on the tortilla chips, I could see Dixon's mind being blown. And yours will too! They bring along extra protein and fibre, so I don't feel like a total glutton when I garnish the nacho platter with generous dollops of sour cream and guacamole. Dixon has an affinity for radishes, and their peppery bite is complemented by the sweetness of the pickled red onions. Once these pretty onions are in your refrigerator, you'll find many uses for them, but I especially love them on a platter of loaded lentil nachos.

Prepare the pickled red onions: Pack the sliced onion into a clean pint jar.

In a small saucepan, combine ½ cup water and everything else except the garlic cloves. Bring to a gentle simmer over medium heat then pour over the onions. Tuck in the garlic cloves. Use a spoon to press the onions under the liquid.

Let the onions come to room temperature, about 30 minutes. Cover with a lid and refrigerate. The pickled onions will last in the refrigerator for 2 weeks. Makes about 2 cups.

Prepare the nachos: In a small bowl, stir the lentils with the chili powder, garlic powder, and salt.

Preheat the oven to 375°F. Lightly grease a 13-inch cast-iron skillet or line a rimmed baking sheet with parchment paper.

Spread the tortilla chips across the pan. Scatter with 1¼ cups of the cheese. Sprinkle the lentils over top, followed by the remaining cheese. Add the jalapeño slices. Put the nachos in the oven and bake until the cheese has melted, about 15 minutes.

Place the nachos on a platter and top with pickled red onions, radish slices, and cilantro. Serve with sour cream, salsa, and guacamole on the side. Devour immediately.

✱ *Use the pickled red onions on tacos, tostadas, chili, enchiladas, sandwiches, burgers, and salads.*

✱ *To cook green lentils: Place 1 cup dried lentils in a fine-mesh sieve and rinse under cool running water. Dump into a medium saucepan and cover with 3 cups of cold water. Bring to a boil over high heat. Cover, turn the heat down to low, and simmer until very tender, about 20 minutes. Drain. Makes about 2½ cups.*

SERVES 2–4

Pickled Red Onions

1 large red onion, peeled and cut in half lengthwise, then sliced into very thin half moons

¼ cup apple cider vinegar (or white vinegar)

¼ cup white vinegar

1 Tbsp honey

1½ tsp salt

½ tsp yellow mustard seeds

¼ tsp red pepper flakes

2 whole garlic cloves

Nachos

1 cup cooked whole green lentils (see note)

1 tsp chili powder

½ tsp garlic powder

¼ tsp salt

⅓ bag of tortilla chips (or thereabouts)

2½ cups grated extra-old cheddar

1 jalapeño pepper, sliced

⅓ cup Pickled Red Onions

4–6 radishes, sliced

2 Tbsp cilantro leaves

For Serving

Sour cream

Salsa

Guacamole

Jammy Upside-Down Onion Tart

Onions are in so many recipes, but rarely are they the star of the show. Well, in this recipe they hog the spotlight! I mean, look at it! I have a soft spot for jammy, caramelized onions, and, while this tart may look like a lot of work, it's really pretty simple. I think the toughest part is inverting it onto a platter, but just take a deep breath and go for it. One of my recipe testers described making this onion tart as a genuine food experience, and when she got it safely onto the platter and saw how gorgeous it was, she was so very proud of herself. I want you to have this experience, too. I love serving this tart with a Sunday roast, be it chicken, beef, or pork. The deep, rich onion flavour is a natural fit for meat, but if you're keen on something lighter, serve it as a main course with a salad of greens on the side. (The Winter Salad on page 139 would be perfect.)

Peel the onions and remove the tops and bottoms. Cut the onions in half crosswise.

Melt the butter in a 10-inch non-stick ovenproof skillet over medium heat. Add the thyme and bay leaves and cook for 1 minute. Stir in the sugar, sherry, and broth. Place the onions in the skillet, cut-side down. It's okay if they overlap slightly as they'll shrink when cooking. Sprinkle on the salt and pepper. Cover with foil, turn down the heat to medium-low, and simmer for 10 minutes.

Preheat the oven to 400°F. Remove the foil and carefully flip the onions over. If any loose bits fall out, try to place them back in the onions. Increase the heat to medium and simmer the onions, uncovered, until most of the liquid has reduced, about 12–17 minutes. Depending on the size of your onions, it may take longer. The main thing is, you still want some liquid coating the bottom of the pan, so don't reduce all of it. The liquid should have the consistency of thin caramel. Turn off the heat.

Roll the puff pastry out into an 11-inch circle, ¼-inch thick. If your sheet of puff pastry is already rolled out, trim it to an 11-inch circle, but don't roll out any further as it may get too thin. Place the pastry on top of the onions, tucking them in snuggly. Try to get the edge of the pastry to fit under the onions a little bit.

Bake on the centre rack of the oven until the pastry is puffed and fully cooked with a lovely golden brown colour, about 22–28 minutes. Remove from the oven and let the tart cool in the pan for a few minutes. Cover the skillet with a larger plate or wooden serving board and carefully invert it. If any onions or herbs stick to the bottom of the skillet, just put them back into place with a fork. I like to use a spatula and scrape any of the caramelized goodness from the skillet back onto the tart. Cut into 8 wedges and serve. Serves 8 as a side dish, or 4 as a main with a salad.

SERVES 8

4 medium yellow onions

¼ cup butter

6 sprigs fresh thyme

3 bay leaves

2½ Tbsp packed brown sugar

¼ cup sherry

⅔ cup low-sodium chicken broth

¾ tsp salt

¼ tsp pepper

1 sheet (8 oz/250 g) puff pastry, thawed in the refrigerator

✳ *If you can't fit 8 onion halves in the skillet, 7 is fine. Some medium onions are larger than others. The main thing is to get the onion halves as snug together as possible.*

The list of vegetables I won't eat is a very short one (rutabaga, I'm looking at you), and, for the longest time, parsnips were on that list. I've since wised up to their elegant, herbal sweetness and now find myself roasting them whenever I get the chance, dicing them into soups for a sneaky mirepoix addition, and pan-frying them à la Dixon. The parsnip is a fabulous companion to salty, smoky bacon, so if you think you don't like this cream-coloured root vegetable, just add a little bacon. Butter never hurts, either. Whenever there's a roast of beef, lamb, or pork headed for the oven, I tuck hefty chunks of parsnip into the pan. Pulled from the roaster and set alongside the glistening meat, the underrated root transforms into sweet nuggets of gold.

This starchy vegetable has a slightly spiced, earthy taste that lends itself well to a variety of recipes. It's also fantastic in baked goods—yes, just like its cousin the carrot—and in breakfast foods, such as waffles. People (parsnip haters) always give me funny looks when I tell them how much I love stirring grated parsnip into delightful scones and waffles. Truth is, I love being sneaky. The subtle sweetness of the parsnip is carried into the batter, and, because the colour is so unassuming, no one but the cook can tell there are parsnips hiding out in their baked goods.

Not only are parsnips delicious, they are also quite good for you—just another reason I hide them in tasty things I like to eat. They're low in calories and rich in potassium, manganese, magnesium, zinc, iron, folate, and phosphorus, as well as vitamins B, C, E, and K. Parsnips have significant anti-inflammatory properties and are helpful for controlling blood sugar levels as well as reducing cholesterol. They are also an excellent source of fibre. A 1-cup serving of parsnip contains 7 grams of dietary fibre. Hooray for the parsnip!

Dixon Says: Parsnips take a very long time to grow, so they are one of the first vegetables we seed in early May. Like carrots, they require moist ground for a couple of weeks to germinate. They're best harvested in late October or early November, and they're the last crop we harvest for winter storage. Before a good hard frost, parsnips taste earthy, but after they've been in the cold ground for most of the autumn, they taste much sweeter and have a more intense flavour. At the market, I'm always asked what to do with parsnips. I think of them as being a great substitute for potatoes. You can fry them, boil them, roast them, scallop them. They're great mashed with gravy or with a creamy mushroom tarragon sauce! I really like parsnips when they're sliced thin and pan-fried in butter until golden brown. They'll be a surprise hit at any dinner table.

PARSNIPS

Roasted Root Vegetable Pot Pie with Gruyère Biscuit Topping

This recipe was inspired by the root cellar built into the side of a small hill at Dixon's family farm. From September to June, it houses tons (literally) of root vegetables. Their superb taste really shines through in this vegetarian pot pie. And no, that is not a typo in the ingredients list. I actually use rutabaga in this! Dixon says that if anyone can make rutabaga taste good, it would be me (yeah, he threw down a challenge—what's a girl to do?), and I find I don't mind it so much when it's mixed with other veg that I adore. Not gonna lie, there's a fair bit of prep here, but it's mostly chopping. The sherry plays a small but vital part—if it's omitted, the flavour will not be the same. Dix literally smacked his lips with pleasure when he first tasted this pot pie. It's got everything you want in a classic comfort food: tender, tasty veg; creamy, delicious gravy; pillowy, yet crispy-topped biscuits. There's enough here for a good-sized gathering, making it perfect for Sunday suppers and holiday feasts.

Prepare the filling: Preheat the oven to 400°F. Line a rimmed baking sheet with parchment paper. Combine the parsnips, carrots, potatoes, and rutabaga in a large bowl with the oil, 1 tsp of the salt, and ¼ tsp of the pepper. Stir well. Spread into a single layer on the baking sheet, scraping out all of the oil, and top with the thyme sprigs. Roast for 30 minutes, stirring occasionally. The vegetables should be fork-tender, but it's okay if they have a little bit of crunch, too. Remove the thyme sprigs and slide the leaves over the roasted vegetables. Leave the veg on the baking sheet and set aside.

Melt the butter in a Dutch oven over medium-high heat. Stir in the diced onion and cook until translucent, about 5 minutes. Stir in the garlic and cook until fragrant, another minute or so. Stir in the flour and cook over low heat, stirring frequently, for 3 minutes, until the roux is lightly browned.

Turn down the heat to medium and gradually stir in the broth, ½ cup at a time. I usually alternate between a wooden spoon and a whisk. Be sure to scrape up any roux clinging to the inside edges of the pot. This whole process takes about 10–12 minutes, and you need to stir frequently until the sauce has somewhat thickened. It's a sauce that's on the thin side, but it shouldn't be watery.

Stir in the cream, sherry, parsley, rosemary, and the remaining ½ tsp of salt and ¼ tsp of pepper. Cook for another 2 minutes. Gently stir in the roasted vegetables. Transfer the mixture to a 3-quart casserole dish or a 9- × 13-inch baking dish—just be sure the sides are at least 2 inches high.

(continued on page 173)

SERVES 8

Filling

2½ cups chopped (½-inch pieces) parsnips

2½ cups chopped (½-inch pieces) carrots

2½ cups chopped (1-inch pieces) red (or Yukon Gold) potatoes

2 cups chopped (½-inch pieces) rutabaga

2½ Tbsp canola oil

1½ tsp salt, divided

½ tsp pepper, divided

6 fresh thyme sprigs

¼ cup butter

1 large yellow onion, diced

3 garlic cloves, minced

⅓ cup all-purpose flour

4 cups low-sodium chicken broth

¼ cup whipping (35%) cream

¼ cup sherry

¼ cup finely chopped fresh parsley (flat-leaf or curly), plus more for garnish

2 tsp finely chopped fresh rosemary

Biscuit Topping

2 cups all-purpose flour

2 tsp baking powder

½ tsp salt

¼ tsp baking soda

⅓ cup cold butter

¾ cup shredded Gruyère cheese

1 cup buttermilk (shaken before measuring)

(continued from page 171)

Prepare the biscuit topping: Combine the flour, baking powder, salt, and baking soda in a large bowl. Use a box grater to grate in the cold butter. Toss with your hands until incorporated. Stir in the cheese. Pour in the buttermilk. Stir just until all of the ingredients are combined. Spoon 9 biscuits over the hot vegetable mixture.

The pot pie may run over, so place a foil-lined baking sheet on the bottom rack of your oven. Bake the pot pie, uncovered, on the middle rack, until the sauce is bubbling and the biscuits are browned, about 30–35 minutes. If you insert a toothpick into the centre of a biscuit, it will come out clean if it's fully cooked. Remove from the oven and let stand 5 minutes before serving. Sprinkle with chopped parsley.

Parsnip and Whole Grain Waffles

To celebrate the dawn of a new year, I often prepare these waffles for brunch on New Year's Day for Dixon and me. It's an easy recipe—probably the trickiest part is whipping the whites by hand. Yes, rather than lug my stand mixer out of the cupboard, I end up whipping the egg whites using just a bowl, whisk, and some elbow grease. I feel like I am back in the olden days, and no doubt my grandmothers and great-grandmothers would be quite proud. The whites billow up after several minutes of heavy whisking, and when I proudly (and slightly out of breath) show the bowl of voluminous whites to Dix, he gives me a standing ovation. I'm not sure if you will get your own standing O with your whites, but one bite of these tender, delicious, and healthy waffles should earn you one. Those lofty whites will ensure fluffy waffles with ever-so-crispy edges. Life is filled with many quiet, joyful moments, and having a plate of waffles set before me is one of them. I'm pretty sure it has something to do with the deep golden brown pockets filled to the brim with butter and maple syrup. What a grand way to start the day—and the year.

Prepare the waffle iron according to its directions. (I use a Belgian waffle maker.)

In a large bowl, combine both flours, the baking powder, ginger, and salt. In a medium bowl, whisk the egg yolks with the oil and milk. Make a well in the centre of the dry ingredients and pour in the egg yolk/milk mixture. Combine with a few swift strokes, being sure not to overmix. Fold in the parsnips.

In a medium bowl, beat the egg whites until stiff, using either a hand mixer, stand mixer, or, if you are feeling very strong, a whisk and some elbow grease. Fold the whipped whites into the batter, just barely blending.

When the waffle iron is hot and ready, spoon about 1 cup of the batter (or the amount stated in your waffle maker's directions) into the centre. Cook until light brown or until the waffle iron indicator light goes off.

Serve immediately with butter, maple syrup, and fresh fruit.

MAKES 6 WAFFLES

1¼ cups all-purpose flour

½ cup barley (or buckwheat, spelt, rye, or whole wheat) flour

2 tsp baking powder

1 tsp ground ginger

½ tsp salt

3 large eggs, separated

½ cup canola oil

1½ cups milk

1 cup peeled and grated parsnips

Butter, maple syrup, and fresh fruit for serving

❋ *Leftovers reheat well in the toaster oven/toaster. You can also pop them in a resealable plastic bag and freeze them for up to 1 month.*

The Cold-Buster Chicken Noodle Soup

There are chicken noodle soups, and then there are Chicken Noodle Soups. This one falls into the latter category. It's not like something you'd see in a box or a can. It's more like something you'd find on a Burmese restaurant menu—and it could be a distant cousin to the soup that Dixon and I shared on our first date, which is another reason I love it so much. This soup has flavour and good things by the truckload, and it's my go-to whenever Dixon or I are under the weather. There's the earthy muskiness of the turmeric, which has all kinds of anti-inflammatory healing powers; the bite of the garlic and ginger; the heat of the chili, which makes the soup spicy, but just enough so that your nose may run, but your mouth won't burn. As far as vegetables go, I generally use what I've got in the crisper, and I love sneaking in the parsnip, as it adds a little sweet herbal action. This soup is a bit of a choose your own adventure when it comes to the vegetables. I like to load it up, but you may want to reduce the variety and even choose different veg altogether.

Warm the oil in a large soup pot over medium-high heat. Stir in the onion, parsnips, carrots, celery, and squash. Add a generous pinch of salt and cook until the vegetables start to soften, about 5 minutes. Add the garlic, ginger, turmeric, coriander, and chili. Cook for 1 minute, then pour in the broth and coconut milk. Stir in the honey and 1 tsp salt. Cover, bring to a boil, then turn the heat to medium-low and simmer, stirring occasionally, until the vegetables are tender, 12–15 minutes.

Add the rice noodles and cook until they're soft, about 5 minutes. Stir in the cooked chicken, zucchini, fish sauce (if using), and juice of 1 lime. Simmer for just a few minutes until the zucchini is tender. Stir in the cilantro, basil, and green onions. Season to taste with more salt, lime juice, pepper, and honey. If you find the soup too thick, thin it out with a little more broth or some water.

Divide the soup into bowls and garnish with cilantro, green onions, and a lime wedge or two. Hot sauce too, if that's how you roll.

---

* To keep the soup vegetarian, substitute chopped tofu for the chicken and use vegetable broth.

* The soup makes a big batch, and it freezes well.

* Mushrooms, chopped kale, or even corn would be delicious in this soup.

SERVES 6–8

2 Tbsp canola oil

1 large onion, diced

1½ cups diced parsnips

1 cup diced carrots

1 cup diced celery

1 cup chopped butternut squash or sweet potato

1 tsp salt, plus a pinch for cooking vegetables and to taste

3 garlic cloves, minced

1 Tbsp minced fresh ginger

1 Tbsp ground turmeric

1 Tbsp ground coriander

1 small red chili such as bird's eye, minced

6–7 cups of chicken broth

1 can (14 oz/398 mL) full-fat coconut milk

1 tsp honey, plus more to taste

4 oz (125 g) wide rice stick noodles

2 cups chopped cooked chicken

1 zucchini, chopped into ¼-inch-thick pieces (about 2 cups)

1 tsp fish sauce (optional)

Juice of 1–2 limes

½ cup chopped cilantro, plus more for garnish

¼ cup chopped fresh basil

3 chopped green onions, plus more for garnish

Pepper

Lime wedges, for garnish

Hot sauce, optional

Parsnip and Cheddar Scones with Sage

I'm always looking for ways to incorporate parsnips into baked goods. Their delicate herbal sweetness deserves to shine in more than just soups and stews, and I think nibbling on something flaky and buttery could be a gateway for even the staunchest non-fan of this humble root vegetable. Instead of going the sweet route, though, I've taken a savoury turn and stirred grated parsnip into absolutely lovely cheddar and sage scones. I swear that sour coffee cream makes the most tender scones, and I often buy a larger container just so some of it can go bad, and I have an excuse to bake. Waste not, want not and all that. These scones are superb when served alongside any of the soups in this book, but Dixon especially loves dipping the buttery edges into a bowl of Cream of Celery and Mashed Potato Soup (page 205).

Preheat the oven to 375°F. Line a baking sheet with parchment paper.

Stir together the dry ingredients in a medium bowl. Use a box grater to grate the butter into them. Using your hands, incorporate the butter into the flour so that there are some pea-sized bits of butter remaining. Mix in the cheese.

Whisk together the egg and sour coffee cream in a small bowl. Pour this into the medium bowl, stir a few times, then add the grated parsnip and sage. Mix (I use my hands) until the dough just comes together.

Dump the dough onto a lightly floured surface. Knead it a few times and shape into a circle about 1-inch thick. Using a sharp knife, cut it into eight equal triangles. Place them on the baking sheet. Brush the tops with the melted butter and sprinkle with flaky salt.

Bake the scones for 25–30 minutes, rotating the pan 180 degrees halfway through the baking time. The scones are done baking when they're flaky and golden brown.

MAKES 8 SCONES

1½ cups all-purpose flour, plus more for the counter

½ cup whole wheat (or spelt or barley) flour

1 Tbsp baking powder

½ tsp baking soda

½ tsp dry mustard powder

½ tsp salt

¼ tsp pepper

½ cup cold butter

½ cup shredded extra-old cheddar cheese

1 large egg

½ cup sour coffee cream (or sour milk or buttermilk)

1½ cups peeled and grated parsnips

2 Tbsp chopped fresh sage

1 Tbsp melted butter or cream

Flaky salt, for sprinkling

✳ *If you're unable to find fresh sage leaves, you can substitute 1 tsp dried sage and add it to the dry ingredients.*

Parsnip Gratin with Bacon and Shallots

The parsnip, that frugal root of the vegetable patch, makes a sensual supper, especially when married with bacon and cream and tucked under a cloak of buttery bread crumbs. The creamy flesh of the parsnip is sweet and earthy, making it a fine match for the smoky richness of the bacon and the subtle bite of Dijon. A gratin wouldn't be a gratin without a crunchy topping, of course, and it provides a welcome textural contrast, not to mention coveted crispy bits. Cozied up to slices of Sunday roast, or a pile of burnished butcher's sausages, I daresay you'll never look at the unassuming parsnip the same way again. Oh! One more thing! This is a dandy dish to serve at Friendsgiving, the neighbourhood potluck, or the family holiday feast. Just be prepared for recipe requests!

Preheat the oven to 350°F.

Place the parsnips and a generous pinch of salt in a medium saucepan. Cover with cold water and bring to a boil over high heat. Cover, turn down the heat to medium-low, and simmer until the parsnips are tender, 6–8 minutes. Drain.

Warm a large skillet over medium-high heat. Fry the bacon until crisp. Remove with a slotted spoon (leaving 2 Tbsp of the fat in the pan) and drain on a paper towel-lined plate. When it's cool, chop it into ½-inch pieces.

Stir the sliced shallots into the reserved fat. If you don't have 2 Tbsp, add some butter to make up the difference. Cook over medium-high heat, until the shallots are golden and smelling great, about 5 minutes. Stir in the cream, mustard, thyme leaves, ½ tsp salt, and pepper. Scrape up any browned bits from the bottom of the skillet. Bring the cream to a boil. Turn down the heat to medium-low and simmer until the cream thickens slightly, about 3–4 minutes. Stir in the chopped bacon. Season to taste.

Arrange the parsnips in a 10-inch gratin dish or baking dish and pour the bacon cream sauce over top, being certain to cover the parsnips completely.

In a small bowl, stir together the bread crumbs, Parmesan, and butter. Sprinkle evenly over the parsnips. Bake until the bread crumb topping is golden brown, about 20–25 minutes.

SERVES 6

2 lb parsnips (about 6–7 medium), peeled and sliced in half lengthwise

½ tsp salt, plus more to taste

5 slices thick-cut bacon

1 Tbsp butter (optional)

3 shallots, sliced

1 cup whipping (35%) cream

1 Tbsp grainy Dijon mustard

1 tsp chopped fresh thyme leaves (or ½ tsp dried thyme)

¼ tsp pepper

½ cup panko bread crumbs

½ cup grated Parmesan cheese

1½ Tbsp melted butter

✳ *If your parsnips are rather fat, slice them in half lengthwise, then in half lengthwise again. Try to have all of the halves about the same size for even cooking.*

Shelling peas is synonymous with summer. Raise your hand if you spent many days of your summertime youth sitting in the shade with your siblings, or cousins, shelling pail after pail of peas freshly picked from the garden plot. As we sipped on lemonade, one by one, the peas would fill up bowls, ever so slowly.

Back then, I'm sure I thought that dealing with the peas was a nuisance. As a grown-up, I'm rather fond of the task, though, and find it all rather therapeutic as I slip the verdant orbs out of their tender shells. It never ceases to amaze me: 1) how few peas you really get out of all those pods, and 2) just how perfectly perfect the insides of a pea pod are.

This cool-season vegetable has been around for thousands of years, even showing up in ancient Egyptian tombs. If you're a fan of Norse mythology, you may know that apparently a grumpy Thor sent flying dragons to drop peas into all of the Earth's wells, thereby filling them up and spoiling the water. But some of the peas missed the wells and sprouted, giving people another food source. To appease (yes, I did just write that) Thor, the mortals ate the peas only on a Thursday, which was dedicated to him. If you've ever had a nasty, dried up, flavourless pea, you know that they can indeed be a weapon, so Thor really wasn't too far off.

When I had a small pea patch in my garden, I particularly loved paying it a visit just as the sun was slipping from the sky. I admired the soft tendrils of the pea plants as they wove their way in and out of the lattice, punctuated by the white pea flowers that added a little magic to the early summer garden. Peas are one of the first vegetables ready in the early part of summer, and it's best to eat them shortly after they've been picked for optimum sweetness. If you let them hang about the refrigerator too long, they get starchy, dry, and bitter. I really only eat fresh peas for a month or two out of the year, and then it's on to the frozen stuff. All that is required is a quick boil, then add a dollop of butter, and away you go. They're affordable, kid-friendly, and gosh darn it, so good for you, being a fantastic provider of fibre and other good things. And the best part—you don't have to beg your kids to shell frozen peas.

✳✳✳✳✳✳✳✳✳✳✳✳✳✳✳✳✳✳✳✳✳✳✳✳✳✳✳✳✳✳✳✳✳✳✳✳

Dixon Says: Around mid-May, we plant peas in rows that are close together, about 1 inch apart so that the vines can support each other. We continue to plant new rows every 2 weeks, so there is a steady supply of peas throughout the summer. Many times, during a hot day in the garden, I've snuck over to the pea patch to poach some for a snack. I like the young, small peas, not quite filled out and fat. Now, as much as I love the different ways that my love prepares peas, my all-time fave is one I learned from my dear deceased dad: Fresh cream of pea soup! Boil the fresh peas. (They have to be fresh! Frozen is just not the same.) Remove from the heat when they are al dente, but save the broth. Add peas and just enough broth to the bowl to make a soup. Add a pat of unsalted butter and about a teaspoon of evaporated milk (or half and half or heavy cream or even milk will do). Salt and pepper to taste. Renée does not care for this oh-so-simple delicacy, but I still love her.

PEAS

Pasta Shells with Minty Peas and Ricotta

I'm gonna come clean with you. Sometimes life is so busy, I cook up some boxed macaroni and cheese for something quick to eat. For real. Not the stuff that starts with a K but the other stuff that is organic and rhymes with fannies. I'll add some frozen peas to the party, just so I feel like I'm eating relatively nutritious food. This recipe uses peas too, but it tastes a million times better than the stuff out of the box, and, honestly, it doesn't take too much longer to prepare. I love how the peas snuggle up inside the shells, trapping them into perfect little bites. Two peas in a pod—just like Dixon and me! There's a creaminess to the sauce, but it's fresh and light, thanks to the lemon and mint. The random package of "cheese powder" has been replaced with ricotta and Parmesan. I know, so fancy, right? The boxed pasta I usually just shovel into my mouth straight out of the pot because I'm classy like that, but this pasta I serve in pretty bowls and, heck, I might even use cloth napkins, too.

SERVES 4 AS SIDE

10 oz (300 g) medium pasta shells

1 Tbsp butter

1 small yellow onion, diced

½ tsp salt, plus more to taste

2 garlic cloves, minced

Grated zest of 1 lemon

½ cup whipping (35%) cream

1 cup ricotta cheese

⅓ cup grated Parmesan cheese, plus more for garnish

1½ cups fresh shelled peas (or frozen peas, thawed)

¼ tsp pepper

Red pepper flakes

⅓ cup chopped fresh mint leaves

Bring a large pot of salted water to boil over high heat. Cook the shells until they're tender but they still have a bit of bite to them, about 5–6 minutes. Drain, reserving ⅔ cup of the pasta water.

In a large non-stick skillet, melt the butter over medium-high heat. Stir in the onion, along with a generous pinch of salt. Cook until the onion is translucent, then stir in the garlic and cook for another minute. Stir in the lemon zest, cream, and reserved pasta water (in that order). Stir well, then add the ricotta and Parmesan. Stir again. Add the pasta shells, peas, ½ tsp salt, pepper, and a pinch of red pepper flakes.

Cook for a couple of minutes until the sauce is thickened, then season again, if necessary. Stir in the mint, then divide the pasta into bowls. Garnish with more Parmesan cheese.

* *Sometimes I like to drizzle a little bit of olive oil over each serving for extra deliciousness.*

* *If you grow your own mint, be sure to use peppermint or spearmint, not something funky like chocolate mint or pineapple mint.*

* *The pasta will thicken up the longer it rests. If you're warming up leftovers, you may want to thin the pasta out with a bit of chicken broth, milk, cream, or even water.*

* *This is tasty alongside chicken, fish, or pork.*

Coconut Rice with Shrimp and Peas

One-pot, 30-minute meals have saved my bacon oh so many times, and I know you feel the same. Every cook needs something they can throw together in minutes, and to be 100% honest, this recipe is why I always have shrimp and peas in the freezer and cans of coconut milk in the pantry. Cooking the curry paste with the aromatics lays down a terrific bedrock of flavour that is enhanced further by the coconut milk and lime juice.

Peas and shrimp add a little sweetness to the pot, and the fresh herbs knock the dish out of the park. This is a simple, delicious, and kid-friendly meal that not only tastes great, it smells darn fine, too. Cleaning up is a breeze (one pot to wash!) because I know all you want to do after a busy day is put up your feet and watch something good on Netflix.

Warm the oil in a Dutch oven over medium-high heat. Stir in the onion and carrot and cook until they're softened, about 5 minutes. Stir in the garlic, ginger, curry paste, salt, and a pinch of cayenne pepper. Cook for another 2 minutes, or until fragrant.

Add the rice, and stir to thoroughly coat. Pour in the coconut milk and scrape up any brown bits from the bottom of the pot. Stir in 1 cup water. Bring to a boil over high heat, then stir once, cover, and turn the heat to low. Cook for 15 minutes.

Stir the rice, scraping up any bits that might be starting to stick to the bottom of the pot. The rice should be completely cooked, or very close to it, at this point. If it's still firm, cover the pot again and cook it a bit longer. Stir in the peas, shrimp, and lime juice. Cover and increase the heat to medium-low. Cook until the shrimp are pink and cooked through, about 5–8 minutes.

Stir in the basil and cilantro, and season to taste with more salt and pepper. Serve immediately, with lime wedges on the side.

* *If you're using frozen shrimp, be sure they are thawed and rinsed.*

* *If you only have hot curry paste, use 1½ tsp.*

* *Look for the blue MSC symbol on the package of shrimp to ensure excellent quality and sustainability.*

* *Use any leftover coconut milk to make Charred Broccoli with Coconut Milk and Peanuts (page 47), add it to smoothies or pancake batter, or freeze for later. If you end up pouring the whole can into the rice, then reduce the amount of water accordingly.*

SERVES 4

2 Tbsp canola oil

1 medium yellow onion, diced

1 medium carrot, diced (about 1 cup)

2 garlic cloves, minced

1 Tbsp minced fresh ginger

1½ Tbsp mild Indian curry paste

¾ tsp salt

Cayenne pepper

1 cup white basmati rice, rinsed

1¼ cups coconut milk

1¼ cups fresh shelled peas (or frozen peas, thawed)

12 oz (350 g) large raw, peeled and deveined shrimp

2 Tbsp fresh lime juice

¼ cup chopped fresh basil

¼ cup chopped fresh cilantro (or mint, or a combo)

Pepper

Lime wedges, for serving

Posh Peas on Toast

Potentially controversial statement: avocado toast is overrated. I love avocados as much as the next person, but hot damn they're expensive. And inconsistent. And I've never really understood the fuss about mashing them on toast. Plus, I can spend $2 on a single avocado, or $2 on a bag of frozen peas. That basic bag will get me a whole lotta posh peas on toast! This recipe has me thinking about peas in a whole new way, as they really can stand alone and you can taste how bright and flavourful they really are. And that colour is just the best, isn't it? I like making posh peas on toast for a light lunch in the spring and summer, and, if I've got people coming over, it makes a dazzling appetizer when slathered on toasted baguette slices. This spread is equally delicious with frozen peas as it is with fresh, but when Dix brings me the little green orbs from his garden, I swear the toast tastes even better. Pricey mascarpone brings the posh to this pea party, but you can save money by making your own. See my note below.

If you're using fresh peas, place them in a saucepan with about 2 cups of water. Bring to a boil then simmer, stirring occasionally, until tender but still bright green, about 3–4 minutes. Drain, then transfer to a bowl of ice water for a few minutes. Drain again. If you're using frozen peas, place them in a medium saucepan and warm them over medium heat (no added water). The peas should be thawed but still cool.

Reserve ½ cup of the peas. Put the remainder in a food processor fitted with a metal blade. Add 3 Tbsp of the oil, the lemon zest, the lemon juice, basil, mint, salt, and pepper. Pulse until the mixture is spreadable but still has some texture. Taste and adjust the seasoning. Scoop the pea mixture into a bowl and stir in the reserved peas.

Preheat the oven to 350°F. Brush the bread with about 4 Tbsp of the oil and toast it on both sides. (I place the bread directly on the oven rack.) Slather the slices with the mascarpone cheese. Spoon the pea spread on top of the bread and garnish with radish slices, chives, and pea shoots. Drizzle with a bit more olive oil and sprinkle with flaky salt. Any leftover pea spread can be kept in the refrigerator for up to 2 days.

MAKES 8 SLICES

2 cups fresh shelled peas or frozen peas (I like the frozen summer sweet peas)

8 Tbsp extra-virgin olive oil, divided

1 tsp grated lemon zest

1½ Tbsp fresh lemon juice

1 Tbsp chopped fresh basil

1 Tbsp chopped fresh mint

½ tsp salt

¼ tsp pepper

8 slices crusty whole grain or sourdough bread, or 16 slices of baguette

½ cup mascarpone cheese (store-bought or homemade, see note below)

4 radishes, thinly sliced

1 Tbsp finely sliced fresh chives

Pea shoots or fresh basil leaves, for garnish

Flaky salt, for sprinkling

Homemade Mascarpone: Warm 2 cups of whipping (35%) cream in a saucepan over medium-high heat. Bring it to the point where bubbles appear at the edge of the pot. (A thermometer will read 185°F.) Don't boil the cream. Add in 1 Tbsp lemon juice and simmer gently for 5–7 minutes. Do not stir. Remove the pan from the heat and cover. Let it rest for 30 minutes. Place a fine-mesh sieve over a bowl and line the sieve with a few layers of damp cheesecloth. Without stirring, gently pour the mixture into the sieve. Sprinkle a pinch of salt over top. Cover loosely with plastic wrap and refrigerate for 24 hours. The longer the cream sits, the thicker it gets. Scrape the mascarpone cheese off the cheesecloth and into a bowl. It can be kept in an airtight container in the refrigerator for 2 weeks. Makes about ¾ cup.

Dixon and I are pretty much on the same page when it comes to likes and dislikes in the vegetable world, with one notable exception: green bell peppers. He admires their crunch and grassy taste. I do not. Yes, they're the more affordable version of their sweeter, ripened, and brightly coloured selves, but even if I can save some money, it still doesn't make me want to eat them. Hard pass.

Sweet bell peppers, on the other hand, are so good when sliced into salads. A Greek salad would not be the same without them. I'm also a fan of cutting them into thick wedges, slicking them with olive oil, and roasting them until there are lovely charred bits on the skins.

One of my favourite ways to cook with red bell peppers is blitzing them into a robust romesco sauce. The Spaniards did a beautiful thing when they created romesco. Fishermen in northern Tarragona concocted this sauce as an accompaniment to fish. A testament to simplicity, romesco is essentially made from roasted red peppers and tomatoes, toasted nuts, stale bread, and olive oil. Toss romesco with hot pasta, or serve it alongside grilled meats, or, yes, fish. Slather it on sandwiches, stir it into stews, and—my favourite—use it as a dip for grilled vegetables. I typically roast 3 whole red peppers, 1 ripe tomato (cored), and 5 garlic cloves in a shallow baking dish at 375°F for 90 minutes. The slow-roasting process produces lovely caramelized goodness, and the house smells heavenly. The roasted vegetables and garlic go into the food processor along with a handful of toasted stale bread, ½ cup toasted sliced almonds, 2 Tbsp red wine vinegar, 2 tsp smoked paprika, and 1 tsp salt. Olive oil is poured in slowly while the motor is running and a lovely emulsion occurs. You'll need about ⅓ cup of oil. I like to make romesco a day in advance of serving, just so all of the flavours have a chance to get to know one another. Gather your favourite fresh vegetables from your garden or market. Toss them in a bit of olive oil and grill them until tender. Serve on a platter with the romesco sauce and plenty of wine. Give a toast to the farmers, the Spaniards, and the talented cook who served you a platter of glorious summer food. If there were a sauce of the summer, romesco would be it. So pretty and tasty, versatile and simple, the only thing better would be a trip to Spain, but I can't give you that. I can, however, share this sauce recipe and hope you love it as much as I do.

✳✳✳✳✳✳✳✳✳✳✳✳✳✳✳✳✳✳✳✳✳✳✳✳✳✳✳✳✳✳✳✳✳✳✳✳✳✳

Dixon Says: Peppers like it hot! Plant them in the sunniest, warmest spot in your garden. They are another of those plants that needs to be started in a greenhouse or sunny window in late winter. When we transplant in the garden, we put them, along with the tomatoes, in between two plantings of corn. This creates a warm, sheltered spot that acts like a sort of microclimate, helping the peppers zip along during the short growing season here in the Prairies.

PEPPERS

Weeknight Warrior Roasted Vegetables and Chickpeas

Dixon and I eat a lot of sheet pan suppers—especially during the summer and fall when he's super busy in the field—and they really are the weeknight warriors when it comes to feeding a hungry family. Assembly is quick and relatively painless. Toss your preferred protein—anything from chicken thighs to chickpeas—with whatever vegetables you have on hand. The vegetables roast up to pretty perfection, and the meat, if you're using any, has lovely crispy bits. Cleaning up is a snap, which, in this day and age, we can all appreciate. I like to go big and use two sheet pans so there are leftovers for later in the week. Cook once, eat twice, and all that. I love how crispy the chickpeas get and how the veg soak up all of the wonderful pan juices. And just look at how photogenic these sheet pans are! Talk about eating the rainbow!

Preheat the oven to 400°F. Line two rimmed baking sheets with parchment paper.

Place the vegetables, chickpeas, garlic, 4 Tbsp of the oil, the vinegar, Italian seasoning, salt, and pepper in a large bowl. Stir to thoroughly combine, then spread evenly between the two baking sheets. Be sure to scrape all of the oil and seasonings from the bowl. Roast for 30 minutes, stirring halfway through. Rotate pans from top to bottom to ensure even roasting.

In the same bowl, toss the kale with the remaining 1 Tbsp oil and a generous pinch of salt. Sprinkle the kale evenly over the two sheet pans. Roast until the kale wilts and becomes crispy and the other vegetables are tender with browned bits, about 7–8 more minutes.

Remove the pans from the oven. Season to taste with more salt and pepper, if you like. Serve in bowls with pasta, quinoa, couscous, or crusty bread. I like to drizzle the bowls with more olive oil or spoonfuls of Gorgeous Greens Pesto (page 85) and top with crumbled feta cheese or Parmesan cheese.

SERVES 6-8

4 bell peppers, assorted colours, sliced into 1-inch strips

1 head broccoli, chopped into florets, stem cut into chunks

6 cocktail tomatoes, halved (or 1½ cups whole cherry tomatoes)

1 medium red onion, cut into ½-inch wedges

1 can (16 oz/540 mL) chickpeas, rinsed and drained

3 garlic cloves, chopped

5 Tbsp extra-virgin olive oil, divided, plus more for drizzling

2 Tbsp balsamic vinegar

2 tsp Italian seasoning (or dried thyme, oregano, or basil)

1 tsp salt, plus more to taste

¼ tsp pepper

1 bunch kale, centre ribs removed, leaves roughly torn and patted dry

Feta cheese or grated Parmesan cheese, for serving

✱ *For the meat lovers, nestle 4–6 Italian or chorizo sausages into the vegetables. Give them a stir when you add the kale. Or use 6–8 skinless, boneless chicken thighs, seasoned with salt and pepper beforehand. Let the pans rest for 5 minutes before serving.*

✱ *Use leftovers in frittata, in pasta, or on top of pizza.*

Mega Veg Black Bean Chili with Chipotle and Chocolate

So you're probably wondering about the chocolate in the chili. For real? Yes, for real. It's just 2 tablespoons of cocoa powder, but it adds a lush richness to the subtle smokiness of the chipotle peppers. The combination makes the chili *smoulder*, not unlike a couple of lovers I know. I first began putting chocolate in my chili after I saw the movie *Like Water for Chocolate*. There's a memorable scene where turkey mole is being prepared, and watching all of that sensuality play out on screen inspired me to up my chili game. I think I succeeded! It's loaded with mega vegetables, beans, and chewy bulgur. I asked Dix if he missed the meat, and he shook his head in the negative. Over the years, I've made this chili with and without meat, and it's delicious either way—especially with all of the fun toppings!

Prepare the chili: In a large pot, warm the oil over medium-high heat. Add the onion, carrots, mushrooms, and jalapeño. Cook until the vegetables are softened and the mushrooms have released most of their liquid, about 5–7 minutes. Stir in the bell peppers, zucchini, and garlic. Cook for a few more minutes, then add the chili powder, cumin, coriander, oregano, salt, and cayenne. Cook for 2 minutes, stirring often.

Stir in the canned tomatoes and scrape up any browned bits from the bottom of the pot. Rinse out each tomato can with about ¾ cup water and add this tomatoey water (about 1½ cups in total) as well. Stir in the black beans, chipotle peppers, cocoa, and honey. Cover, bring to a boil, then turn down the heat to medium-low and simmer, uncovered, for 25 minutes, stirring often.

Stir in the cooked bulgur, corn, and cilantro. Simmer for 5 more minutes. Season to taste with more salt, pepper, and hot sauce, if you like. Spoon into bowls and garnish with any or all of the toppings listed.

✳ *For the carnivores, brown 1 lb of ground beef, chicken, or turkey, and then proceed with the recipe above. You may need to add more water or omit the bulgur if the chili is too thick.*

✳ *If mushrooms are a controversial ingredient in chili for you, substitute 1½ cups chopped sweet potato, or just leave them out and don't add anything as a substitute.*

SERVES 6–8

Chili

2 Tbsp canola oil

1 large yellow onion, diced

3 medium carrots, grated

1½ cups sliced button mushrooms

1 jalapeño pepper, diced (some seeds removed)

2 red bell peppers, chopped

2 medium zucchini, chopped

3 garlic cloves, minced

1½ Tbsp chili powder

1 Tbsp ground cumin

1 Tbsp ground coriander

1 Tbsp oregano

1½ tsp salt, plus more to taste

½ tsp cayenne pepper

1 can (28 oz/798 mL) crushed tomatoes

1 can (28 oz/798 mL) diced tomatoes

2 cans (each 19 oz/540mL) black beans, rinsed and drained

3–4 canned chipotle peppers in adobo sauce, minced

2 Tbsp cocoa powder

1½ Tbsp honey

1½ cups cooked bulgur wheat (see page 261)

1 cup frozen corn, thawed

½ cup chopped cilantro

Pepper

Hot sauce (optional)

Toppings

Chopped cilantro

Lime wedges

Diced avocado

Sour cream

Shredded cheddar cheese

Pickled Red Onions (page 165)

Tortilla chips

Roasted Vegetable Sandwich with Pesto Mayonnaise

I love this combination of roasted vegetables. Their flavours are highly compatible, which means they make a pretty great vegetarian sandwich, especially with a pesto mayonnaise and melty cheese along for the ride. This sandwich was on the menu at Rutherford House—a tea room in Edmonton where I was the chef in the mid-2000s—and was super popular among customers and staff alike. Every time we considered taking it off the menu, an uprising ensued. And so the sandwich remained. Feel free to use whatever cheese you love. I'm partial to provolone, one of my recipe testers went bonkers for brie, and another was gaga for Gouda. I know some folks will grimace at the thought of eating eggplant, in which case you can roast more of the other veg, or even some sliced butternut squash or sweet potato.

Prepare the vegetables: Preheat the oven to 425°F. Line two rimmed baking sheets with parchment paper.

In a large bowl, toss the vegetables with the oil, salt, oregano, basil, and pepper. Spread them into an even layer on each baking sheet. Place one pan on the top rack of the oven and the other on the bottom rack. Roast for 45 minutes, stirring once and rotating the pans from top to bottom halfway through. You want the vegetables to have some crispy, deeply caramelized bits. Remove from the oven.

Prepare the pesto mayonnaise: While the vegetables are in the oven, mix together the mayonnaise, pesto, lemon zest, and lemon juice in a small bowl. Season with pinches of salt and pepper. Refrigerate until you're ready to make the sandwiches.

Assemble the sandwiches: Toast the buns until nice and crispy, then spread pesto mayonnaise on both sides. On the bottom half, pile on some roasted vegetables and top with 2 slices of cheese. Place under a preheated broiler and keep it there until the cheese is melted and slightly browned, about 2–3 minutes. Remove from the broiler and top with the other half of the bun. Tuck in a few fresh basil leaves, if you have them around. Eat immediately.

* *If you don't eat all of the vegetables at once, refrigerate them for up to 2 days. Just reheat in the oven or microwave and assemble the sandwiches as above.*

* *The vegetables can also be grilled on the barbecue, sliced into thicker pieces. The zucchini would be best sliced lengthwise so it doesn't burn.*

* *Use basil pesto instead of the Gorgeous Greens Pesto. Or skip the pesto mayonnaise entirely and just slather the toasted bread with the Gorgeous Greens Pesto.*

MAKES 6 SANDWICHES

Vegetables

3 sweet bell peppers, assorted colours, sliced into 1-inch-thick wedges

2 medium zucchini, sliced on the diagonal into ½-inch-thick pieces

1 medium eggplant, sliced into ½-inch-thick rounds

1 small red onion, sliced into wedges

⅓ cup extra-virgin olive oil

¾ tsp salt

½ tsp dried oregano

½ tsp dried basil

¼ tsp pepper

Pesto Mayonnaise

⅓ cup mayonnaise

3 Tbsp Gorgeous Greens Pesto (page 85)

Grated zest of ½ lemon

1 Tbsp fresh lemon juice

Salt and pepper

To Assemble

6 ciabatta buns

12 slices provolone, Gouda, Swiss, or brie cheese

Small handful fresh basil leaves (optional)

quite enjoy eating potatoes. Dixon, how-ever, knows practically everything there is to know about potatoes, so I'm turning the rest of the page over to him.

* *

Dixon Says: One of the most often asked questions at the farmers' market is "Which potato is best?" Well, we grow six varieties of potatoes, and they're all good, although some are a little better than others, depending on what you're using them for. The waxy varieties such as Red Bliss, Fingerlings, baby potatoes, and creamers are good for soups, stews, scalloped potatoes, and so forth as they hold their shape really well. The drier, starchier ones, like russets, are great for deep-frying, mashing, and baking. Russian Blues are great pan-fried or tossed in oil and roasted, and they contain anthocyanins, the same antioxidant that blueberries are famous for. But I always qualify any response with "But . . . my favourite is Yukon Gold."

Yukon Gold is a Canadian variety developed in Ontario during the 1960s. They have an amazing flavour, easily the best among any variety we grow. There are some new yellow varieties that are much higher producing and disease resistant, and we've grown a few. Every time, I've decided "in flavour" of Yukon Gold.

Potatoes, any variety, are fairly easy to grow, even for a backyard gardener. Aim for planting them around the end of May, though you can plant earlier if the weather is nice and the soil is warm. We have successfully harvested potatoes planted as late as early July, so there's a fairly wide window. Potatoes can be used as their own seed. Leave them out in a warm room until sprouts start to grow out of their eyes. (You don't need to do this, but they'll grow faster if you do.) If the potatoes are big, you may wish to get more bang for your buck by cutting them into smaller pieces, taking care not to damage those sprouts. Just remember that each piece should be no smaller than 2 inches on every side and have at least two eyes on it. I call this Darth Bintje's Rule of Two (a little geeky *Star Wars* potato pun for you). In a sunny part of the garden, dig a trench about 4–6 inches deep and carefully pile the soil along-side, as you'll need it later. Place the potato seed pieces about 10–14 inches apart—closer for more potatoes, farther apart for ease of digging. Then, cover them up. When they start to grow leaves, hill them up with more soil. While you can grow potatoes without irrigation, you won't be happy with the results. You'll likely get small soft, mushy potatoes with little flavour. Potatoes need a good amount of water to develop a nice texture and excellent flavour. Remember too that the water will tend to run off the hill, so you will need to give them a good soaking once a week. About 2 inches' worth should do it. When the plants start to flower, the tubers are ready. Harvest now if you like the little baby potatoes. You can tell potatoes are sizing up as the soil on the hills will start to crack as they grow bigger. Carefully dig around where the soil is cracked with your hands to pick potatoes without digging up the plant. If you're harvesting potatoes for storage, cut the tops off the plants and wait a week before harvesting. This lets the skins toughen up or "cure" so they won't scratch and bruise while being harvested and spoil in storage. The ideal storage is dark, dry, and 8°–10°C (also known as 50°F).

POTATOES

Ode to the Potato

Let's start at the beginning. One of my earliest memories is digging into the earth, searching for potatoes buried below the surface. The sky is bright blue, like it is on most summer days in Saskatchewan, and the air is warm, smelling like wheat and sunshine. My little hands have the best time as I find one nugget, then another. Into the pail they go, and onto the next hill I go. These small, very new potatoes will be gently boiled in their paper-thin skins and tumbled in glorious amounts of melted butter, chopped dill, salt, and pepper. My mom likes to keep their preparation simple, as these tiny tubers are pure and simple goodness all on their own. Because they've been harvested before they're fully grown, their sugars haven't turned to starch. Thus, they're more delicate, creamier, even a bit sweeter than their grown-up versions. In summer, this is how I want my potatoes to be. Nothing more, nothing less. Four decades later, much has changed, but not this.

At the opposite end of the spectrum is the simple baked potato. Large unassuming russets lack the cuteness of the creamers, but when done right, their skins are slightly crispy, shimmering with salt, and their tender flesh pillowy soft. A sharp knife slides through the hot potato with no resistance. No firm chunks are allowed in baked potatoes. The steam escapes, wafting up to greet my nose. Butter is the first layer of flavour, evenly and decadently applied. Next is a good amount of shredded cheddar, followed by chopped, crispy bacon (no substitutes from a plastic container, please). You gotta have a heaping dollop or two of sour cream (go full-fat or go home), and, finally, a smattering of sliced green onions. No potato, however it's cooked, is complete without salt and pepper. Behold, a masterpiece of culinary creation. This humble spud is transformed into something spectacular with the simple application of heat. And fat. And salt. On days when I've come home late from work, with no idea about what to make for dinner, I reach for a russet. A heaping, hot baked potato is a solo diner's best friend, skin and all.

Dixon says he knew he loved me when I told him I would never cook plain boiled potatoes for supper. As someone who was raised in a family that grows the tubers for a living, Dixon has consumed more potatoes in a lifetime than anyone probably should. More often than not, the potatoes served by his mom were the plain boiled sort, where you had to pat them down flat and mash in the butter with your fork to make them somewhat palatable. I too know these potatoes well, and they certainly weren't my favourite as a kid either. They were bland. They were boring. As an adult, I can appreciate that both of our moms just wanted to feed their families quickly, and some nights, dinner had to be straightforward and fuss-free. Hence, the plain boiled potatoes. These potatoes were often sidelined to the edge of the plate, where they were left to go cold. And the only thing worse than a plain boiled potato is a cold boiled potato.

THE POTATO HAS LONG BEEN ADMIRED FOR ITS VERSATILITY AND ABILITY TO FILL UP OUR BELLIES RATHER CHEAPLY. I'M FOND OF ALL THE WAYS IT SOOTHES AND SATISFIES US . . .

The potato has long been admired for its versatility and ability to fill up our bellies rather cheaply. I'm fond of all the ways it soothes and satisfies us, with the power to offer calm and comfort more than any other vegetable I know. Slice Yukon Golds into cubes or wedges, toss them in olive oil, garlic, salt, and pepper, and roast at high heat until the edges are crispy and the centres are soft. These are the perfect potatoes for dunking into spicy mayonnaise. And I never, ever need an excuse to eat creamy, buttery mashed potatoes. If gravy is involved, the more the merrier. I love potatoes when they're shredded into frilly latkes and rösti, sour cream on the side, please. I love them pan-fried in bacon fat, snuggled up to a couple of sunny-side-up eggs. I love them scalloped with plenty of cream—a perfect accompaniment to baked ham, if there ever was one. I love them deep-fried into French fries, sprinkled with sea salt, and drizzled with vinegar. And, because we're all friends here, I want you to know that there is a bag of Tater Tots in my freezer at all times, ready to be baked at 425°F for 25 minutes, then dusted with smoked paprika and salt. This is my favourite 2 AM insomnia snack, often consumed while watching a rerun of *Seinfeld* with a cat on my lap. The potato is my constant carb, the food I reach for in moments that are joyful and not so joyful. It is always there, in my kitchen, and in my heart. Just don't ask me to eat it boiled.

Lemon Roasted Potatoes

I wish I had a story to share with you about that time I went to Greece, stayed in a seaside villa, and fell in love with lemon roasted potatoes. Maybe in my dreams! Note to Dixon: Go ahead and surprise me with a trip anytime! Truth is, I just love a good lemon roasted potato. One that walks the line of being almost too tart but pulls back just in time. One that is terrifically soft but still has some crispy bits clinging to the edges. One that has so much flavour, you'll think that maybe you've been magically transported to Greece to your own seaside villa. Serve these super-lemony potatoes with any roasted/grilled meat or fish.

Preheat the oven to 400°F.

Place the potatoes in a 9- × 13-inch glass, enamel, or ceramic baking dish. Drizzle the oil over them and season with the oregano, salt, and pepper. Stir to evenly coat. Place in the oven and roast for 15 minutes.

Add the broth, stir, and roast for 10 more minutes. Stir in the lemon juice and lemon slices, if using, and roast for another 15 minutes. Stir the potatoes, then put them back in the oven and increase the heat to 500°F. Roast until most of the liquid has been absorbed, another 15 minutes or so. A little will remain and that's okay.

For some crispy bits, place the potatoes under the broiler for about 3–4 minutes.

Remove from the oven, spoon the potatoes into a serving dish (be sure to get all of the lemony goodness out of the pan), sprinkle with parsley, and serve.

SERVES 6–8

4 lb (about 8 medium) russet potatoes, peeled and quartered

½ cup extra-virgin olive oil

1 Tbsp dried oregano

1¾ tsp salt

¼ tsp pepper

1 cup low-sodium chicken (or vegetable) broth

½ cup fresh lemon juice (from 2–3 lemons)

½ lemon, sliced (optional)

2 Tbsp chopped fresh parsley (flat-leaf or curly), for garnish

✳ *If you're using large russet potatoes (4 lb = about 5 potatoes), cut them into 8 pieces.*

✳ *Leftovers make great hash browns for breakfast.*

Cream of Celery and Mashed Potato Soup

This is one of my favourite soups that Mom would make when I was a kid. It's simple, home-style goodness that only takes 30 minutes from start to finish. When I watched Mom make it, I was always super impressed that she stirred leftover mashed potatoes into it. Such a good idea, as the creaminess and flavour are already there, as opposed to just raw potatoes, which lack the richness and texture of the mashed. If you don't have mashed potatoes on hand, just make some as you normally would (I always use butter and sour cream), then let them cool to room temperature, and proceed with the recipe. This soup is a tasty way to use up celery that's lingering in the crisper when you don't quite know what to do with it. It's not a vegetable known to take the spotlight, but it surely shines here.

Warm the butter in a Dutch oven over medium-high heat. Stir in the leek and cook until softened, about 5 minutes. Stir in the celery. Sauté until the celery is softened, 5 minutes, then stir in the garlic and salt. Cook for another minute, then stir in the broth.

Cover and bring to a boil. Turn down the heat to medium, simmer for 5 minutes, then stir in the mashed potatoes, a large serving spoonful at a time, making sure they are dissolved before adding another spoonful. After all of the potatoes have been added, simmer the soup, uncovered, for about 5 minutes. Remove from the heat and use an immersion blender to purée it. I like to have some bits of celery remain, so I don't purée it until it's super creamy, only a little creamy.

Put the pot back onto low heat and stir in the cream, dill, and pepper. Cook for another few minutes. Season to taste. Ladle the soup into bowls and garnish with a few celery leaves.

SERVES 4–6

2 Tbsp butter

1 leek, cleaned and sliced (about 2 cups)

7 celery stalks, diced (about 3 cups)

2 garlic cloves, minced

½ tsp salt

4 cups low-sodium chicken (or vegetable) broth

3 cups leftover mashed potatoes

½ cup whipping (35%) cream

2 Tbsp finely chopped fresh dill

¼ tsp pepper

Celery leaves, for garnish

* Substitute a diced yellow onion for the leek.

* When preparing leeks, cut them in half lengthwise and run each half under cool running water so as to remove any grit or sand that may be trapped.

* If you're making the mashed potatoes specifically for this soup, be sure that they are seasoned with butter, cream, salt, and pepper, like they are in the recipe on page 129, but minus the cheese and roasted garlic.

Dutch Oven Potato Bread

I know this is a book about vegetables, but once a baker, always a baker! And with that, I give you bread! Well, a recipe for bread, using a little bit of mashed potato and the water it was cooked in. Baking bread always makes me feel like I'm a grown-up, like I've somehow got this adulting thing figured out. This is not a no-knead recipe, but I let my trusty stand mixer do all of the kneading. The loaf is baked in a very hot pot, so do take care when moving it in and out of the oven. This is a lovely yeasty soft bread with a light-textured crumb and a good chew factor. There is just a whisper of potato flavour, and the crust is crispy, just how I like it. While the bread is delicious when fresh and warm and slathered with salted butter, I really do make it just for the superior toast it produces. When we're dunking the toasty slices into our runny yolks, Dixon always leans over to me and says, "Babe, you make great bread."

MAKES 1 LOAF

½ lb peeled russet potatoes, chopped into large chunks

2 tsp active dry yeast

Sugar

1 tsp salt

3–3½ cups all-purpose or bread flour

Extra-virgin olive oil

Boil the potato chunks in a small pot with plenty of salted water until tender. Reserve 2 cups of the cooking water and drain off the rest. Mash the potato (don't add anything) until smooth. You'll have about 1 cup of mashed potatoes.

Pour 1 cup of the cooking water into a small bowl. When it's cooled down to the point where it's warm but not hot, stir in the yeast and a pinch of sugar. It should froth up in about 5 minutes; but if not, start over with more yeast and the remaining warm cooking water.

In a large mixing bowl, use your fingertips to work the mashed potato and salt into 3 cups of flour. It will be coarse, but you're just looking to combine them. Dump the yeast mixture into the bowl of a stand mixer fitted with a dough hook. With the motor running on medium/low speed, gradually add the flour/potato mixture. The dough should be loose and sticky, but if you find it too wet, gradually add more flour. If you find it too dry, add a little more potato water (or warm tap water if you've used up all your potato water). Knead with the dough hook for about 5 minutes, until it transforms into a smooth elastic ball. If you're doing this by hand, add the yeast mixture to the bowl of flour/potato dough and mix until it comes together into a ball. Transfer the ball to a lightly floured surface and knead for about 8 minutes (this is why I use my stand mixer) until the dough is smooth and elastic. You may need to add more flour. It's good if it's still a little sticky!

Lightly grease a large bowl with olive oil and set the dough inside, turning to coat the top. Cover with a clean kitchen towel and let rise in a warm, draft-free space until the dough has doubled in size, about 1 hour.

Gently punch the dough down and shape it into a round. Sprinkle a piece of parchment paper (about 15 inches square) with flour and set the round on top. Cover with a clean kitchen towel and let rise for another hour or so. You'll know it's ready when the round has doubled in size and when you gently press the top with your thumb, a small imprint remains. If not, let it rise for another 15 minutes. Lightly dust the top with flour and use a very sharp knife to score the loaf.

(continued on page 209)

(continued from page 207)

   Move a rack into the middle of the oven. Half an hour before the dough is ready, place a 5- to 6-quart Dutch oven fitted with its lid inside the oven as it preheats to 450°F. The oven should be preheating for at least 30 minutes. When the loaf has risen and is dusted with flour and scored, carefully set it inside the very hot pot, parchment paper and all. Cover with the lid and carefully put it in the oven. Bake for 30 minutes. Remove the lid and bake for another 15–25 minutes, until the bread is crusty and a deep golden brown on top. It should also sound hollow when tapped. Remove the pot to a cooling rack and let the bread cool inside the pot for at least 45 minutes before slicing. Willpower!

Pommes Anna

I first began crushing hard on Pommes Anna when I first began crushing hard on Gilbert (yes, the same Gilbert from *All the Sweet Things*). The handsome French chef would prepare these fancy spuds at least once a week during the summer we worked in the Yukon together. He would slide thin wedges over to my cutting board so I could have a taste. I don't know what gave me the butterflies more—the potatoes or the chef. Pommes Anna is like the Cinderella of the potato world. It's hard to imagine that something so utterly beige and basic as a potato could be transformed into something so ethereal and elegant as this dish. Butter, salt, a very sharp knife, and a little care and attention are all you need to have these sumptuous potatoes on your dinner table. I brown the butter first so that there is a deeper, richer flavour happening here. Inverting them onto a platter is the best part. No, I take that back. Eating them is the best part.

Preheat the oven to 425°F.

Using a very sharp knife or mandolin, slice the potatoes ⅛-inch thick. Do not rinse or soak the slices in water. The starch is what binds the layers.

In a small saucepan, melt the butter over medium heat and cook, swirling the pan. The butter will bubble and froth up and eventually turn light brown and nutty. Remove from the heat immediately. If you happen to burn the butter (happens to the best of us), you'll have to start over.

Using a pastry brush, generously grease the bottom and sides of a well-seasoned 10-inch cast-iron skillet with about 2½ Tbsp of the brown butter. Cover the bottom of the pan with one-third of the best-looking potato slices, arranging them in a slightly overlapping circular pattern, working from the outside edge of the skillet toward the centre. Brush with about 1 Tbsp of the remaining butter and sprinkle with ½ tsp of the salt and some of the pepper. Make two or three more layers, depending on how many potato slices you have left. Remember to brush butter on each layer and sprinkle with the salt and pepper.

Set the skillet over medium heat and let the potatoes cook, without touching them, for about 4 minutes. You'll hear a sizzling sound. This is when you set your timer. We want to initiate browning on the bottom layer of potatoes. Cover the skillet loosely with foil and transfer to the oven. Bake for 30 minutes on the centre rack. Remove the foil and bake until the top is browned and crispy and the potatoes can be pierced easily with a fork, about 20–25 more minutes. Remove the potatoes from the oven and let rest for 5 minutes. Place a small sheet of aluminum foil on top of the potatoes and add something heavy to weigh them down. This will help compress the potatoes. Let them rest like this for another 5 minutes.

Run a spatula around the edge of the skillet. Hold a serving plate against the skillet and carefully flip so that the golden bottom is facing up. If any potatoes stick to the bottom of the skillet, pick them off and place them where they belong. Sprinkle with thyme leaves and flaky salt, if you like. Slice into wedges and serve.

SERVES 6

2½ lb medium Yukon Gold potatoes, peeled

7 Tbsp unsalted butter

1½ tsp salt, divided

¼ tsp pepper, divided

Fresh thyme leaves

Flaky salt

* *You don't have to invert the potatoes, if you don't want to. You can slice and serve the wedges from the skillet.*

* *Leftover wedges make great crispy hash browns.*

* *If you can't find Yukon Golds, use russet potatoes.*

Lazy Perogie Casserole

I feel like there should be a warning attached to this recipe: Caution! This is one buttery decadent casserole that is so darn good, but if you're afraid of carbs or pools of melted butter, then maybe flip the page. If you're still with me, hello! I have a real treat for you perogie-loving people! My mom has been making this casserole for ages, and every time she would serve it, my heart would skip a beat. (Note to self: maybe it was all of that butter.) This recipe has everything you love about perogies, made in a fraction of the time. Dixon is in love with this casserole, too. He said the only thing that would make it better is a garnish of chopped bacon. Is he my kindred spirit, or what?!

Preheat the oven to 350°F. Lightly grease a 3-quart casserole dish. Depending on the shape and size of your casserole dish, you may use fewer than 12 noodles. A 9- × 13-inch baking dish, for example, will use fewer noodles than the deep 3-quart dish in the photo.

Cook the lasagna noodles in salted, boiling water according to the package directions. Rinse under cool water and drain.

Stir 2 cups of the cheddar cheese into the mashed potatoes.

In a medium bowl, combine the cottage cheese, egg, green onions, salt, and pepper.

In the same pot you cooked the noodles in, melt the butter over medium-high heat. Add the onion and sauté until translucent, about 5 minutes.

Spread about 1 cup of the cottage cheese mixture on the bottom of the baking dish. Top with 4 noodles, then half the mashed potatoes. Add another layer of the cottage cheese mixture, 4 noodles, and the rest of the potatoes. Finish with the last of the cottage cheese mixture and noodles.

Pour the hot buttery onions over the noodles. Scatter the remaining cheddar cheese on top and bake, uncovered, until the cheese is golden and gooey and the edges of the casserole are bubbly, about 30–35 minutes. Remove from the oven and let the casserole stand for 10 minutes before serving. There will be butter lingering on top, but it will eventually be absorbed by the casserole. Like I said, there will be pools of butter! Garnish with chopped chives.

SERVES 6–8

9–12 lasagna noodles

3 cups extra-old cheddar cheese, divided

2 cups warm mashed potatoes (see note)

1 container (16 oz/ 500 g) creamed cottage cheese

1 large egg, lightly beaten

3 green onions, finely chopped

½ tsp salt

¼ tsp pepper

½ cup butter

1 medium yellow onion, diced

1 Tbsp chopped chives, for garnish

* *Prepare tasty, creamy, well-seasoned mashed potatoes for this casserole, like the recipe from the Very Veggie Shepherd's Pie on page 129.*

* *You can trim the noodles to fit the dish exactly or leave them freestyle and rustic like I did here.*

Curried Potato Salad

I'm all about the potato salad. If you ever see me at a backyard barbecue, chances are I'll be hovering over the buffet table and loading my plate up with this summertime staple. This recipe has warm and vibrant curry spices instead of the usual creamy dill or spiky vinaigrette dressings. It's a bit of a twist, but those I served it to uttered no complaints, and I even heard a few murmurs of "This is the best potato salad I've ever tasted." There are a couple of things to point out about this recipe. First, the potatoes are boiled whole, then chopped after they have cooled down. This provides an excellent texture for the salad, avoiding the dreaded scenarios of either underdone or mushy potatoes. Second, the spices are toasted in a skillet for a few minutes. This step brings out so much flavour! I add the dressing to the potatoes while they're still slightly warm so they can absorb more of that gorgeous seasoning. I find that the potato salad tastes even better the next day, after the flavours have gotten to know each other a little better. This is a great dish to take to all of your potluck events. If you invite me, you know where I'll be!

In a large Dutch oven, pour in enough cold water to come at least 1 inch above the potatoes. Add a generous pinch of salt and bring to a boil over high heat. Turn down the heat to medium. Cook, partially covered, until the potatoes are tender, about 20–40 minutes, depending on the size of your potatoes. Drain and let cool slightly. Peel if you like, but I leave the skins on. Cut the potatoes into 1-inch chunks and place them in a large bowl.

Meanwhile, in a small skillet over medium-low heat, warm the curry powder, coriander, and turmeric until fragrant and lightly toasted, about 3 minutes. Cool to room temperature.

In a medium bowl, whisk together the mayonnaise, yogurt, vinegar, honey, 1¼ tsp salt, and pepper. Add the toasted spices. Whisk well. Pour the dressing over the potatoes and stir to combine. Add the vegetables, chopped eggs, and cilantro. Stir well. Season to taste with salt and pepper.

Cover and refrigerate for at least 4 hours before serving. You may have to adjust the seasonings after it is chilled. Garnish with more chopped cilantro. You can refrigerate this for up to 2 days.

SERVES 12

3 lb medium waxy white potatoes, of a similar size

1¼ tsp salt, and to taste

2½ tsp curry powder (mild, medium, whatever you prefer)

1 tsp ground coriander

1 tsp ground turmeric

½ cup mayonnaise

½ cup plain Greek yogurt

⅓ cup apple cider vinegar

2 tsp liquid honey

½ tsp pepper

2 celery stalks, diced

1 red bell pepper, diced

4 radishes, sliced

2 green onions, finely chopped

4 hard-boiled eggs, chopped

¼ cup chopped cilantro (or parsley, flat-leaf or curly), plus more for garnish

✳ *Use 2 Tbsp finely chopped chives in place of the green onions.*

There comes a point in September when it feels like I blinked and suddenly I'm enveloped by autumn. It's the time of cozy sweaters and scarves, mugs of assorted warm beverages (pumpkin spice latte, anyone?), and an abundance of winter squash. The farmers' market is bursting with various varieties, and it's fun to ask the farmers about them, as they all have their personal favourites. Buttercup, Hubbard, butternut, acorn, festival, and spaghetti are available aplenty. Then there are the different kinds of pumpkins; some perfect for carving and others more suited for pies.

I love squash in everything from ravioli to risotto, fries to frittatas, pastries to pizza. You can stuff it, roast it, slice it, and dice it. Sometimes slicing open a butternut, or any other large squash, can be a tad daunting, especially if you know your knives aren't the sharpest. The exterior of the squash can be really firm, and a dull knife has no chance of getting through to the inside. Plus, you have to put more pressure on the darn thing to get it open, which increases the chance you'll need a Band-Aid or two. A word to the wise: dull knives are bad; sharp knives are good. To avoid any kitchen mishaps, just throw the whole darn squash on a baking sheet and roast it whole. You don't have to worry about hacking off a hand. In fact, the only thing you have to worry about is what to make with it once it has slumped and softened, the skin so tender you could actually eat it as is, if you choose. I like to sneak the pulp into gooey macaroni and cheese or slip it into soups. Heck, you can even blitz it into hummus, or bake it into loaves and muffins, like you would with good ol' pumpkin.

Spaghetti squash is one of the neatest vegetables. Cut it in half, scoop out the seeds and other gunk, then drizzle it with a bit of olive oil, season with salt and pepper, and roast at 375°F for about an hour, give or take, depending on its size. Use a fork to loosen the yellow strands that, you guessed it, resemble real spaghetti. High in beta carotene, fibre, potassium, and other good things, it makes a mighty fine vehicle for your favourite meat sauce. The texture holds up well, as long as you don't overcook it. You want tender strands, not mushy strands. Plus, the combination of a somewhat sweet squash pairs really well with a savoury meat sauce. Scatter some mozzarella and meat sauce on top of the squash. Place the whole deal under the broiler and, oh gracious, the cheese bubbles and browns and is a lovely sight to behold.

****

Dixon Says: Squash of all sorts like to have room to grow, so give them plenty of space to vine out. Because young squash plants are very delicate, it's a good plan to plant two or three in the same hill so they can mutually support each other when they're small and vulnerable to damage. When they start flowering, they'll be better pollinated, as the flowers will be in closer proximity to each other. Water a little more often when they start to set fruit. Squash are ready to harvest when they develop small cracks in the stem.

SQUASH

Cheesy Butternut Squash Rigatoni

For many of us, mac and cheese is life. When I was a kid, I loved the days when Mom would whisk her hot and creamy cheese sauce over macaroni and I would devour it in no time. Pasta and melty cheese is just so good, no matter how old you are. Over the years, I've played around with many variations on the comfort food classic, but I think I hit it out of the park with this one. The addition of vitamin-rich roasted squash to cheesy, gooey rigatoni makes it essentially health food. I see you all nodding your heads in agreement. Good! I used extra-old sharp cheddar and Parmesan, but Gruyère, fontina, or Asiago would all be acceptable substitutes. I love how the sauce fills the tubular rigatoni, but you can use any shape you like—even the classic macaroni! The buttery bread crumbs add a nice bit of crunch, and, at my house, some of us love this pasta with hot sauce (me) or ketchup drizzled on top (Dixon).

Preheat the oven to 400°F. Line a rimmed baking sheet with aluminum foil.

Scrub the butternut squash. Place it on the baking sheet and roast whole until it is easily pierced with a fork, 60–75 minutes. Let cool for 10 minutes, then slice it in half and let cool until it can be easily handled. Scoop out the seeds and stringy bits, then scrape the cooked pulp into a bowl. This step can be done a few days ahead of time. You need about 2–2½ cups of squash for this recipe. You can mash it with a fork until smooth.

Cook the rigatoni according to package directions, shaving off 3 minutes of cooking time. The pasta will cook further in the oven. Drain the pasta then place it in a greased 3-quart casserole dish, a 12-inch braising pan, or a 9-× 13-inch baking dish.

Warm a large saucepan over medium-high heat. Add the bacon and cook until crisp, stirring often. Remove the bacon with a slotted spoon and drain on paper towels. Remove all but 2 Tbsp of bacon fat from the pan. (If vegetarian, use 2 Tbsp butter instead.)

Stir the onion into the bacon fat. Cook until translucent, about 5 minutes, then stir in the garlic and sage. Cook until fragrant, another minute. Stir the flour into this mixture and cook for 1 minute over medium heat. Gradually whisk in the broth, then the evaporated milk and cream. Whisk constantly so there are no lumps. The sauce takes about 5 minutes to thicken. Stir the sauce with a wooden spoon, then swipe your finger across the spoon. If the line holds, the sauce is thick enough.

Stir the butternut squash purée into the sauce along with 1 cup of the cheddar cheese and the Parmesan. Stir until it's creamy and smooth. Add the Dijon, hot sauce, salt, and pepper. Stir in the cooked bacon.

Preheat the oven to 400°F.

Stir the cheese sauce into the cooked pasta so it's evenly coated. Scatter the remaining 1 cup of cheddar over top. Combine the panko crumbs with the melted butter and sprinkle on top of the pasta. Bake until the bread crumbs are golden and the cheese is melted, about 17–20 minutes. Remove from the oven and let stand 5 minutes before serving.

SERVES 6–8

1 medium (about 2–2½ lb) butternut squash

1 lb rigatoni pasta

5 slices thick-cut bacon, chopped

1 small onion, diced

2 garlic cloves, minced

1 Tbsp fresh sage leaves, chopped

¼ cup all-purpose flour

1½ cups low-sodium chicken or vegetable broth

1 can (12 oz/345 mL) evaporated milk

¼ cup whipping (35%) cream

2 cups shredded extra-old cheddar cheese, divided

1 cup grated Parmesan cheese

2 tsp Dijon mustard

1–2 tsp hot sauce

1 tsp salt

¼ tsp pepper

½ cup panko bread crumbs

1½ Tbsp melted butter

Roasted Acorn Squash with Maple Goat Cheese and Pecans

This is a fantastic way to celebrate the delicate sweetness of acorn squash. It's quite pretty to look at too, making this side dish a desirable addition to any autumn and winter feast. Combining brown sugar, butter, and squash is nothing new, but I've sweetened some goat cheese and added that to the mix for a delicious twist. Pecans add some welcome texture, especially for those of us who have "texture issues" with squash. I love seeing those gathered around my table tuck into their individual squash, my mom marvelling at how it's almost like dessert. These roasted squash halves are quite delightful when served alongside juicy ham, tantalizing roast turkey, or even a platter of pot roast. They make a welcome contribution to any vegetarian feast, too.

Preheat the oven to 425°F.

Cut each squash in half lengthwise. Scoop out and discard the seeds. Carefully trim about ⅛ inch off the bottom of each half so each squash will sit flat, cut-side up, in a 12-inch cast-iron skillet or on a rimmed baking sheet lined with parchment paper. Using a sharp knife, score the flesh of each squash. Rub with the butter, sprinkle with the sugar, and generously season with salt and pepper.

Bake the squash until tender, about 45–55 minutes, depending on their thickness. Using a pastry brush, baste each half at the 30-minute mark with the brown sugar butter juice that will pool in the middle of each squash. When the squash halves are roasted and tender, let them cool in the pan for 10 minutes.

In a medium bowl, beat together the goat cheese, maple syrup, and the ¼ tsp salt.

Place the nuts in a small bowl. Remove the brown sugar syrup from each squash half (a ¼ cup measure works well for this) and pour it over the pecans, tossing to coat.

Fill each squash half with some of the maple goat cheese. Top with the pecans, leaving the brown sugar syrup in the bowl. Return the squash to the oven and roast until the pecans are toasted, another 7–8 minutes. Remove from the oven and drizzle the remaining brown sugar syrup from the bowl over each squash half. Garnish with fresh thyme leaves, if desired.

SERVES 4

2 small (each about 1¼ lb) acorn squash, scrubbed

2 Tbsp butter

¼ cup firmly packed brown sugar

¼ tsp salt, plus more to taste

Pepper

1 package (5 oz/140 g) goat cheese, softened

2 Tbsp maple syrup

⅓ cup pecan halves

Fresh thyme leaves, for garnish (optional)

✱ *For even cooking, be sure the squash are of a similar size.*

Curried Butternut Squash Soup with Coconut Milk

Butternut squash soup is one of my favourite things about autumn and winter. I get all the cozy feels just thinking about it. Peeling squash can be a pain in the neck, so save yourself the grief and roast the whole thing in the oven. It tastes so much better, too! For this soup I use a mild Indian curry paste, because that's what I usually have in my refrigerator, but I have made it with a hot Thai red curry paste with equally delicious results. I always have a couple of Dixon's carrots in the crisper, and sneaking them into the soup didn't compromise the flavour either. Drizzling in a bit of maple syrup for a touch of sweetness and finishing the whole thing off with an infusion of lime juice really sends this soup to squash-lover's paradise.

Preheat the oven to 400°F. Line a rimmed baking sheet with aluminum foil.

Scrub the butternut squash, and place it on the baking sheet. Roast the whole thing until fork-tender, anywhere from 60–90 minutes. When it's done roasting, slice it in half and let it cool until you can handle it comfortably. Scoop out and discard the seeds. Scrape the peel away from the flesh and discard. Put the butternut squash pulp into a bowl. You need about 3 cups for this recipe. This step can be done a few days ahead of time.

In a large soup pot, warm the oil over medium-high heat. Add the onion and cook until it is softened and translucent, 3–5 minutes. Stir in the garlic, ginger, and a generous pinch of salt. Cook for a couple more minutes until fragrant. Add the curry paste and stir for another minute. Add the butternut squash and carrots. Pour in 4 cups of broth. Cover and bring to a boil over high heat. Turn down the heat to medium-low and simmer until the vegetables are tender, about 15 minutes.

Remove from the heat, and, using an immersion blender, purée the soup until smooth. Place the pot back on medium heat and add the coconut milk, lime juice, maple syrup, and cilantro. Add salt and pepper to taste and adjust the seasonings, including more lime juice and maple syrup, if necessary. If the soup is too thick, add more broth or water. Ladle into bowls and garnish with swirls of reserved coconut milk, hot sauce, and cilantro leaves. This soup freezes very well, and it tastes even better the next day.

SERVES 6

1 large (about 3 lb) butternut squash

2 Tbsp canola oil

1 large onion, chopped

2 garlic cloves, minced

1 Tbsp minced fresh ginger

Salt, to taste

2 Tbsp mild Indian (or 2 tsp Thai red) curry paste

2 medium carrots, chopped

4–5 cups low-sodium chicken (or vegetable) broth

1 can (14 oz/398 mL) full-fat coconut milk (reserve 2 Tbsp for garnish)

2 Tbsp fresh lime juice, plus more to taste

2 tsp maple syrup, plus more to taste

2 Tbsp chopped fresh cilantro or basil

Pepper, to taste

Hot sauce and cilantro leaves, for garnish

Stuffed Squash with Greens and Grains

This recipe was 100 percent inspired by the stunning squash Dixon grows every year. The red kuri are my favourite—not only because of their lovely burnt orange colour but their cute rotund shape, too. And that little knobby bit at the top makes the perfect lid for a squash just crying out to be stuffed. Their flavour is relatively delicate, with a subtle nuttiness, so I've punched up the grains and greens filling with plenty of garlic, herbs, cranberries, nuts, and cheese. As far as grains go, I went with basmati rice and red quinoa (it's actually a seed that acts like a grain), but cooked millet, wild rice, bulgur, or barley would be tasty as well. This is a fun recipe to play around with and customize as you see fit. Instead of kale, swap in chard or spinach. Instead of mushrooms, do zucchini. There is a bit of prep involved, but the presentation is quite lovely. For an impressive vegetarian, or even vegan, main course at holiday gatherings, look no further.

Preheat the oven to 400°F. Line a baking sheet with parchment paper.

Using a sharp paring knife, cut the tops off each squash. Scoop out and discard the seeds from the lids and the insides of each squash. Trim the bottoms off each squash so they lie flat on the baking sheet. Lightly brush inside each squash with 1 Tbsp of the canola oil and season each with a little salt and pepper. Roast the lids and the individual squashes for 25–35 minutes, depending on the thickness of the squash. They should be close to being cooked through. To test for doneness, pierce the thickest part of each squash with a fork. It should offer little resistance. The squash will continue to cook through when stuffed. Turn down the oven to 375°F.

Meanwhile, warm the remaining 2 Tbsp of canola oil in a large skillet over medium-high heat. Stir in the onion, garlic, and mushrooms. Cook until the vegetables are softened and the mushrooms have some colour, about 5 minutes. Stir in the kale, vinegar, salt, pepper, thyme leaves, and a pinch of red pepper flakes. Cook until the kale is softened, another 3 minutes or so. Remove from the heat and place the mixture in a large bowl.

Stir the cooked rice, quinoa, dried cranberries, almonds, feta, and parsley into the kale mixture. Season to taste with more salt and pepper.

Remove the squash from the oven and stuff each one with the greens and grains mixture. Top each with its respective lid and bake until each squash is easily pierced in the thickest part by a fork, 25–35 minutes. Remove from the oven and let the squash rest for 5 minutes before serving. Serves 4 as a main course or 8 as a side dish.

✳ *A substitute for the kuri squash would be anything relatively round and small, like hokkaido pumpkins. Check your local farmers' market for the best variety of winter squash.*

✳ *Omit the feta cheese for a vegan dish.*

✳ *The stuffing is delicious on its own and makes an excellent side dish.*

SERVES 4

4 (each about 1½ lb) red kuri squash

3 Tbsp canola oil, divided

1 tsp salt, plus more to taste

¼ tsp pepper, plus more to taste

1 medium yellow onion, diced

2 garlic cloves, minced

8 oz button mushrooms, quartered

1 bunch kale, centre ribs removed, leaves chopped (about 3 cups packed)

1 Tbsp apple cider vinegar

2 tsp chopped fresh thyme leaves (or 1 tsp dried thyme)

Red pepper flakes

2 cups cooked white basmati rice

1¼ cups cooked red or white quinoa (see page 229)

¾ cup dried cranberries

¾ cup toasted, slivered or sliced almonds

¾ cup crumbled feta cheese

¼ cup chopped parsley (flat-leaf or curly)

Before I wrote this cookbook, I didn't eat enough sweet potatoes. After doing some research, I'm loving them way more often. These guys are bursting with vitamins and minerals and are generally known as a superfood. You need more beta carotene in your life? Say hello to a sweet potato. Sweet potatoes are also chock full of carotenoids, which help strengthen our eyesight and may boost our resistance to disease, and powerful antioxidants that may help us on our journey of healthy aging. I'm down with that. Plus, sweet potatoes are generally affordable and readily available at the grocery store year-round, not to mention versatile and super tasty. I'm now a full-fledged member of Team Sweet Potato. I've even got the T-shirt to prove it.

There seems to be a certain amount of confusion circulating around sweet potatoes. First off, their name. Being a root vegetable, sweet potatoes are actually completely unrelated to regular potatoes. Then there is the whole "Is it a yam or is it a sweet potato?" debate. While both are root vegetables, they're completely unrelated plants. Yams are grown in Africa, where they originated, as well as in Southeast Asia, Central America, and the Caribbean. True yams are difficult to find outside of specialty grocery stores and are always imported into North America. Sweet potatoes are largely grown in southern parts of the United States, due to their requirement of needing a lot of heat and a lot of sun. While yams are cylindrical, with pale flesh and rough, almost hairy skin (sounds like me in the dead of winter), sweet potatoes have tapered ends, smooth skin, and a deep burnished orange flesh, though there are purple and creamy yellow varieties, too. Yams taste starchy and dry, while sweet potatoes are moist and, well, sweet. To add to the confusion, there are firm sweet potatoes, which have golden skin and pale flesh, and soft sweet potatoes, which have copper skin and orange flesh. The former remain firm and a little waxy after cooking, while the latter become creamy and fluffy. The firm variety was the first type to be introduced to the United States, so when soft sweet potatoes began to be produced commercially, there was a need to somehow differentiate between the two. Since the soft sweet potatoes vaguely resembled yams, producers and shippers chose the English form of the African word "nyami" and labelled them as yams. That's what you see labelled as "yams" in most grocery stores, but they're really soft sweet potatoes. The recipes in this cookbook call for the copper-skinned, orange-fleshed sweet potatoes, though they very well may be labelled as yams. Whelp! That's a lot to take in. I hope I haven't confused the bejeezus out of you.

Dixon Says: Sweet potatoes generally don't fare too well when grown on the Canadian Prairies. The season is just a little too short for them with not enough hot days. It is possible, though, to grow them in a greenhouse or a hoophouse. Cover the soil early with black plastic to preheat it and plant early. Cover them up again until they start to emerge. Water regularly, about 1 inch a week. When the soil starts to crack, the tubers are growing! Hopefully.

SWEET

POTATOES

Supersonic Power Bowl
with Sun-Dried Tomato Dressing

When we first started dating, Dixon took me to all of the superhero movies. *Avengers. Iron Man. Thor. Guardians of the Galaxy.* So many dudes trying to save the world! I can't guarantee that you'll save the universe by eating this super-healthy power bowl, but with the amount of vegetables consumed in one sitting, you may feel like you've gained some superpowers of your own. I know the ingredient list is long and the prep will take some time, but the great thing is that once it's done, it's so easy to throw the bowl together during the week when you're super busy. Let's talk about the sun-dried tomato dressing for a second. I added turmeric and flaxseed, which are nutritional powerhouses in their own right. It's super good when drizzled on greens or roasted vegetables and as a marinade for chicken. Now, if only I can muster some superpowers to do the dishes . . .

Prepare the roasted sweet potato: Preheat the oven to 375°F. Line a rimmed baking sheet with parchment paper.

In a medium bowl, toss together the sweet potato, oil, paprika, garlic powder, salt, and pepper. Toss to coat evenly. Spread in an even layer on the prepared baking sheet and roast until tender, about 30 minutes. Set aside.

Prepare the dressing: Place the dressing ingredients, plus ¼ cup water in a blender and process until smooth.

Divide the roasted sweet potato, black beans, quinoa, cabbage, greens, avocado, and feta, if using, into bowls. Drizzle with the sun-dried tomato dressing.

* *For the olive oil, try using some oil from the sun-dried tomato jar.*

* *To cook quinoa, place 1 cup of quinoa (any variety) into a fine-mesh strainer and rinse thoroughly under cool running water. Drain. Place in a medium saucepan and add 1¾ cups low-sodium chicken or vegetable broth. Bring to a rolling boil over high heat. Turn down the heat to low, cover, and cook for 15 minutes. Remove the pot from the heat and let stand, covered, for 5 minutes. Fluff with a fork. If any liquid remains, or the quinoa is still crunchy, return the pot to low heat and cook, covered, until the water is absorbed.*

* *If you're using kale, be sure to massage it with a bit of olive oil and salt before adding it to the power bowl.*

* *Instead of black beans, use chickpeas or lentils.*

* *To make even tastier roasted sweet potatoes, add ½ cup grated Parmesan to the party. This is great for breakfast hash browns, too.*

SERVES 4-6

Roasted Sweet Potato

1 large sweet potato, peeled and cut into ½-inch cubes (about 5 cups)

2 Tbsp canola oil

1 tsp smoked paprika

1 tsp garlic powder

¾ tsp salt

¼ tsp pepper

Sun-Dried Tomato Dressing

10 oil-packed sun-dried tomato halves

½ cup packed fresh basil leaves

½ cup extra-virgin olive oil (see note)

¼ cup ground flaxseed

3 garlic cloves, smashed

6 Tbsp apple cider vinegar

2 tsp ground turmeric

2 tsp pure maple syrup

1 tsp salt

¼ tsp cayenne pepper

¼ tsp pepper

Power Bowl Toppings

1 can (19 oz/540 mL) black beans, rinsed and drained

3 cups cooked red or white quinoa (see note)

2 cups shredded red cabbage

2 cups fresh greens (kale, arugula, spinach)

1 avocado, sliced

1 cup crumbled feta cheese (optional)

Roasted Sweet Potato and Lentil Hummus

This beautiful dip has the nutritional strength of sweet potatoes and red lentils, as well as warm and earthy Middle Eastern flavours. It's a fixture in my kitchen over the holidays as it's just so darn attractive when garnished with pomegranate arils. But given its healthfulness, it's a good idea to have this dip hanging out in the refrigerator all year-round. As with any hummus, you can make a batch and freeze some for later if you don't think you can gobble it up within a few days. I usually serve this with warm pita bread for a tasty appetizer or snack. It's also quite excellent when slathered on sandwiches and wraps and as a dip for fresh vegetables, like Dixon's extra-sweet carrots.

Preheat the oven to 375°F. Line a rimmed baking sheet with parchment paper.

In a large bowl, toss together the sweet potato, canola oil, salt, and pepper. Spread the sweet potato in a single layer on the prepared baking sheet and roast for about 30 minutes, stirring occasionally. It will be golden and tender when done. Remove from the oven and let cool to room temperature.

Place the roasted sweet potato, cooked split red lentils, lemon juice, olive oil, tahini, garlic, za'atar, sumac, and red pepper flakes in a food processor fitted with a metal blade. Process until smooth, scraping down the bowl once. If you find the hummus is too thick, add a splash or two of water. Adjust the seasoning with more salt and pepper, if needed.

Scrape the hummus into a shallow serving bowl. Drizzle with more olive oil and sprinkle with some red pepper flakes, sumac, and za'atar. Garnish with pomegranate arils and cilantro. Serve with plenty of warm pita bread, crackers, and fresh vegetables. You can refrigerate the hummus for up to 3 days or freeze it for up to 3 months.

MAKES 2½ CUPS

1 medium/large sweet potato, peeled and chopped into ½-inch cubes (about 4 cups)

1 Tbsp canola oil

½ tsp salt

¼ tsp pepper

1 cup cooked room-temperature split red lentils (see note)

¼ cup fresh lemon juice

¼ cup extra-virgin olive oil, plus more for drizzling

2 Tbsp tahini

2 garlic cloves, chopped

1 tsp za'atar, plus more for sprinkling

1 tsp sumac, plus more for sprinkling

¼ tsp red pepper flakes (or cayenne pepper), plus more for sprinkling

Pomegranate arils, for garnish

Cilantro or flat-leaf parsley leaves, for garnish

✳ *To cook split red lentils: Place 1 cup lentils in a fine-mesh sieve and rinse under cool running water. Dump them into a medium saucepan and cover with 3 cups cold water. Bring to a boil over high heat, cover, turn the heat to low, and simmer until the lentils are very tender, 5–7 minutes. Drain. This makes about 3 cups of cooked lentils. What you don't use for this recipe can be refrigerated for up to 5 days or frozen for up to 3 months. Alternatively, you could use 1 cup of canned lentils, rinsed and drained, though the colour of the hummus may be different.*

✳ *Look for za'atar (see page 53), sumac, and tahini in the international foods aisle of the supermarket. Sumac has a bright flavour reminiscent of vinegar or lemon.*

Smoky and Spicy Sweet Potato Soup

Delicious and nutritious, this pretty soup is spiced up with smoky canned chipotle peppers, while maple syrup and lime juice round out its flavours in a very agreeable way. This soup does take a little bit of effort, but the rewards are worth it. The sweet potatoes caramelize a little bit, deepening their flavour, while cloves of garlic soften in their papery skins. That smell alone is why you should try this soup. For those out there who think puréed soups are akin to baby food, I've added some garnishes with texture and tang. This is a big batch of soup, so freeze some for the days when you don't feel like cooking. Your future self thanks you already!

Preheat the oven to 400°F. Line two rimmed baking sheets with parchment paper.

Peel and chop the sweet potatoes into 1-inch cubes. Place them in a large bowl. Toss with 3 Tbsp of the oil and season generously with salt and pepper. Divide evenly between the baking sheets. Nestle in the garlic cloves. Cut the peppers in half and discard the seeds. Place them in the bowl and drizzle with 1½ Tbsp of the oil. Snuggle the peppers in with the sweet potatoes.

Place one pan on the top rack of the oven and the other on the bottom. Roast until the peppers' skins puff and turn brown and the sweet potatoes and garlic are golden and tender, about 40–45 minutes, stirring halfway through and rotating the pans from top to bottom. If the peppers and garlic are getting too dark, pull them off the sheet pan before the sweet potatoes are done cooking.

Transfer the roasted red peppers to a bowl, cover with plastic wrap, and let them sit for 20 minutes. Peel away the skins and discard, dice the flesh, and set aside. Squeeze the garlic out of its skin and set aside.

Heat the remaining 2 Tbsp oil in a large soup pot over medium-high heat. Add the onion and sauté until translucent. Add the 1 tsp salt, sage, oregano, cumin, and chili powder and cook for a minute or two. Stir in the roasted sweet potatoes and red peppers, garlic, chipotle peppers and some adobo sauce, diced tomatoes with their juice, and broth. Rinse out the tomato can with about 1 cup water and add this tomatoey water as well. Cover, bring to a boil, then turn down the heat to medium-low and simmer, covered, for 20 minutes.

Remove the pot from the heat. Purée the soup with an immersion blender, and stir in the maple syrup and lime juice. If it seems too thick, add more broth or water. Season with salt and pepper, and adjust the seasonings with more maple syrup, lime juice, or some hot sauce. Ladle the soup into bowls and garnish with crumbled feta cheese, cilantro, tortilla chips, and lime wedges.

*   *Three canned chipotle peppers will give you mild heat; 4 will give more kick. If you're preparing this for kids, drop it down to just 1 or 2.*

*   *Omit the feta and this is a vegan soup. It's gluten-free if you choose corn tortilla chips!*

SERVES 8

2 large sweet potatoes (3 lb total)

6½ Tbsp canola oil, divided

1 tsp salt, plus more to taste

Pepper, to taste

8 whole garlic cloves, unpeeled

3 red bell peppers

1 large yellow onion, diced

1 tsp ground sage

1 tsp dried oregano

1 tsp ground cumin

1 tsp chili powder

4 canned chipotle peppers in adobo sauce, minced (see note)

1 can (19 oz/540 mL) diced tomatoes

8 cups vegetable (or low-sodium chicken) broth

2 Tbsp maple syrup

Juice of 2 limes

Your favourite hot sauce (optional)

½ cup crumbled feta cheese, for garnish

Chopped cilantro, tortilla chips, and lime wedges, for garnish

Sweet Potato Biscuit Rolls with Honey Butter Glaze

When life gives you leftover mashed sweet potato, you make light-as-a-feather biscuit rolls. At least, that's how I roll. These are the love child (children?) of a crispy biscuit and a soft bun, and, unlike some blended families, everyone gets along nicely. They're also a great way to use up any leftover sweet potato in the refrigerator, though I do declare once you've had a taste, you'll intentionally be mashing the orange root vegetable on the regular. Delicate and yeasty, with a tender crumb, these rolls are quite a delight when fresh out of the oven, especially with the honey butter glaze. These are fabulous at any time of the year but particularly around the holidays when you want to push the boat out a little. Dixon likes to tuck cold sliced ham inside his for a dandy little sandwich. He's a smart one, that man of mine.

Prepare the biscuit rolls: In a small bowl, stir the yeast into the warm water. Let stand until bubbly, about 5 minutes. (If it doesn't bubble, you'll have to start again.)

In a medium bowl, whisk together the flour, sugar, baking powder, salt, and paprika. Cut in the cold butter (I just use my hands) until the mixture is crumbly, with pea-sized bits of butter showing. Stir in the yeast mixture and the sweet potato, until the dough forms a ball. I typically use my hands for this step as well.

Turn the dough out onto a lightly floured surface. Knead until smooth and elastic, about 5 minutes. The dough will be quite soft and sticky, so you'll need to keep the counter lightly floured as you knead. Lightly grease a large bowl with olive oil and place the dough inside, turning to coat the top. Cover with plastic wrap and let the dough rise in a warm, draft-free space for about 1–2 hours, until it has doubled in size.

Punch the dough down. On a lightly floured surface, pat the dough into a ¾-inch-thick circle. Using a 2½-inch round cutter, cut the dough into rounds, rerolling the scraps once. You should get about 12 biscuit rolls. Place the biscuits into a lightly greased 9- × 13-inch baking dish, aiming for three rows of 4 biscuits. It's fine if they're snuggled up against each other. If you have more than 12 rolls, fit the extras into a smaller baking dish (baking time stays the same). Cover with plastic wrap and let rise in the same warm place until doubled in size, about 40–50 minutes.

Preheat the oven to 400°F. Bake the biscuit rolls for 15 minutes, then turn down the heat to 375°F. Bake until deeply golden brown, about 10–12 minutes.

Remove the pan from the oven and let the rolls cool for 5 minutes.

Prepare the glaze: Combine the melted butter and honey in a small bowl. Bush the tops of the warm rolls with the glaze and sprinkle with flaky salt. Let the rolls cool until barely warm before eating. These are best eaten the day they are made, but leftovers can be warmed the next day in the oven at 300°F with excellent results.

MAKES 12 ROLLS

Biscuit Rolls

2 tsp active dry yeast

⅓ cup warm water (110°–120°F)

2½ cups all-purpose flour, plus more for the counter

½ cup granulated sugar

1 tsp baking powder

1 tsp salt

¼ tsp paprika

½ cup cold butter, cubed

1 cup cold plain mashed sweet potato

Extra-virgin olive oil, for bowl and pan

Glaze

3 Tbsp butter, melted

1½ Tbsp honey

Flaky salt

This earthy-tasting leafy green is a member of the gooseroot family—aptly named because the Swiss chard's leaves resemble a goose's foot. Other members include spinach and beets. Swiss chard is loaded with good things like vitamins K, A, and C, as well as a healthy dose of iron and fibre. High in anti-inflammatory compounds, it's right up there with kale on the list of foods to eat to keep you bright-eyed and bushy-tailed. This slightly bitter green can come in an assortment of stem colours, with white being the classic variety. Rainbow chard has jewel-coloured stems that are not unlike the candles on a birthday cake, and, in the summer, it's one of the most eye-catching vegetables in the garden and at the farmers' market. I love how the bright colours weave their way up from the stems to the tiny veins in the leaves, making them almost too pretty to eat. I've been known to take bundles of fresh rainbow chard home from the market and photograph them in all of their colourful glory. I'm a total veg nerd, in case you hadn't guessed already.

When I grew rows of chard in my own kitchen garden, I'd marvel at how quickly it would shoot up after a bit of heat and rain. If you like to grow your own food, you'll know that there is a point in the summer when your Swiss chard plants have exceeded your expectations. You forget to pick it for a day, and the next day it's gone wild. If you're the generous sort, you can parcel it up and give it to unsuspecting neighbours before the slugs have their way with it. Tuck in a few recipes, too. People often don't know what to do with chard. You're performing a community service!

Rainbow chard is the photogenic show-off in the garden, but it's also a treat to eat! The small chard leaves are a great addition to salads and sandwiches, and the larger leaves are lovely when sautéed with garlic and olive oil. Adding a splash of cream will help tame its earthy mineral notes. A whole lotta chard cooks down relatively quickly, and, because of my spinach intolerance, I often use it as a spinach substitute in pastas, quiches, savoury tarts, and what have you. I've also added chopped chard to soups, stews, chili, and pasta sauces in place of kale, and it worked well. The stems can be a little tough, so be sure to chop them finer than the leaves, or you can remove them completely and cook them like you would asparagus.

❋❋❋❋❋❋❋❋❋❋❋❋❋❋❋❋❋❋❋❋❋❋❋❋❋❋❋❋❋❋❋❋❋❋❋❋❋

Dixon Says: Swiss chard can be grown directly in the garden or in a container. It needs plenty of sun and regular watering. Caterpillars really like chard, so it should be covered with netting. Here's a weird thing: I like the stems of Swiss chard. When picked fresh, they're crisp and crunchy and juicy. Slightly salty, they make a great snack eaten raw like celery sticks. Who'da thunk it?

SWISS

CHARD

Swiss Chard and Cherry Tomato Pie

This is a fantastic savoury pie to make in the summer, as it uses up a bunch of chard and is crowned with those delicious tiny tomatoes that taste like candy. I like to cook some onion with the bacon first, because they are big-time BFFs when it comes to building flavour. I used whatever hard cheese was lingering in the refrigerator when I created this—you can't go wrong with any of them. This pretty pie is superb fresh out of the oven, as the puff pastry is crispy and buttery. The slightly bitter notes of the chard are tempered by the creamy custard and sweet tomatoes. This would not be out of place on a brunch table or served as a light supper with salad on the side. Dixon also loves it cold, so I often pack up a slice for him to take to the field, and he can munch on it for his lunch.

Preheat the oven to 425°F.

The sheet of puff pastry should measure 10 × 12 inches and be about ⅛-inch thick. Fit it into a 9-inch glass pie plate. Trim the overhang and crimp the edges. Place the pastry shell in the refrigerator while you work on the filling.

Melt the butter in a large skillet over medium-high heat. Stir in the onion and bacon, cooking for a minute or two. Add the chard and let it cook down, stirring often. When it's nice and wilted, about 3–4 minutes, remove from the heat and let it cool in the pan to room temperature.

In a medium bowl, whisk together the eggs, cream, salt, pepper, mustard, a pinch of nutmeg, and the dill. Stir in the chard mixture, along with ½ cup of the cheese. Pour this into the prepared puff pastry shell. Top with the remaining cheese and sliced tomatoes.

Bake for 20 minutes at 425°F, then turn down the heat to 350°F and bake until the tart is golden and puffed up, and the custard is set, about 25 minutes. Let it cool for 10 minutes before serving.

SERVES 4

1 sheet (8 oz/250 g) frozen puff pastry, thawed in the refrigerator

2 Tbsp butter

½ cup diced onion

5 slices thick-cut bacon, cooked and chopped

1 bunch chopped Swiss chard, stems chopped very small (about 3 cups)

4 large eggs

1 cup whipping (35%) cream

1 tsp salt

¼ tsp pepper

¼ tsp dry mustard powder

Ground nutmeg

2 Tbsp chopped fresh dill

¾ cup grated hard cheese, such as Gruyère, extra-old cheddar, or Parmesan, divided

12–14 cherry tomatoes, cut in half

Chorizo and Swiss Chard Pizza

Dixon and I love pizza. I mean, *really* love pizza. When I'm not rolling out balls of my go-to dough, we're spreading all kinds of toppings on naan for quick suppers. Pizza is life, after all. It's also a great way to use up the bounty of vegetable goodness in your gardens, CSA baskets, or farmers' market purchases in the summer. Along with Swiss chard, this pizza has corn straight off the cob, super-sweet cherry tomatoes, and heaps of basil—both fresh and in pesto form. I used mozzarella and bocconcini for the cheese, but goat cheese or feta would be great substitutions. It's pizza, so feel free to play around. If you're not crazy about the chorizo, I won't say a word if you add cooked bacon instead. If you want to go the meatless route, I would sauté some diced onion, garlic, and chili flakes with the chard, just for extra flavour. Savoury, spicy, with a hint of sweet, it's a perfect pizza party! The last slice will disappear and you'll be sad. But you've got more dough in the freezer, so you can make this pizza again and again.

Prepare the pizza dough: In the bowl of a stand mixer fitted with a dough hook, use a spoon to stir the yeast into 1 cup warm water (110°–120°F) until it dissolves. It should get foamy and frothy up. This will take about 5 minutes. If your yeast doesn't froth up, you'll have to start over with a new package of yeast.

Add the remaining dough ingredients, plus 1 cup cool water to the bowl. Knead on medium-low speed for 5–6 minutes, until the dough is smooth and elastic. Or you can knead the dough by hand for about 7 minutes.

Place the dough in a large greased bowl, turning to coat, and cover with a clean tea towel. Let rise in a warm, draft-free spot until the dough has doubled in size, about 50–60 minutes.

Punch down the dough and divide it into three portions. Keep one portion for this recipe. Wrap the other two in plastic wrap and place them in a resealable plastic bag. Refrigerate for 2 days or freeze for up to 3 months. To use, just thaw in the refrigerator for 8–12 hours before you want to use it.

Prepare the toppings: Warm a large skillet over medium-high heat. Squeeze the sausage meat from its casings into the hot skillet and cook, stirring occasionally, until no longer pink, about 8–10 minutes. Depending on how fatty the sausage is, you may have to add some canola oil to the skillet while it's cooking. Transfer the meat to a clean plate to cool.

If there's no fat left in the skillet, add 1 Tbsp canola oil. Stir in the corn, and sauté for about 3 minutes, scraping up all of the brown bits. Remove to a plate to cool. Add the chard to the skillet and cook

SERVES 3–4

Whole Wheat Dough

2 Tbsp active dry yeast

3 cups all-purpose flour

2 cups whole wheat flour

¼ cup extra-virgin olive oil, plus more for bowl

2 Tbsp liquid honey

1½ tsp salt

Toppings

1 lb fresh chorizo sausage

3–4 Tbsp canola oil

1 cup fresh or frozen (thawed) corn kernels, or leftover cooked corn

2 bunches chopped Swiss chard, stems chopped very small (about 6 cups)

½ tsp salt

¼ tsp pepper

1½ cups shredded mozzarella

1 cup halved cherry tomatoes

Handful (about 4 oz/125 g) bocconcini cheese, torn

⅓ cup basil pesto (or Gorgeous Greens Pesto, page 85)

Handful fresh basil leaves, torn

for about 3 minutes, stirring until wilted. Remove to a separate plate to cool. Season the corn and chard with salt and pepper.

Preheat the oven to 450°F. Grease a rimmed baking sheet with 2 Tbsp canola oil, being sure to get right into the corners.

On a lightly floured surface, roll one ball of the pizza dough out into a large, thin oval, about 11 × 14 inches. Transfer the dough to the baking sheet. Remember, it's pizza, so it doesn't have to be a perfect shape.

Scatter the shredded mozzarella on top of the dough. Top with the cooked chorizo, corn, chard, cherry tomatoes, and bocconcini. Dollop with pesto. Slide into the oven and bake until the cheese is golden brown and melted and the crust is cooked through in the centre, about 20 minutes. Let the pizza rest for a few minutes, then scatter fresh basil leaves on top. Slice into wedges.

Swiss Chard and Ricotta Stuffed Jumbo Pasta Shells in Marinara Sauce

The first meal you cook for a potential mate is a big deal. If you're a good cook, you want to show off a little. If you're not a good cook, you want a recipe that is straightforward and can hide any unfortunate mishaps. This recipe is great for both types of cooks, and I have a particular fondness for it, as this is what I served Dixon when he ate at my table for the very first time. I was in the midst of recipe development for Sask Pulse Growers (Hi, Rachel and Amber!) and some lentils snuck their way into the filling for extra protein, fibre, and nutritional goodness. Dixon loved this pasta very much, and, to this day, it's one of his most requested dinner recipes. We have it as either a vegetarian main course or a side dish with some grilled sausages. There are a few steps, but you can easily prepare the sauce and filling ahead of time, so there's no need to stress so much on the day of the big date. And let's not forget that melty cheese covers all of the imperfections, should any emerge.

Prepare the sauce: Place a Dutch oven over medium-high heat and add the oil. When it's hot, stir in the onion and sauté for about 5 minutes, until it is soft. Stir in the garlic, and cook for another minute. Stir in the crushed tomatoes (rinse out the can with about ½ cup water and add the tomatoey water as well), honey, salt, pepper, and red pepper flakes. Cover and bring it to a simmer. Turn down the heat to low and simmer the sauce, uncovered, for 20 minutes. Remove from the heat and adjust the seasonings with more salt and pepper, if needed.

Prepare the filling: Place a large skillet over medium-high heat. Add the chopped chard to the skillet and cook it until it wilts down, about 3–4 minutes. There's no need to add anything else to the skillet as long as there is still water clinging to the leaves. Let the chard cool in the pan to room temperature.

In a large bowl, stir together the ricotta, 1 cup of the mozzarella, the lentils, ¼ cup of the Parmesan, the eggs, basil, salt, pepper, and a pinch of nutmeg. Stir in the Swiss chard once it has cooled.

Bring a large pot of salted water to a boil. Cook the shells according to the package directions, shaving 2 minutes off of the cooking time. Drain, reserving ½ cup of the pasta water. Stir the pasta water into the tomato sauce. Rinse the shells with cold water. Some shells may break. That's why you're cooking the whole package, even though you won't use them all.

Preheat the oven to 375°F. Place the filling in a resealable plastic bag and snip off one corner. Just make a small cut that's large enough to squeeze the filling out to fill the shells. Spread about 2 cups of the tomato sauce in the bottom of a shallow 13-inch round baking dish that will hold 36 shells.

(continued on page 245)

SERVES 6

Marinara Sauce

2 Tbsp extra-virgin olive oil

1 medium yellow onion, diced

3 garlic cloves, minced

1 can (28 oz/798 mL) crushed tomatoes

2 tsp honey

1 tsp salt

¼ tsp pepper

¼ tsp red pepper flakes

Filling

1 bunch chopped Swiss chard, stems chopped very small (about 3 cups)

2 cups ricotta cheese

2½ cups mozzarella cheese, divided

1 cup cooked red lentils (see page 231)

¾ cup grated Parmesan cheese, divided

2 large eggs, beaten

½ cup chopped fresh basil or 2 tsp dried basil

1 tsp salt

¼ tsp pepper

Ground nutmeg

1 package (1 lb/500 g) jumbo shells or conchiglie

2 Tbsp chopped parsley (flat-leaf or curly), for garnish (optional)

Pipe the filling inside the shells, laying them down in an even layer in the sauce once they're filled. Alternatively, you can use a heaping teaspoon to fill the shells.

Spoon the remaining tomato sauce over the shells and top with the remaining cheese. Cover tightly with foil and bake for 25 minutes. Remove the foil and bake until the cheese is browned and the sauce is bubbling, another 20–25 minutes. Let the pasta rest for 5 minutes before serving. Garnish with chopped parsley, if you like.

* *The marinara sauce can be made up to 4 days ahead. The lentil and ricotta filling can be made up to 1 day ahead.*

* *For the meat lovers, brown 1 lb of ground beef, chicken, or turkey before proceeding with the marinara sauce recipe.*

* *A 9- × 13-inch baking dish works fine, too. It will hold 26 shells, which means you can fit the other 10 shells in an 8- × 8-inch baking dish. You could potentially freeze this smaller dish for later (cover with some marinara sauce and cheese first).*

Phyllo Tart with Swiss Chard and Feta

The first cookbook I ever bought was *The Enchanted Broccoli Forest* by Mollie Katzen. I was 20 years old and about to leave home for the first time, embarking on my cross-Canada trek to art school. What I loved about this book then, as I do now, are the whimsical drawings that accompany every recipe. Leafing through the pages, it was impossible to not be inspired by vegetables. Her rendering of a bunch of tomatoes or a head of cauliflower spoke to my inner art nerd and to my desire to learn how to cook for and feed my friends. This buttery, crispy phyllo tart was inspired by Mollie's Greek Pizza—a recipe I made countless times in that Montreal walk-up apartment. I swapped Swiss chard for spinach (because intolerant!), amped up the flavour with lemon and pesto, and dialled back the butter. (No, I can't believe I just wrote that either.) This is a creative and delicious way to get more chard into your life.

Preheat the oven to 400°F.

Prepare the pastry: In a small bowl, combine the melted butter and olive oil.

Prepare the topping: In a large skillet, warm 2 Tbsp of the canola oil over medium-high heat. Cook the onion and garlic with the salt until the onion is translucent. Add the oregano, basil, red pepper flakes, and lemon zest and juice. Stir well. Add the chard and cook until the greens are wilted and all of the liquid is evaporated. Stir in the pesto.

Assemble the tart: Grease a rimmed baking sheet with the remaining 1½ Tbsp canola oil. Place a damp dishtowel over the phyllo pastry. Fit one sheet of the phyllo pastry into the pan and brush it with the melted butter and olive oil mixture. Repeat with the rest of the phyllo, being careful to keep the remainder covered while you work so it doesn't dry out. Brush the last sheet of phyllo in the pan with the oil/butter mixture. Use a slotted spoon to transfer the greens mixture to the phyllo. Spread them out evenly, leaving a ½-inch border of naked pastry.

Sprinkle half the mozzarella and all of the feta over top. Arrange the tomato slices on top of the cheese. Toss the remaining mozzarella over the tomatoes. Bake until the cheese is melted and the edge of the pastry is golden brown, about 25–30 minutes. Let the tart rest for 5 minutes before slicing into 8 pieces. Garnish with the basil leaves.

SERVES 4

Pastry

8 oz (or ½ package) frozen phyllo pastry, thawed

¼ cup melted butter

¼ cup extra-virgin olive oil

Topping

3½ Tbsp canola oil, divided

1 medium onion, chopped

3 cloves garlic, smashed

¼ tsp salt

1 tsp dried oregano

½ tsp dried basil

¼ tsp red pepper flakes

Grated zest and juice from 1 lemon

2 bunches chopped Swiss chard, stems sliced very small (about 6 cups)

¼ cup Gorgeous Greens Pesto (page 85)

Finishing the Tart

3 cups shredded mozzarella cheese, divided

1½ cups crumbled feta

2 medium tomatoes, sliced and patted dry

Fresh basil leaves, for garnish

✳ *Try basil pesto instead of the Gorgeous Greens Pesto.*

When you read the following recipes, I'm certain that my love for all things tomato will shine through. Picking the little cherry guys off the vine while they're still warm from the sun and popping them straight into my mouth is one of my favourite things to do from July to September. The large, fat heirloom variety I slice thickly, and their juices run off my cutting board. I arrange the slices on a pretty plate, drizzle them with a bit of good olive oil and sprinkle with a flutter of flaky salt. I cut them with my fork, savouring the sweetness of a fine summer tomato. Sometimes, if I'm feeling fancy, I'll slip in some leaves of fresh basil and torn shards of fresh, milky mozzarella. A flourish of reduced balsamic vinegar is an extra step, but one worth taking. And let's not forget summer's finest sandwich: lightly toasted bread, slathered with mayonnaise, and topped with slim slices of your favourite tomato. Cracked pepper and sea salt are the only necessary additions. Bonus points if you make your own mayonnaise. High-five if you bake your own bread. I could eat this sandwich every day until my supply of fresh tomatoes runs out. If I'm fortunate enough to have a bumper crop of cherry tomatoes, I'll roast them slowly with olive oil, salt, and whatever herbs I have about. When they've slumped out of their burnished skins, I love to heap them high on thick slices of sourdough toast that has been kissed with a layer of ricotta cheese. Oh là là. Now that is a sandwich and a half.

As the September days get shorter and the night air has a bit of a chill to it, I'll pick off the remaining tomatoes when they're just blushing with pink and let them ripen inside the house in a box covered with newspaper. As a kid, I would find it odd to see these same boxes tucked into a closet. But now I get it. Tomatoes ripen faster in the dark.

Oh, the melancholia I feel when the last of the summer tomatoes are gone. The pallid grocery store imposter is left there on the shelves for most of the winter months. The only tomatoes that come home with me are the Canadian-grown hothouse variety. I find the small grape/cherry varieties are enough to satisfy my winter tomato hankerings, and even delicious if they're roasted. Winter and spring are prime time for making good use of canned tomatoes. Cans of whole tomatoes are a pantry staple in my house and probably in your house, too. You can purée them into sauce or squish them with your bare hands into soups and stews. I take great pleasure in feeling the juices slip through my fingers as the flesh drops into the bubbling pot of goodness below. I think of how once upon a time that tomato grew in a sunny garden plot, maybe by a woman who had an unabashed adoration for tomatoes, too.

✳✳✳

Dixon Says: I just love Renée from way up high down to-ma-toes! Here's a fun fact about tomatoes. They can internalize water and possibly bacterial pathogens when the water is colder than the tomato. For this reason, when you wash tomatoes, it is a good idea to use water that is warmer than the internal temperature of the tomato. I go by the following: for refrigerated tomatoes, water should be lukewarm or warmer; for room-temperature tomatoes, water should be warm to the touch but not scalding.

TOMATOES

Creamy Roasted Tomato Soup
with Cheesy Croutons

Raise your hand if you grew up dunking the crispy edges of your grilled cheese sandwich into a bowl of cream of tomato soup. Me too! Maybe the soup was the out-of-the-can-just-add-milk variety but it doesn't matter. It was comforting and filled my belly as I watched *All My Children* before heading back to high school for the afternoon. I no longer go to school (hooray!) and no longer watch soap operas (RIP *AMC*, *Another World*), but I sure do still love a bowl of creamy tomato soup. My version consists of roasting the toma-toes Dixon brings to me in the late summer and early autumn, when they're at their sweetest and most divine. Roasting enhances the flavours of all of the vegetables in this soup, and it's important to scrape off all of those glorious brown bits from the pan into the blender. Brown bits = flavour! With just a bit of broth and cream, this is a tomato-forward soup that tastes familiar and wholesome, especially when combined with crunchy, cheesy croutons.

Preheat the oven to 400°F. Combine the tomatoes, onion, garlic, carrots, oil, rosemary, and thyme in a 9- × 13-inch roasting pan. Season with the salt and pepper. Toss well. Roast, stirring once or twice, until the vegetables are charred in places and nicely softened, about 25–30 minutes.

Remove the roasted vegetables from the oven and let cool for 5 minutes. Discard the sprigs of rosemary and thyme. Using a blender (be careful, hot liquid!), purée the vegetables, then dump them into a Dutch oven or other soup pot.

Stir in the broth, then cover the pot with a lid. Bring the soup to a simmer over medium-high heat. Let it cook for about 10 minutes, then turn down the heat to low and stir in the cream. Season to taste with more salt and pepper, and stir in the fresh herbs.

Ladle the soup into bowls and garnish with plenty of cheesy croutons.

SERVES 4 *28g canned toms*

2 lb fresh plum tomatoes, such as Roma, cut in half lengthwise

1 large onion, sliced into 8 wedges

4 whole garlic cloves

1 cup chopped (about ½-inch-thick pieces) carrots

¼ cup extra-virgin olive oil

4 sprigs fresh rosemary

4 sprigs fresh thyme

1 tsp salt, plus more to taste

¼ tsp pepper, plus more to taste

1½ cups low-sodium chicken (or vegetable) broth

¼ cup whipping (35%) cream

¼ cup chopped fresh herbs, such as basil or dill

✱ *When I don't have access to ample fresh tomatoes (like in the winter and spring), I prepare this soup with 1 can (28 oz/798 mL) of crushed or whole tomatoes instead of the fresh. Sauté the onion and minced garlic in 2 Tbsp olive oil in a Dutch oven. Grate in 1 carrot. Cook until soft, about 5 minutes. Stir in the tomatoes and broth. Bring to a simmer over medium-high heat. Cook for 15 minutes. Remove from the heat, purée if using whole tomatoes, and stir in the cream. Season to taste with salt, pepper, and herbs. If you find the soup too thick, thin it out with a bit of water or broth.*

Cheesy Croutons

These are super fun to snack on in their own right, but if you happen to save some for garnishing soups, consider it a win in the self-control department. Feel free to swap out the Parmesan for sharp cheddar cheese.

Preheat the oven to 400°F. Line a rimmed baking sheet with parchment paper.

In a medium bowl, toss together the bread cubes with the oil. Spread in an even layer on the baking sheet, then sprinkle with the Parmesan. Season with generous pinches of salt and pepper. Bake until the bread is toasted, the cheese is melted, and the croutons are clumping together, about 12–14 minutes. Give them a stir, then bake a few more minutes until the croutons are golden brown.

Remove from the oven and let cool for a bit, then scatter them over the bowls of tomato soup. Store in an airtight container for 1 day.

3 cups cubed crusty day-old bread, such as baguette or sourdough

1 Tbsp extra-virgin olive oil

½ cup grated Parmesan cheese

Salt and pepper

Heirloom Tomato Galette

This galette shows off the best of your homegrown heirloom tomatoes—the ones you watered just enough and trimmed back the leaves like the gardening pros tell you to. I know you too ran out in the middle of a hail storm, clad in a rain jacket and jean shorts, just so you could move your pots of tomatoes under the awning so those evil white balls of ice falling from the sky would not smash your precious plants. Those carefully grown tomatoes require something a little special to show off their deliciousness. This simple galette does just that. But beware: If you find yourself all alone in the house after it comes out of the oven, the temptation will be to eat the whole darn thing, which is fine and I salute you. Hot tip: If you want to show someone you love them, like *really* love them, dish them up a slice of this rustic tomato-filled pastry. Dixon always gives me extra kisses when tomato galette is for dinner.

Prepare the pastry: In a large bowl, combine the flour and salt. Using a box grater, grate the butter into the flour mixture. Mix with your hands for a few seconds until it resembles coarse meal and there are some pea-sized bits of butter remaining. Drizzle with the vinegar and ⅓ cup ice-cold water. Mix with a fork, adding a little more ice-cold water until a shaggy dough comes together.

Turn out onto a lightly floured work surface and gently knead until there are no dry floury bits left behind. But be careful not to overwork it. Shape the dough into a disc, wrap in plastic, and chill in the refrigerator for at least 1 hour. Bring it out of the refrigerator to sit at room temperature for 15 minutes before using. It can be made up to 5 days ahead or frozen for up to 1 month. If you freeze it, let it thaw in the refrigerator before using.

Prepare the topping: In a medium bowl, gently toss together the tomato slices and salt. Let stand for 10 minutes, then drain in a single layer on paper towels. Blot the tops of the tomatoes, too. This will help remove excess moisture so you don't have a juicy tart.

Meanwhile, roll the pastry into a 14-inch circle or thereabouts. It doesn't have to be perfect, but it does have to be about ⅛-inch thick. Prick the pastry with a fork, leaving a 1½-inch border. Place the rolled-out pastry on a parchment-lined baking sheet.

Scatter the Parmesan over the pastry, avoiding the border. Dollop the pesto over the cheese. Layer in the slices of tomatoes in a concentric circle, working from the outer edge into the centre. Tuck the thin slices of feta cheese in between the tomatoes. Be sure to leave a 1½-inch border around the edge of the galette.

Preheat the oven to 400°F. Place one oven rack in the lower half of the oven and one in the middle.

In a small bowl, combine the cherry tomatoes, garlic, and pepper. Spoon these over the sliced tomatoes. Fold the edges of the pastry up and over the sliced tomatoes,

SERVES 4

Pastry

1½ cups all-purpose flour, plus more for sprinkling

½ tsp salt

½ cup cold butter

1 Tbsp vinegar

Topping

1¾ lb garden-fresh heirloom tomatoes, sliced ¼-inch thick

1 tsp salt

½ cup grated Parmesan cheese

3 Tbsp basil pesto or Gorgeous Greens Pesto (page 85)

½ cup thinly sliced feta cheese

1¼ cups sliced cherry/grape tomatoes

1 garlic clove, minced

¼ tsp pepper

1 large egg, beaten with 1 Tbsp water, for egg wash

1 Tbsp cornmeal

Fresh basil leaves, for garnish

Flaky salt

tucking in any that go rogue. Brush the edge of the galette with egg wash. Sprinkle the pastry with cornmeal.

Bake the galette on the lower rack for 35 minutes. Move it up to the middle rack and bake until the pastry is golden brown, 15–20 more minutes. Remove from the oven and let rest for 10 minutes before slicing. Garnish with basil leaves and flaky salt.

I used Brandywine, Cherokee Purple, Yellow Pear, Black Krim, and Green Zebra heirloom tomatoes. If you're unable to find heirloom tomatoes, then any tomatoes off the vine will work.

A Simple Tomato Bread Salad

When I was first learning to cook for myself, way, way back when I lived in Montreal in the early 1990s, this salad (otherwise known as panzanella) was a summertime staple. Who knew toasted stale bread tossed with heaps of fresh tomatoes, olive oil, and basil could be so delicious? Not yet into gardening (or gardeners), I bought the tomatoes at the market and the bread from a wonderful bakery around the corner. I would devour the whole thing while sitting in the sunshine on my balcony, watching the world go by down below. Back then, this conglomeration of good simple ingredients made my life, and I was so proud that I could concoct something so darn satisfying. Flash forward almost 30 years (I just gasped out loud!) and this salad still makes my life. I love how the bread absorbs the juices from the ripe tomatoes, and the feta sails along with the saltiness, while the basil assures us that, yes, this is summer, and we need to eat this way for as long as we possibly can.

Warm a large skillet over medium heat. Pour in 2½ Tbsp of the oil. When it's warm, add the garlic and give it a stir. When it starts to sizzle, stir in the bread cubes and turn down the heat to medium-low. Cook until the bread is crispy and lightly golden and all of the oil has been absorbed. Remove from the heat. Let the bread cool just until it's still slightly warm.

Place the bread in a medium bowl. Pour the tomatoes over the bread and gently press down onto the bread. Add the remaining 1 Tbsp oil, the feta, basil, and vinegar. Gently toss. Season to taste with salt and pepper. This salad tastes best the day it's made. Makes enough for 1 hungry person, but 2 could share.

SERVES 1–2

3½ Tbsp extra-virgin olive oil, divided

2 garlic cloves, thinly sliced

2 cups (1-inch cubes) day-old sourdough bread

2 heaping cups chopped summer-fresh tomatoes

½ cup crumbled feta cheese

2 Tbsp chopped fresh basil

1 Tbsp red wine vinegar

Salt and pepper

✳ *The recipe can be easily doubled or tripled.*

✳ *Be sure to use a loaf of good crusty bread such as sourdough or a French loaf.*

✳ *To bulk up the salad, add other grilled summer vegetables such as red onion, zucchini, eggplant, or peppers. Or add 1 cup of cooked white beans or chickpeas for extra fibre and protein.*

Spaghetti with Balsamic Roasted Tomatoes and Chickpeas

I really like using whole grain spaghetti with this robust sauce of balsamic roasted tomatoes and fibre-rich chickpeas. There's something quite wonderful about how the nuttiness of the pasta dances around with the subtle sweetness of the sauce. This simple, delicious, and healthful pasta comes together in under 30 minutes, so when Dixon calls and says he's on his way to see me, I start preheating the oven and putting water on to boil. I could rave for days about how glorious roasted cherry tomatoes are, but I especially love them when it's not quite tomato season and I've got a craving like nobody's business. Roasting the tomatoes intensifies their flavour, and, if you close your eyes, they kind of taste like summer.

Preheat the oven to 425°F. Line a rimmed baking sheet with parchment paper.

I like to leave half of the tomatoes whole and cut the rest in half. Place the tomatoes, chickpeas, garlic, oil, vinegar, salt, pepper, and a pinch of red pepper flakes in a large bowl. Gently toss.

Scrape the tomato mixture onto the prepared pan and roast until the tomatoes are softened and have some caramelized bits, about 25 minutes.

Meanwhile, in a large pot of salted boiling water, cook the pasta according to the package directions. You want it al dente. Drain, reserving ½ cup of the pasta water.

Place the pasta in a large bowl, adding in the roasted tomato mixture (be sure to get all of the pan juices), reserved pasta water, and fresh basil. Gently toss.

Divide the pasta into bowls and garnish with fresh basil leaves and cheese. Drizzle the pasta with a bit more olive oil, if you like.

SERVES 4

6 cups cherry or grape tomatoes

1 can (19 oz/540 mL) chickpeas, drained and rinsed

4 garlic cloves, chopped

3 Tbsp extra-virgin olive oil, plus more for serving

3 Tbsp balsamic vinegar

1 tsp salt

¼ tsp pepper

Red pepper flakes

1 box (13 oz/375 g) whole grain spaghetti

½ cup chopped fresh basil, plus more for garnish

½ cup crumbled feta cheese or grated Parmesan cheese

✳ *I usually use a variety of yellow, orange, and red cherry/grape tomatoes, but all red is fine, too.*

✳ *You can also use regular spaghetti instead of whole grain spaghetti.*

Lemony Barley and Bulgur Salad with Tomatoes and Herbs

If you have Go On A Picnic on your summer to-do list, then I have a wonderful salad for you to pack along. This hearty whole grain salad was on heavy rotation during my summers of the mid-1990s, and the page in my coil-bound recipe notebook is so splattered and stained, you know it was well-loved. More or less a riff on tabbouleh, this salad is a grand way of using up your out-of-control parsley plant and summer-fresh tomatoes. If you're not familiar with bulgur wheat, it's made by parboiling, drying, then coarsely grinding wheat berries. It has a satisfying, chewy texture and a mild nuttiness. You can find it in the bulk section of most supermarkets or natural food stores. Barley needs no introduction, I'm sure. I'm a big fan of the texture and flavour it brings to the salad. Both bulgur and barley are high in fibre and other nutrients, so this salad packs a nutritional punch. Serve it alongside anything that comes off the grill, or as part of a picnic or potluck.

Place the bulgur in a medium bowl and cover with 1½ cups boiling water. Let stand, uncovered, for about 1½ hours, until tender yet chewy. Drain, rinse, drain. (Or, to speed things up, place the bulgur in a medium saucepan and cover with 1 cup of cold water. Bring to a boil over medium-high heat, cover, turn down the heat to low, and simmer for 12 minutes. Remove from the heat, fluff with a fork, and transfer to a large mixing bowl. Let cool to room temperature.)

Meanwhile, place 3 cups of water and the barley in a medium saucepan and bring to a boil. Cover, turn down the heat to low, and cook until tender, about 25–30 minutes. Drain, let cool to room temperature, and add to the bulgur wheat.

Add the remaining ingredients to the bowl and stir well. Season to taste with more salt and pepper, if you like. Cover and refrigerate for at least 1 hour before serving.

SERVES 4-6

½ cup bulgur wheat

½ cup pearl barley

3 cups halved cherry tomatoes

¾ cup flat-leaf parsley, finely chopped

¼ cup packed fresh mint leaves, finely chopped

3 green onions, finely chopped

2 garlic cloves, minced

Grated zest and juice of 1-2 lemons (about ¼ cup juice)

¼ cup extra-virgin olive oil

½ tsp salt, and to taste

¼ tsp pepper, and to taste

✳ *Substitute 3 large ripe tomatoes (chopped) in place of the cherry tomatoes.*

✳ *You can cook the grains up to 3 days before assembling the salad.*

Tomato Jam

Tomato jam is a sticky, sweet, tangy spread that's a fancier take on ketchup and a wonderful way to use up all of the beautiful fresh Roma tomatoes in the autumn. The tomatoes don't have to be perfect—they're just going to get smooshed into jam—so you can use ones that are a little bruised or disfigured. Dix doesn't really grow Romas, so I'll ask the tomato man at the farmers' market for any sorta sad tomatoes, and he often cuts me a deal. I like deals! This savoury jam is simple to prepare: just dump all of the ingredients into a large pot, and stir, stir, stir. It does take some time to cook the tomatoes down to a jammy consistency, but apparently patience is a virtue, so hang in there. There's a little bit of a kick to the jam, thanks to the lime juice, ginger, and red pepper flakes, and it really adds character to grilled cheese sandwiches, scrambled eggs, grilled sausages, and charcuterie boards. Dixon especially loves it when I mix a few spoonfuls of tomato jam with mayonnaise, thereby creating a dipping sauce for crispy roasted potatoes. Once you have a jar of this jam in your refrigerator, you'll find so many delicious ways to use it.

Combine all of the ingredients in a very large heavy-bottomed, non-reactive pot. Bring to a boil over high heat, stirring often, and then turn down the heat to low. Simmer the jam, stirring regularly, until it reduces to a sticky, jammy consistency. Toward the end of cooking, be super vigilant about stirring, as it burns easily when it's nearly finished. When the tomato jam is done, it should look glossy and not runny at all. The jam is finished when you can run your mixing spoon through the pot and the jam doesn't immediately run back to the middle of the pot. This process takes about 2½–3 hours.

Funnel the jam into five sterilized jars (the dishwasher works great for this), wipe the rims, let the jam cool down for 5 minutes, then screw on the sterilized lids. Allow the jars to come to room temperature on the counter and then pop them in the back of the refrigerator.

This jam keeps for 3 months in the refrigerator. However, if you'd like to preserve it for longer, or give it away as a gift, here's what you do: When the jam is nearly done, prepare a boiling water bath and sterilize five ½-pint jars. Place the lids in a small saucepan, cover them with water, and simmer over very low heat for at least 3 minutes. Or you can put the jars and lids in the dishwasher. When the jam has cooked down sufficiently, remove the pot from the heat and ladle the jam into the prepared jars, using a wide-mouth funnel. Wipe the rims, put on the lids and rings, being sure not to twist the rings on too tight, and process in a boiling water bath for 20 minutes (be sure to cover the pot with a lid), timing from the moment the water comes back to a boil after you add the jars. Turn the heat off at 20 minutes, uncover, and let the jars stand for 5 minutes longer. Carefully remove the jars from the hot water and let cool on the counter for 24 hours. You should hear a popping sound when they're sealed. Preserved in this manner, unopened jars of tomato jam will last for up to 2 years.

MAKES 5 (½-PINT) JARS

5 lb Roma tomatoes, cored and chopped

2¾ cups granulated sugar

⅔ cup bottled lime juice

1 Tbsp salt

2½ tsp red pepper flakes

2 tsp minced fresh ginger

1 tsp ground cinnamon

½ tsp ground cloves

✽   *Use bottled lime juice for preserving, not the fresh stuff.*

If you've ever grown zucchini, you'll know there comes a time in the summer when this prolific vegetable is growing fast and furious, and you're at a loss for what to do with it. I don't have scientific proof, but I'm almost certain they multiply overnight. In August and September, the chances of you finding zucchini on your doorstep are high, no matter where you live. The question I hear a lot is "What in the world can I do with them?" Luckily, they're exceptionally versatile. Zucchini can be made into almost anything. Seriously. Roast them with other seasonal veg for a great side dish. Add them to stir-fries and stews. Purée them into soup. Slice them into casseroles and gratins. Cut them in half and stuff them. Spiralize them into zoodles. Fry them into fritters. Preserve them as a tangy relish. Grate them into cakes and muffins, loaves and brownies. There are those who believe they can eat only so much chocolate zucchini bread. I'm not one of those people.

Grating and freezing zucchini is another option when it comes to dealing with your bounty. Just lightly pack it into resealable plastic bags—no need to squeeze the moisture out, as this will help prevent freezer burn. Once it's thawed, you can add it to baked goods, though I usually squeeze out some of the liquid first. Be sure to use the frozen zucchini within 3 to 4 months. More often than not, I forget that it's even in the freezer until I find a package mid-May, by which point it looks like something out of a sci-fi novel.

Young, small zucchini have a wonderful mild-tasting flavour that is further enhanced by slicing, tossing with olive oil, and seasoning with salt and pepper. Roast them at 425°F until they are deeply golden, 12–15 minutes, then remove from the oven, and toss with lemon juice and feta cheese. Drizzle on more olive oil and add whatever herbs you still have in the garden. Mint is especially lovely. The mid-size zucchini are great when deseeded and filled with a savoury ground meat/herb/cheese filling. A comforting dish, I've yet to meet a version of it that I don't like. And then there are the monsters of the garden. Those great big, dark green zucchini that have had the run of the plot. Admit it: you keep letting them grow just to see how big they can get before the frost arrives. When it comes time to cook with them, the skin will be firm and thick. It's best to chop such beasts into several pieces, then peel. Scoop out the seeds and then grate the flesh for baked goods, fritters, or even soup.

If you grow your own zucchini, don't forget how wondrous and delicious the blossoms can be. Battered and deep-fried, these golden clouds are little pieces of summer heaven, especially if they're still sizzling from the hot oil.

Dixon Says: We start zucchini plants in the greenhouse with two plants in a small starter tray. They are put into the garden in early to mid-June, when the plants are 6 inches or taller, and are spaced about 3–4 feet apart. Zucchini can be harvested at any size, but we generally prefer to pick them at 6 inches or longer for the market. In order for the plants to continue producing, the zucchini need to be cut every day or every other day. I use a long, sharp knife to cut the zucchini at the stem, although they break off with a gentle twist as well. Be sure to wear long sleeves while doing so, as the leaves can be scratchy.

ZUCCHINI

Zesty Zucchini Salmon Cakes

These light and lovely cakes use budget-friendly canned fish and mild yet marvellous zucchini. There are plenty of flavourful add-ins, not to mention the golden crust that makes these cakes so fun to cut into. I've slid these into buns alongside lettuce and tomatoes for tasty fish burgers. I've nestled them into pita bread with cucumbers and sprouts. I've served them alongside a big green salad. I've even plated them up for breakfast alongside sunny-side-up eggs. Feel free to switch up the herbs with whatever you have on hand, and, if you have salmon left over from last night's dinner, you can use that instead of canned.

Prepare the salmon cakes: Squeeze as much liquid as you can from the grated zucchini and place it in a large bowl along with the salmon, eggs, ⅔ cup of the bread crumbs, green onions, garlic, dill, lemon zest, mustard, mayonnaise, turmeric, salt, and pepper. Stir well to incorporate, but try not to overmix.

Shape the mixture into ¾-inch-thick cakes. I eyeball the amount, but it's about ½ cup for each cake. Place the remaining bread crumbs on a plate and carefully coat both sides of each cake, then place on a baking tray. Refrigerate the cakes, uncovered, for 20 minutes. Freeze any leftover panko for future use.

Prepare the sauce: While the salmon cakes are chilling, whisk all of the sauce ingredients together. If you don't have dill pickle juice, add 2 tsp more lemon juice. Season to taste, adding a few drops of your favourite hot sauce.

Warm 2 Tbsp of the oil in a 12-inch skillet over medium heat. Carefully slide half of the cakes into the hot oil and cook until golden brown, about 4 minutes per side. If the cakes are getting too dark, turn down the heat. Remove the cakes from the pan and place on a paper towel–lined plate. Wipe the skillet (turn off the heat first!) of any burnt crumbs, add the remaining 2 Tbsp of oil, and fry the remaining cakes. To make the process go faster, you can have two skillets going at once.

Serve the salmon cakes warm, with the dill sauce. If the first batch of cakes has cooled down too much, warm them in a 250°F oven for a few minutes.

* *I like to keep the salmon bones in the mix for extra nutrition, and, more often than not, a few flecks of fish will fall down into my cats' dishes, as they love salmon as much as I do.*

* *Use 1 Tbsp chopped chives instead of green onion, if you like.*

* *That sauce is so dilly good, try serving it with slices of fresh garden cucumbers and tomatoes.*

* *Look for the MSC blue fish label on all canned fish to ensure sustainability and quality.*

MAKES 6–8 CAKES

Salmon Cakes

1½ cups grated zucchini

1 can (7 oz/213 g) sockeye salmon, drained

1 can (7 oz/213 g) pink salmon, drained

2 large eggs, beaten

1⅔ cups panko bread crumbs, divided

3 green onions, finely chopped

1 garlic clove, minced

2 Tbsp finely chopped fresh dill

Grated zest of 1 lemon

1 Tbsp grainy Dijon mustard

1 Tbsp mayonnaise

½ tsp ground turmeric

½ tsp salt

¼ tsp pepper

4 Tbsp canola oil, divided

Dill Sauce

2 Tbsp mayonnaise

2 Tbsp plain Greek yogurt

2 Tbsp sour cream

1 Tbsp finely chopped fresh dill

2 tsp fresh lemon juice

2 tsp dill pickle juice

¼ tsp salt

Your favourite hot sauce

Zucchini Blossoms Stuffed with Bocconcini and Lemon

When the zucchini plants begin to bloom, Dixon knows to set aside some of the pretty yellow blossoms for me. They should be picked in the early morning light, as the cheerful flowers will be wide awake by then. As the heat of the day descends upon the garden, the blossoms softly shutter, more often than not slumping into soggy blobs by bedtime. Inside my little green kitchen, I gingerly ease open the zucchini flowers and fill them with a mixture of fresh bocconcini, lemon zest, and herbs, then dip them in a light tempura batter. They're given a bath in hot oil and pulled out when they are golden and glorious. Sprinkled with salt and drizzled with lemon juice, these stuffed blossoms are utterly delectable. Salty, crispy, and cheesy, with a mild hint of squashness, if you have access to zucchini flowers, it would be so wrong if you didn't make these summertime snacks.

Whisk together the flour and olive oil in a large bowl. It will be pebbly. Whisk the fizzy water into the mixture until the batter is smooth. Season with ½ tsp of the salt and ¼ tsp of the pepper. Cover with plastic wrap and let sit at room temperature for 30 minutes.

Meanwhile, mix together the cheese, lemon zest, lemon juice, herbs, the ¼ tsp of salt, and ¼ tsp of pepper. Carefully open each flower and stuff a heaping teaspoon of filling inside. Some will tear, but do your best. Gently twist the tops to keep everything inside.

In a large heavy saucepan or Dutch oven, warm up 2 inches of canola oil over medium heat to around 360°F. When a small cube of bread sizzles in the hot oil, you're ready to fry.

Carefully dip each flower into the batter, shaking off any excess, and slip it into the hot oil. You're using your hands for this step, so be very careful you don't burn your fingers. Fill the pan with 4–5 blossoms to create a single layer, being mindful not to overcrowd the pan. Fry the blossoms until golden brown, about 1–2 minutes per side. Remove them with a slotted spoon and drain on paper towels. Repeat with the remaining blossoms. Serve hot, with a sprinkle of flaky salt and a squeeze of lemon juice. Garnish with lemon slices.

SERVES 4

Batter

1 cup all-purpose flour

2 Tbsp extra-virgin olive oil

1 cup ice-cold sparkling water (I use Perrier)

½ tsp salt

¼ tsp pepper

Filling and Frying Blossoms

6 oz (170 g) bocconcini, coarsely chopped

Grated zest of 1 lemon

1 Tbsp fresh lemon juice

1 Tbsp chopped fresh herbs, such as dill, parsley, or basil

¼ tsp salt

¼ tsp pepper

20–25 fresh zucchini blossoms

3–4 cups canola oil, for frying

Flaky salt, for serving

Juice from ½ lemon, for serving

Lemon slices, for serving

✳ *You'll want to carefully look the blossoms over for bugs, such as ants. And while it may sound gross, I don't typically rinse the blossoms before stuffing them, as the batter will cling to dry leaves better than wet. If your blossoms appear to have dirt on them, by all means, gently rinse with water and pat dry with a paper towel before dipping, or better yet, give them a gentle shake to rid them of any debris.*

Broken Enchiladas with Zucchini and Black Beans

When I was a wee wisp of a lass just learning how to cook, and, really, just learning how to be a grown-up, this recipe for enchiladas was a frequent feature on my Montreal kitchen table. My roommate and good friend Josée and I turned out this delicious Mexican-inspired fare for good friends and potential boyfriends alike. The zucchini soaks up loads of flavour from the spices and is anything but boring here. The sauce is a little spicy, and so good you'll be dipping your spoon into the pot several times just for "quality control." I've filled flour tortillas with the zucchini mixture before but find they get too gummy and soft when baked in the sauce. Crisping up the corn tortillas yields a better texture, and takes the pressure off trying to roll perfect enchiladas. Both the sauce and the filling can be made a few days ahead, so assembling this casserole will take mere minutes on busy weeknights. This is a fun dish to put in the middle of the table and let everyone dress it up however they like.

Prepare the sauce: Place the quartered onion, garlic, and chipotle pepper in a food processor fitted with the steel blade. Pulse until finely chopped, but not mushy. In a Dutch oven, warm the oil over medium-high heat. Cook the onion mixture for 2 minutes, stirring often. Stir in the chili powder, cumin, sugar, and ½ tsp salt. Cook for another 2 minutes. Stir in the crushed tomatoes. Rinse out the tomato can with about ½ cup water and add this tomatoey water as well. Cover, bring to a simmer, then turn down the heat to low and cook for 15 minutes, stirring frequently. Remove from the heat and stir in the cream. Season to taste. The sauce can be made up to 3 days ahead.

Prepare the filling: In a large skillet, warm 2 Tbsp oil over medium-high heat. Stir in the diced onion and sauté until soft and translucent, 5 minutes. Stir in the garlic, zucchini, chili powder, oregano, red pepper flakes, and ½ tsp salt. Cook until the zucchini is slightly softened, 3 minutes. Stir in the black beans. Cook for another minute. Season to taste. The filling can be made up to 3 days ahead.

Preheat the oven to 375°F. Line two rimmed baking sheets with parchment paper. Place the cut tortilla pieces in a large bowl and drizzle with the remaining 2 Tbsp oil. Rub the tortillas with the oil so they're evenly coated. Place them on the baking sheets in a single layer. Bake for about 15–17 minutes, with one sheet on the top rack and the other on the bottom, rotating the pans halfway through the cooking time. The tortilla chips will be very crispy and will make a

SERVES 6

Sauce

1 medium yellow onion, quartered

2 garlic cloves

1 canned chipotle pepper in adobo sauce

2 Tbsp canola oil

1 Tbsp chili powder

1 Tbsp ground cumin

1 tsp sugar

½ tsp salt

1 can (28 oz/798 mL) crushed tomatoes

½ cup whipping (35%) cream

Filling

4 Tbsp canola oil, divided

1 medium yellow onion, diced

2 garlic cloves, minced

3 medium zucchini, quartered and sliced into ½-inch pieces (about 4 cups)

1 tsp chili powder

1 tsp dried oregano

½ tsp red pepper flakes

½ tsp salt

1 can (19 oz/540 mL) black beans, drained and rinsed

12 (each 6-inch) soft corn tortillas, cut into quarters

2 cups shredded extra-old cheddar cheese

Garnishes

1 avocado, sliced

8 radishes, sliced

1 jalapeño pepper, sliced

1 lime, cut into wedges

Cilantro leaves

Sour cream

Pickled Red Onions (page 165)

snapping sound when you break them in half. Remove from the oven and let cool. These can be made 1 day ahead.

In a large bowl, combine the zucchini/black bean mixture with the tortilla chips. Pour the sauce over top and mix evenly. Transfer all of this into a greased 9-×13-inch baking dish and bake for 10 minutes. Sprinkle with cheese and bake until the cheese is melted, another 5–7 minutes. Place under the broiler for 2–3 minutes for extra-crispy bits.

Have bowls of garnishes on the table and let everyone dress up their broken enchiladas as they like.

* *Add cooked, shredded chicken to the enchiladas for extra protein.*

* *For huevos rancheros the next day, serve leftovers alongside eggs and bacon.*

* *Once you've opened up a can of chipotle peppers in adobo sauce, use them in the Mega Veg Black Bean Chili with Chipotle and Chocolate on page 195 or the Smoky and Spicy Sweet Potato Soup on page 233. You can also freeze them for up to 3 months.*

"Babe, I'll Cook Dinner Tonight"

After dropping a couple of subtle hints to my darling D about how fantastic it would be if he cooked us dinner sometime, one evening in the late summer of 2016, he showed up at my doorstep with a basket bursting with zucchini, peppers, tomatoes, onions, and dill. "Babe, I'll cook dinner tonight" are some of the sweetest words in the English language, are they not? Beaming with pride, Dixon had the fixings for a fine supper of zucchini goulash. His recipe is a family favourite, one he's loved for years and years, and he wanted me to be let in on the love. I poured us glasses of red wine while I sat on a stool and watched him chop and mince and stir and taste. What a lovely sight, indeed. As you may have guessed, I do the bulk of the cooking in this relationship. Dix will occasionally make us pancakes or eggs and toast for breakfast, and he's also an excellent maker of nachos and sandwiches, but before the night of the goulash, dinner was really my territory. He says that he felt intimidated about cooking for someone with cheffy skills, and I always remind him that I'm just a girl who likes to eat—and even I need a night off once in a while!

While Dixon put the finishing flourishes on our dinner, I made the table look pretty and topped up the wine glasses. When offered a taste of the goulash, I suggested a tad more of this and a pinch of that. Dixon isn't a "clean as you go" cook, and while I thought about giving him some helpful kitchen tips, I also didn't want to step on his toes. Having someone cook for you is a testament to their love for you. Knowing when to keep mum about the clutter on the counter and general kitchen disarray is a good skill to have in a relationship. And so, the goulash sputtered on the stove and the dishes piled up in the sink. It didn't really matter. There was a lovely man making me dinner. I would find another time to clean the sauce off the ceiling.

It's always fun to learn and observe something new about your partner, and I have to say I was quite delighted by the way my love would move around the kitchen in an apron that was a little too small for him, a dish towel casually slung over his shoulder. We were listening to a '70s playlist, and every once in a while Dixon would take a break from the stove and scoop me into his arms and we'd groove to the Stones or Chicago. I'd be like "Babe! The sauce!" and he'd be like "Just a few more minutes! I can't let you go just yet." That's the thing with Dixon. He says the most romantic things like this to me all day, every day. I hope that when I'm old and grey (or older and greyer), this memory of us dancing and laughing in my kitchen, as the pot burbles away with zucchini and tomatoes, won't ever leave me. To find someone who makes your heart full and light is like having all of those wishes you cast upon stars come true. Sure, he takes forever to do the dishes and forgets to wipe down the stove and the counters. But he sure can make a mean zucchini goulash and twirl a girl around a room.

Once Dixon was satisfied with his vegetable medley, he spooned the zucchini goulash over slices of toasted sourdough, and I put on the finishing touch of crumbled feta. We tucked into the meal with forks and knives, and, after one bite, I too fell in love with this humble, simple meal. Dixon has since made the goulash for me on several occasions, but we really love to eat this homey yet delicious fare on warm, late summer nights just as the sun is setting and the stars are beginning to pop out of the night sky. The kitchen is full of dirty dishes, but they can wait. A summer moment with your love, the one who has made you dinner, is a moment to be savoured and cherished.

THE KITCHEN IS FULL OF DIRTY DISHES, BUT THEY CAN WAIT. A SUMMER MOMENT WITH YOUR LOVE, THE ONE WHO HAS MADE YOU DINNER, IS A MOMENT TO BE SAVOURED AND CHERISHED.

Dixon's Zucchini Goulash

Dixon's Goulash is not a fancy or fussy recipe, but one of fresh, seasonal ingredients simmered and stewed until the zucchini is soft and silky and the tomatoes are bursting with their juices. You'll notice that there's quite a bit of fresh dill, but as Dix says, the dill really makes the dish. And chances are, if you have a lot of zucchini in your garden, you also have dill. Dixon's family always eats the goulash over toast, so I brush some sourdough bread on both sides with olive oil and let that crisp up in the oven. We heap the goulash high on the bread, drizzle each slice with more olive oil, and let loose a generous sprinkling of feta. (The feta is my addition to the recipe, and Dix loves it.) I adore the simplicity of this rustic dish, and I hope it becomes a favourite in your kitchen, too.

Warm the oil in a Dutch oven or very large skillet over medium-high heat. Add the onion and cook until softened, about 4 minutes. Stir in the garlic, cook for another minute, then stir in the peppers. Cook just until everything starts to soften, about 3 minutes.

Stir in the zucchini and cook for another few minutes until they begin to soften as well. Stir in the tomatoes, paprika, cayenne, salt, and pepper. Turn down the heat to medium-low and cook, uncovered, until the tomatoes have released their juices and the sauce has thickened, about 20–25 minutes. Stir it occasionally as it cooks, but you don't need to hover over it.

Stir in the dill and season to taste with more salt and pepper. Serve the goulash over thick-cut toast brushed with olive oil or pasta. Drizzle with olive oil and sprinkle with plenty of crumbled feta cheese.

SERVES 4–6

2 Tbsp canola oil

1 large yellow onion, diced

2 garlic cloves, minced

1 orange bell pepper, chopped

1 yellow bell pepper, chopped

4 small zucchini, sliced ¼-inch thick (about 4 cups)

8 large plum tomatoes, chopped

1 tsp smoked paprika

¼–½ tsp cayenne pepper (or less if you don't want it spicy)

½ tsp salt, plus more to taste

¼ tsp pepper, plus more to taste

½ cup finely chopped fresh dill

Extra-virgin olive oil, for drizzling

Crumbled feta cheese, for serving

HOW TO WRITE A COOKBOOK DURING A PANDEMIC

My plan at the beginning of 2020 was to hunker down for the first seven months of the year and work on *Vegetables: A Love Story*. Money was saved. Time off work was arranged. When the first COVID-19 cases in Saskatoon started emerging in mid-March, my game plan didn't really change that much. Aside from not seeing dear friends (Mom and Dixon were in my bubble from the beginning), the biggest hurdle was grocery shopping. Not only was it super stressful, as I'm sure you all experienced, but I had to have a major plan so I could go to just one grocery store every two weeks. I wasn't just buying food to eat, I was buying food to create a cookbook. I therefore had to arrange my recipe testing accordingly. Fortunately, Dixon could bring me root vegetables, and so I worked on those recipes, and any recipes where the vegetables could last for about two weeks in the refrigerator or pantry, things like cabbage, sweet potatoes, or squash. I would work on the more perishable vegetable recipes (mushrooms, peppers, Brussels sprouts, kale, and broccoli) at the beginning of the two weeks, and the remainder was spent testing the more pantry-stable veg recipes until I could go grocery shopping again. I don't think I've ever been more organized as far as stocking my pantry and refrigerator goes. And my grocery lists! They were written on a full sheet of paper, broken down into six categories. There may have been highlighter involved. If the store I visited did not have a certain ingredient I needed, then that recipe didn't get tested until the next round of shopping. I had to be flexible, patient, and terribly organized. It all paid off in the end.

Those first several weeks of lockdown were pretty intense, and I'm so thankful that I had a massive project to throw myself into. While most things were out of my control, the one thing I did have control of was writing this cookbook, and I think it really protected my mental health. I'd look forward to getting up every day, knowing that I had to cook something delicious, and so that's what I did. And I stayed home. I'm so lucky that I didn't need anyone else to help with the food styling or the photography. Just like in my first cookbook, I did all of the creative work by myself, and all of the photos were shot on my iPhone XR. No fancy equipment or lighting over here! Just good ol' natural light and a steady hand. Dixon was by my side through it all, thank goodness, and so he was the taster of many recipes and a helpful washer of dishes and folder of laundry. As things opened up during the middle of the year, and cases dropped in Saskatoon, I was able to go out and grocery shop every week, all while wearing a mask and covered in hand sanitizer. My mind was more relaxed by then, and so I was able to escape into writing the stories and the introductions to the vegetable chapters. While at the beginning of the year I had pretty much planned on self-isolating for a good chunk of it, I didn't think think the rest of the world would also be self-isolating. As this manuscript is ready to crystallize into a full-fledged book, I'm so very proud of the work I accomplished, all while accommodating a pandemic and dodging those unmasked folks in the grocery store who refused to stay 6 feet away from me. Now, maybe I'll get around to baking with that jar of sourdough starter that's been stuck in the back of my refrigerator since April. Quentin Quarantino, if you're still alive, I'm finally ready for you.

LOVE NOTES

It's an honour and a privilege to write a book of recipes and stories. I hope you've enjoyed what you've read so far! Now that we are at the back of the cookbook, I get to thank those that helped me reach this tremendous goal.

Much love to those dear friends who cheered me on, and said, "Yes, you must write this!" when *Vegetables: A Love Story* was just an idea floating around in my brain. Josée, Mel, Chelsey, Kim, Grace, Jenni, Sonia, Stacy: You are my chosen family; your encouragement and support mean the world to me. Some of you live way across the country, and I can't wait to hop a plane so I can see you again! Thank you to my amazing team of recipe testers, who gave such valuable feedback. I had chefs, home cooks, professional home economists, registered dieticians, cookbook authors, people who lived alone, and people with a caboodle of kids cook my recipes in their kitchens. Much love to: Kim Fehr, Donna Pelech, Stacy Deschamps, Josée Johnston, Peter Graefe, Jenni Lessard, Leanne Kohlman, Ashley Markus, Grace Thompson, Chelsey Bast, Kathlin Simpkins, Dan Clapson, Carol Harrison, Emily Richards, Sylvia Kong, Dorothy Long, Tiffany Mayer, Kelly Neil, Trish Galenza, Zannat Reza, Fiona Odlum, Erika Quiring, Noelle Chorney, Heather

Bekar-Schulte, Nicole Harling, and my mom, Lorna Boser. A special shout-out goes to Candus Hunter for not only testing the most recipes (you're a machine!) but also for your thoughtful, concise, and super thorough test results, which enabled me to be a better recipe writer. Seriously, if anyone out there needs recipes tested, Candus is your person.

Thank you to Bob Deutscher for lending me gorgeous props once again. I think I gave them all back! Special thanks to Coralee Abbot, who graciously granted me time off from my part-time baking job at the beginning of the year, and then hired me back when the manuscript was completed, many months later. Thank you for being so flexible and understanding. To my sister Juanita, your strength is so inspiring. No one puts Baby in a corner. Big love to my Aunt Helen, who gave me the Caesar salad recipe, and to Dixon for the goulash recipe. You need to make it for me again, babe! Mom, you are the best cook I know, and I can't thank you enough for sharing those family-favourite recipes with me. It makes me so happy to see them in print!

Thank you to the farmers and producers all across Canada who work tirelessly to put safe, affordable, and nutritious food on our tables. From kale to canola, lettuce to lentils, and beans to barley, I am grateful to have such excellent ingredients to work with.

Because COVID-19 made going grocery shopping such a pain in the bum, I want to thank those folks who stocked shelves and rang in my purchases. It couldn't have been easy to work during such stressful times, and I just want you to know that I appreciate you.

Thank you to Karlynn Johnston, Aimée Wimbush-Bourque, and Mairlyn Smith for writing such beautiful blurbs for the cookbook. You know that I'm in awe of you, right? Thank you for sharing your wit and wisdom with me!

Taryn Boyd, you are a rock star of a publisher. I'll never forget sitting with you and Dixon in that hotel bar the night I won my Taste Canada Award. We were on cloud nine! You asked what my thoughts were on another project, and you didn't flinch one bit when I said I wanted to write a cookbook devoted to vegetables. It took a year for me to get that proposal to you, but here we are! Thank you for believing in me, and for working so hard to publish another beautiful cookbook of mine. To the stellar team at TouchWood, thank you for all the things. One day I need to visit your office so we can have a big group hug. To my editor, Lesley Cameron, thank you for giving me the idea for Dixon Says way back when we had lunch in May of 2018. Having Dixon's insight into growing veg was a brilliant idea—thanks for planting the seed. And, of course, thank you for going through my manuscript, ensuring that this cookbook is the best it could be. Special thanks to Tree Abraham, designer extra-ordinaire. You made my recipes and stories come to life, with your artistry and skill. Thanks for sharing your talent on these pages.

To Audrey Simpkins, thank you for welcoming me into your family. I can't thank you enough for raising such a kind-hearted, good man.

To my dear, sweet mom (again!). Thank you for everything. It's been a pleasure being your daughter. I'll cherish our time in the kitchen forever.

And finally, to my darling Dixon. Without you this cookbook would not have happened. Thank you for the first-date asparagus, and every other vegetable you've brought my way since May of 2016. You've made all my dreams come true, and then some. Thank you for being my partner in this love story. You know the best part? There are so many chapters still to be written, and, for that, I can't wait.

METRIC CONVERSION TABLE

Volume

IMPERIAL	METRIC
⅛ tsp	0.5 mL
¼ tsp	1 mL
½ tsp	2.5 mL
¾ tsp	4 mL
1 tsp	5 mL
½ Tbsp	8 mL
1 Tbsp	15 mL
1½ Tbsp	23 mL
2 Tbsp	30 mL
2½ Tbsp	38 mL
¼ cup	60 mL
⅓ cup	80 mL
½ cup	125 mL
⅔ cup	165 mL
¾ cup	185 mL
1 cup	250 mL
1¼ cups	310 mL
1⅓ cups	330 mL
1½ cups	375 mL
1⅔ cups	415 mL
1¾ cups	435 mL
2 cups/ 1 pint	500 mL
2¼ cups	560 mL
2⅓ cups	580 mL
2½ cups	625 mL
2⅔ cups	665 mL
2¾ cups	690 mL
3 cups	750 mL
3½ cups	875 mL
4 cups	1 L
5 cups	1.25 L
6 cups	1.5 L
8 cups / 2 quarts	2 L
25 cups	6 L

Weight

IMPERIAL	METRIC
1 oz	30 g
4 oz	115 g
8 oz	225 g
10 oz	250 g
12 oz	340 g
1 lb (16 oz)	450 g

Cans

IMPERIAL	METRIC
6 oz	177 mL
10 oz	284 mL
14 oz	398 mL
16 oz	480 mL
28 oz	796 mL

Length

IMPERIAL	METRIC
1/12 inch	2 mm
⅛ inch	3 mm
⅙ inch	4 mm
¼ inch	6 mm
½ inch	12 mm
¾ inch	2 cm
1 inch	2.5 cm
1¼ inches	3 cm
1½ inches	3.5 cm
1¾ inches	4.5 cm
2 inches	5 cm
2½ inches	6.5 cm
3 inches	7.5 cm
3½ inches	9 cm
4 inches	10 cm
5 inches	12.5 cm
6 inches	15 cm
7 inches	18 cm
8 inches	20 cm
9 inches	23 cm
10 inches	25 cm
11 inches	28 cm
12 inches	30 cm
17 inches	43 cm
18 inches	46 cm
20 inches	50 cm

Temperature

(For oven temperatures, see chart below)

IMPERIAL	METRIC
115°F	46°C
150°F	66°C
160°F	71°C
170°F	77°C
180°F	82°C
185°F	85°C
190°F	88°C
200°F	93°C
240°F	116°C
247°F	119°C
250°F	121°C
290°F	143°C
300°F	149°C
350°F	177°C
360°F	182°C
370°F	188°C

Oven Temperature

IMPERIAL	METRIC
200°F	95°C
225°F	105°C
250°F	120°C
275°F	135°C
300°F	150°C
325°F	160°C
350°F	180°C
375°F	190°C
400°F	200°C
425°F	220°C
450°F	230°C

INDEX

(handwritten annotations: "FREEZES WELL" next to Cold-Buster Chicken Noodle Soup, 177)